Structures of Domination and
Peasant Movements in Latin America

Structures of Domination and Peasant Movements in Latin America

Peter Singelmann

University of Missouri Press
Columbia & London, 1981

Copyright © 1981 by the Curators of the University of Missouri, University of
Missouri Press, Columbia, Missouri 65211

Library of Congress Catalog Card Number 79–48030

Printed and bound in the United States of America

LIBRARY OF CONGRESS CATALOGING IN PUBLICATION DATA

Singelmann, Peter, 1942–
    Structures of Domination and Peasant Movements in
Latin America.
    Bibliography: p.
    Includes index.
    1. Peasantry—Latin America. 2. Latin America—
Rural conditions. 3. Dominance (Psychology) I. Title.
HD320.5.S55   302   79–48030
ISBN 0–8262–0307–8

In Dank und Anerkunnung widme ich dieses Buch meinen
Eltern Peter und Gisela Singelmann in Hamburg

Acknowledgments

My work on structures of domination in Latin America began with my Ph.D. dissertation at the University of Texas–Austin. Therefore, I owe my first recognition and appreciation to the members of my dissertation committee. Joseph Lopreato has been not only a helpful and critical supervisor, but also a good friend who has encouraged my work from its beginning. Walter Firey has been instrumental in enabling my studies at the University of Texas, and his helpful suggestions significantly improved my study. To Jack Gibbs I am grateful for his critical suggestions during all phases of the work; my methodological thinking has been profoundly influenced by my participation in his seminars, although this work may hardly do justice to his influence. Russell Curtis and John Higley have given a great deal of their time to discuss the project with me and to make valuable suggestions on parts or all of the original manuscript. Anthony Leeds has been a fine friend whose office and library, as well as my various discussions with him, greatly stimulated and facilitated my work. My brother, Joachim, helped me when I needed it most by relieving me from many of the lesser chores that make getting a Ph.D. such a tedious affair.

I owe a great deal to my colleagues of the University of Missouri, especially chairmen Phil Olson and Neil Bull for a variety of administrative supports, both for the original dissertation and the current book. I also greatly appreciate Joan Davis's supportive, flexible, and professionally qualified help as a secretary.

In academia it is difficult to separate work hours from leisure time. My wife, María Elena, and our children, Claudia, Jan, and Mario, have shared with me some of the more strenuous parts of academic careers. They have been understanding and helpful, and I owe them much in exchange for their company.

Contents

PART I

The Theoretical Problem

CHAPTER I

Introduction

Latin American societies have had a long history of Indian and peasant revolts dating back to the beginnings of the Spanish and Portuguese conquest, but not until the twentieth century have peasant movements contributed to major social dislocations and reorganizations throughout the continent. In 1910 the peasant armies of Emiliano Zapata and Pancho Villa came to dominate large parts of Mexico and were instrumental in the pressure for large-scale agrarian reforms. In the middle of the century peasants were the main participants and victims of Colombia's *violencia;* they participated in the Bolivian revolution of 1952–1953 and formed leagues and syndicates in northeast Brazil against the violent repressions of the ruling landed elite. In Peru peasant organizations have gained recognition for some time in the coastal zone, while in the sierra militant peasant movements at times secured substantial gains in the face of often violent opposition. Before the military coup of September 1973, Chile had experienced a major upsurge of peasant movements, and in Venezuela a coalition of government and peasant unions has led to large-scale land redistribution programs.[1]

Although the results of Latin American peasant movements appeared particularly impressive in the 1960s and the 1970s, the end of the decade witnessed the progressive repression of the major movements on the continent. Military dictatorships choked autonomous campesino mobilization in Bolivia, Guatemala, Chile, and Brazil. In Mexico, campesino organizations were either co-opted or repressed. In Colombia peasant organizations had little room to maneuver without encountering police sanctions. Furthermore, there have been in the past many futile peasant rebellions in Latin America as well as substantial evidence that many peasants have been forced to accept a status quo.

Latin American peasant movements, thus, have to be understood in terms of their conditions, their accomplishments in terms

3

of potential class emancipation, and alternative outcomes such as repression, reform, and co-optation. One of the complex issues that needs to be resolved entails the interconnection between varying concrete historical conditions and events and their varying implications on the one hand, and the possibility of explanatory generalizations on the other. Such generalizations should seek to account for revolutionary successes as well as for alternative patterns and outcomes of social movements.

GENERALIZATIONS AND HISTORICAL CASE STUDIES

Since the mid-1960s historians and social scientists have increasingly developed interest in understanding the basic causes and structural implications of peasant movements, both in the classical transition from feudalism to capitalism and in contemporary Third World nations. There have been a variety of regional and national case studies as well as some brilliant attempts to outline larger, international historical conditions that have promoted radical peasant revolutions in the nineteenth and twentieth centuries (Moore, 1966; Wolf, 1969; Paige, 1975; and Skocpol, 1979). Historically, however, the vast majority of peasant resistances to landholders have entailed not radical transformations of peasant functions within a qualitative restructuring of the macrosociety, but rather repression, token concessions, and reformist movements in the twentieth century that essentially resulted in readjustments within a class structure that maintained the peasantry as a subordinate class under "modernized" mechanisms of exploitation (Singelmann, 1976; and Chapter 15 below). This historical evidence, of course, does not support generalized arguments suggesting that peasants are inherently incapable of developing successful revolutionary movements; rather, it invites analysts to relate the variable and historically unique conditions and patterns of peasant movements to some degree of abstract generalizability (Skocpol, 1979: 33–40). For a general understanding, however, it is not only necessary to investigate the specific conditions under which peasants get involved in revolutionary movements and when they are likely to succeed or fail; it is also necessary to establish a more general theoretical approach that begins with the question of why humans tend to act the way they do within given cultural frameworks and under given external conditions of opportunities and constraints. The relatively abstract propositions that attempt to answer such questions then have to be applied to concrete historical conditions, which, in turn, lead to more specialized propositions concerning alternative responses of actors under differentiated structural conditions.

The theoretical approach presented in this book does not take its point of departure in specific subsets of conditions under which peasant resistance leads to revolutionary transformation; the book will focus, rather, on more generic structural processes applying to a variety of historical and cultural conditions and corresponding human responses. Generally, studies of peasantries and their revolutionary potentials have focused either on varieties in terms of typologies based on a combination of historically unique conditions and generalizations that explain the presence or absence of peasant revolutions (Moore, 1966; Wolf, 1969; Skocpol, 1979), or on two-by-two classifications with corresponding hypotheses concerning the category of peasantry with the greatest potential for effective revolutionary mobilization (Paige, 1975). I suggest that (1) such explanations based on classification are most promising in detailed comparisons of case studies (Moore and Skocpol), although it is precisely those studies that emphasize the historical uniqueness that will always point to the limitations of any generalization, but (2) these explanations also risk oversimplification and misinterpretation when offering generalizations based on classifications and a large number of case studies (see the critical discussions of Paige; Wolf, 1977; and I.J. Schulman, 1978). This study will attempt to avoid such "fallacy of misplaced abstraction" without, however, avoiding the search for generalized propositions. I will take previous approaches as a point of departure and then reapproach the issue of Latin American peasant movements. Different theoretical approaches have offered a variety of explanations that, in part, supplement one another but have also led frequently to radically contradictory interpretations and causal analyses. As has been argued by Skocpol (1979: 33–40) and Moore (1966), any explanation of peasant mobilizations and their revolutionary potential requires the application of general theoretical perspectives to the concrete variability of given cases with their unique, and possibly unrepeatable, historical conditions.

Hence, the complexity of historical variations need not result in conditions that tend to promote revolutions; it is equally important to recognize that the general conditions of revolutions may, under certain historical conditions, lead to no movements at all, to a search for improvement within the given social structure, or to successful repression on the part of the ruling classes.

Hence, this study will attempt to expand the theoretical generalizations about revolutionary movements and the conditions under which they may or may not occur and will focus on a more generalized explanation of the conditions under which peasants tend to resist landlords. This approach necessarily requires a more general theoretical approach that, I would argue, not only transcends historical case analyses and comparisons but also requires a more generic theoretical approach than the ones represented, for example, by theories of class analysis, political mobilization, and social revolution. Such a more generic approach may, in fact, precisely integrate different and contradictory explanations based on more specific macrostructural dimensions of unique historical processes; or, phrased differently, this approach may also explain the exceptions that have not fitted into previous theoretical approaches (Landsberger, 1969a: 27–28).

THEORIES OF PEASANT REVOLUTION

There have been a variety of theoretical approaches to explain successful peasant revolutions. In very general terms, the major explanatory approaches have been identified by Skocpol (1979: 9–12) as focusing on (1) psychological motivations, (2) ideologies reacting against severe social disequilibration, and (3) the political relationships between governmental and nongovernmental organizations.[2] For the purposes of this book, a number of issues and dimensions, along which theories of peasant revolutions differ, can be outlined.

1. Peasant mobilizations have been classified in multiple stages of increasing radicalization; generally, peasants tend to fall short of the last stage, which entails a radical transformation of rural-class structures within larger social contexts (Migdal, 1974: 251–52, 259–60; Landsberger, 1969a: 10–11).

2. There are different interpretations concerning the basis of peasant revolutions. They may be more likely to occur in traditional, relatively isolated, and self-sufficient middle-peasant communities exposed to increasing exploitation from the outside (Stinchcombe, 1961; Landsberger, 1969a: 39; Wolf, 1969) or in areas characterized by poor families with no or minimal land (Paige, 1975; see also the responses to Paige, for example, Skocpol, 1980; Schulman, 1978; and Wolf, 1977).

3. There are different interpretations with regard to internal and external social processes in peasant communities and how they function to promote revolutions; a related issue concerns the formation of institutional links between peasant communities and the outside world. While some authors emphasize the importance of integrated movements that link the peasant with outside allies (Landsberger, 1969a: 59; Wolf, 1969; Fowler, 1978; Migdal, 1974), others have emphasized the significance of independent peasant mobilization from within the villages (Moore, 1966). Skocpol

(1979), on the other hand, has emphasized the variability of combinations of social dimensions that may entail different facilitating conditions of peasant revolutions.

4. Modernization has frequently been connected with increased freedom for peasant mobilization and the breakup of landlord monopolization over economic and political resources (Migdal, 1974: 258; Landsberger, 1969a: 59–60). Modernization as such, however, has more frequently led to the emergence of new *patrones* who have tended to replace traditional landlords within competitive political frameworks without, however, changing the exploitation of the peasants (Petras and Haven, 1980; Singelmann, 1975b; Chapter 15 below).

5. While most scholars emphasize the significance of peasant integration into larger commercialized economies that exert increasing pressure on peasant subsistence, others (Moore, 1966) emphasize the lack of agricultural commercialization as crucial for promoting peasant revolutions in the nineteenth and twentieth centuries.

6. There are opposing theoretical approaches, on the one hand emphasizing the importance of wider political or institutional links between peasants and outside social forces (Migdal, 1974; Landsberger, 1969a; Wolf, 1969), and on the other hand arguing that lacking or weak institutional links between peasants and the outside tend to promote revolutions (Moore, 1966). Others (Skocpol, 1979) have developed a more flexible perspective according to which institutional links with the outside are more important when revolutionary movements have their principal basis in political organizations outside the countryside; under different historical conditions, relatively independent peasant mobilizations can be the primary revolutionary force.

7. Some authors have emphasized the differential likelihood of peasant revolutions within given qualitative types of societies or subsocieties (Paige, 1975; Moore, 1966; Stinchcombe, 1961), while others have focused on quantitative increases or declines in peasant outcomes either using psychological approaches (Davies, 1962; Gurr, 1968; Geschwender, 1968; Schwartz, 1971; Scott, 1977) or approaches emphasizing sociostructural dimensions (Singelmann, 1974; also Eisenstadt and Roniger, 1980).

8. Authors have approached the explanation of peasant revolutions differently, either by focusing on peasant involvements in political mobilization on the basis of class relations (Paige, 1975) or, conversely, by emphasizing that the outcomes of class conflicts

themselves are to a significant extent shaped by political processes (Skocpol, 1979).

Some of these controversies may be appropriately classified as disagreements over a specific subject where eventually one interpretation will be accepted as more appropriate—a case in point would be Wolf's (1977) disagreement with Paige's (1975: chap. 5) explanation of the South Vietnamese revolution as based on impoverished sharecroppers and migrant laborers or traditional middle-peasants (see also Skocpol, 1980: 10–19, for a critical review). I suggest, however, that many of the contradictions involved in the explanation of peasant revolutions are founded not on differences in data interpretation but rather on differences in initial theoretical approaches as well as on the investigators' failure to move from the interpretation of their data to sufficiently generic levels of social theory, which would increase the possibilities for explaining historical variants within a common theoretical framework.

The contradictory arguments listed above can, thus, be put into a more general perspective. Within both traditional and modernized agrarian structures, for example, peasant mobilization depends on concrete responses to the outcomes of social actions, on degrees of exploitation, or on changing expectations. Modernization as such can be interconnected with refined patterns of exploitation within a given system of agrarian production (for example, the four types identified by Paige) and may be more conducive to violent peasant mobilization than the structure of their respective internal organization; the outcome then does not depend on the type of peasantry engaged in revolts but, rather, on the macrostructural support they obtain. Similarly the relationship between internal and external village forces not only varies according to concrete historical contexts (Skocpol, 1979) but, moreover, tends to entail dialectic interrelationships. The same argument applies to the interrelationships between political systems and class structure. While it is, thus, legitimate either to focus on primary control variables of the investigators' interests or to emphasize the relatively crucial importance of certain variables within a dialectic process (for example, the more sophisticated Marxian approaches), the very principle of dialectic analysis is incompatible with unidirectional explanation. A similar argument can be made with regard to the false dichotomy of qualitative and quantitative variables.

This argument can, then, be summarized so far as follows: (1) many alternative theories tend to be founded on different foci in terms of causal factors under consideration; (2) regardless of general explanations, differences in concrete structural contexts entail different motivations, constraints, and opportunities with regard to revolutionary movements; (3) different historical coincidences, such as ingenious leaders or incompetent administrators in power, offer concrete stimulations and outcomes of peasant movements; (4) structurally similar societies can contain quantitative differences, for example, in peasant outcomes, which may lead to revolutionary mobilizations in some but not other societies.

The issues involved in these debates, then, suggest that theories focusing on macrostructural processes leading to peasant revolutions can be complemented by a more generic approach beginning with assumptions about human conduct that are subsequently applied to variable historical conditions that may result in a variety of peasant reactions and results within given social structures.

SOCIAL EXCHANGES IN PEASANT SOCIETIES:
MICRO- AND MACROSOCIAL DIMENSIONS

The argument I am making here, then, is not that the explanation of macrostructural processes can be redirected to microsocial phenomena. I am suggesting, rather, that (1) micro- and macrostructural phenomena are interdependent, (2) microstructural processes tend to have a greater potential for generalization, and (3) microstructural propositions can, hence, explain "why people act the way they do" in general and specifically in the case of peasant resistance.

The generic microstructural basis I take as my point of departure is that of social exchange. There are, of course, dimensions of social structure and social interrelations that do not fit into this category. This does not deny, however, that exchanges are a fundamental basis of any social order, the significance of which can be shown specifically in the integration and tensions within peasant societies and their larger social frameworks.[3] The universal significance of exchange in peasant societies is reflected by Barrington Moore's (1966: 496) observation that "where the links arising out of the relationship between lord and peasant community are strong, the tendency toward peasant rebellion (and later revolution) is feeble." In qualifying the nature of these links, Moore suggests, "Political stability requires the inclusion of the overlord and/or priest as members of the village community who perform services necessary for the agricultural cycle and the social cohesion of the village for which they receive roughly commensurate privileges and material rewards" (1966: 470).

What Moore points out here is not only the central importance of exchange mechanisms in which peasants are engaged within a larger societal context, but also a fundamental problem to which peasantries are generally exposed: under conditions of scarcity and repression, they have to choose between either "horizontal" solidarity with other members of their class or "vertical" solidarity with their landlords. *Solidarity* in this sense is understood not so much in emotional terms, but rather as peasant recognition that cooperation with the landlord is vital for survival. Historically, the balance of vertical solidarity between landlords and peasants has always been tenuous (Eisenstadt and Roniger, 1980: 49–50, 59). Yet, these balances have tended to be maintained through coercion and dependence until the late nineteenth and the twentieth centuries.[4]

Exchange balances do not necessarily entail equality. Rather, they entail a tentative equilibrium in terms of which actors consider their returns to be fair in relation to their contributions in given social relationships (Blau, 1964a). Inequality entails balanced social relations to the extent that (1) each actor considers his rewards to adequately correspond to his costs or contributions in social relations, and (2) some actors are willing to "overpay" others as a way to balance their dependence (Blau, 1964a: chap. 5).

The historical conditions of peasantries in general, and those of Latin America in particular, can be seen as extremely unequal exchanges that tend to be maintained by coercion (or threats of coercion) and by the peasants' dependence on the landowners for their means of subsistence.[5] It is this process of dependence that links an analysis of local peasant-landlord relations with the more complex macrostructural developments, since the dependence of peasants on landlords is founded on their differential access to economic, political, and military resources linked with the larger society. The ideal-typical model of balanced peasant-landlord relations is based on the observation that traditional landlords have tended to regionally monopolize the access of rival populations to these vital resources and thus maintain exclusive "brokerage" positions whereby the peasantry was integrated into an exploitative macrostructural framework.[6] Under different historical conditions, either the landlords have eliminated the peasants completely from exchanges with elements outside the hacienda (and, hence, forced them to subsist on resources produced within the property), or they have monopolized the controls over exchanges with the outside. The effect was the same (Migdal, 1974: chap. 7). The peasants could leave the area or revolt, but they could also submit to subordination and exploitation. When the decision was made to submit to the landlord, the most rational adaptation was to receive the greatest returns by offering not only obedience and labor, but also the only gifts that the landlords could not get except from their subordinates: symbolic gestures expressing the peasants' personal recognition of, and affection to, the landlords as the fathers to whom they owed their physical existence and spiritual inspiration. These symbolic resources were not only among the few available to the peasants, but they also added a crucial dimension to the social status of the traditional *patrón,* which was reflected in his personal respectability as well as in his expected (or hoped for) generosity of helping his subordinates in cases of emergency with small amounts of cash, a day off work, or by straightening out legal conflicts with the outside without demanding a direct return. The indirect return to such occasional favors was the strengthening of loyalty.

The motivation of peasant loyalty to the *patrón* under such constraints also constituted an obstacle to potential class solidarity among the peasants, as it was in the interest of each individual to seek his most favorable results by demonstrating his loyalty and utility to the landlord. That meant that it was in the interests of peasants to betray their fellow peasants, if necessary, to abuse them as low-ranking supervisors, to try to outweigh their fellow peasants in their utility and loyalty to the landlord—in short, to win in a zero-sum game where the winning of one member within a social class entails a corresponding loss of the others. This pattern of solidarity across class lines between landlords and peasants is reflected in the model of the "open triangle" that has been suggested for traditional patterns of peasant domination by the landlords. The openness of this triangle entails the lack of horizontal solidarity at the bottom between any two peasants who are each, however, engaged in vertical solidarity with the landlord at the top of the triangle.[7]

In these terms, the question of peasant solidarity and mobilization is addressed to the conditions under which such triangles may "close," whether they will, in fact, remain triangular interrelations, whether they can be converted to simple linear horizontal relations between peasants without higher-level *patrones,* whether a variety of triangular alternatives can put the peasants into a superior bargaining position, and whether triangular alternatives as such are likely to promote the emancipation of peasantries as a class. The triangular model thus enables us to connect microstructural patterns of interaction with larger social processes that are conducive to structural changes at the local level.[8]

The recognition that peasant-landlord relationships have been founded on the mutual but unequal reception of rewards and punishments and that the nature of the benefits peasants received from the landlords affected the nature of the solidarity among the peasants leads to the major theses of this study:

1. class solidarity among peasants has traditionally been constrained by the scarcity of rewards available from intraclass (horizontal) exchanges;

2. vertical solidarity between peasants and landholders (or other *patrones*) has traditionally been promoted
    a. by the relative gains peasants can receive from interclass exchanges, and
    b. by the relative dependency of the peasants on the landholders (or other *patrones*);

3. in traditional rural Latin America, peasants have been caught in a network of competing solidarities where vertical solidarities with *patrones* were usually incompatible with horizontal solidarities among the peasants; and

4. peasant movements have arisen in Latin America when
    a. the rewards from vertical solidarities decreased relative to the rewards from horizontal solidarities for the peasants,
    b. the dependence of the peasants on their landholders decreased, and/or
    c. alternative vertical solidarities emerged that were compatible with horizontal solidarities for the peasants.

ON PEASANT CONSCIOUSNESS

It is appropriate for any theoretical approach that takes its point of departure at the microstructural level of peasant interactions to incorporate information on cultural values and socially shared consciousnesses that underlie concrete peasant acts. While it is possible to examine peasant consciousness in terms of its potential for correct class consciousness,[9] an alternative approach would assume that peasant behaviors tend to be realistic responses to objective constraints and opportunities as well as subjectively meaningful within the context of culturally shared "definitions of the situation." With this approach, the problem of "correct" or "false" consciousness is quite irrelevant, since humans act in terms of cognitive orientations in the light of which

both in an abstract philosophical sense and in the view of the individual of himself, all behavior is 'rational' and sense-making. 'Irrational' behavior can be spoken of only in the context of a cognitive view which did not give rise to that behavior. (Foster, 1967b: 302)

Such an approach can account for human actions by referring to situationally specific motivating cognitions and is thus appropriate for the analysis of microsocial phenomena. But, in turn, this approach is incapable of handling the objective structural implications of social action; furthermore, it treats every act as equally valid and thus cannot differentiate between acts that have a truly emancipatory potential and others that lead to co-optation and subtler forms of alienation. What is needed, therefore, is an approach that permits a dialectic analysis of the interdependence between the objective and subjective dimensions of human action (Berger and Luckmann, 1966).

While cultural and psychological aspects are no doubt in themselves to a large extent adaptive responses to the objective environment in which the peasants exist, they nevertheless provide the direct motivations for the peasants' behaviors and thus, in contrast to the Marxist type of "class consciousness," include the directly measurable historical manifestations of the peasants' self-awareness. Such psychological and cultural configurations, while arising out of the concrete existential conditions of humanity, can become "objectified" *(versachlicht)* and outlast the structural context within which they have developed. In such a case they become autonomized and stand in contradiction to political and economic realities.[10]

This study will proceed from the assumption that such autonomization of cultural and psychological factors is possible and that, therefore, cognitive and cultural patterns persist and change at least partially independent of their economic substructure; they thus have to be included in our theories as explanatory variables. Our analysis will acknowledge, then, the concrete reality of human existence as it is reflected in the perceptions and goals of the actors, although by itself such an approach will not help us in formulating theories about the structural interrelationships between institutions, which constitute the outcomes of human actions. As Engels (in Marx and Engels, 1966, vol. 1: 212) wrote on the interrelationships between consciousness and objective constraints:

In history the actors all are men who are capable of consciousness, who act with reflection or passion, and who work toward definite goals; nothing happens without conscious purpose or desired goals. But this . . . , *as important as it is for the historical analysis especially of single eras and events,* cannot change the fact that the course of history is ruled by inherent general laws. Because here, too, on the whole, chance appears to rule on the surface, in spite of the consciously desired goals of the individuals. Only rarely the desired (events) happen. . . . The purposes of the actions are willed, but the results that really follow these actions are not willed; or, if at first they appear to correspond to the desired purpose, they eventually have consequences completely different from the ones intended. (My translation and italics)

This brilliant statement of the dialectics inherent in the objective and subjective dimensions of social action provides also an important clarification of historical materialism. Although the dynamics of macrosocial structures will thus have to be analyzed in terms of objective social and economic relations, our explanation of concrete human acts will proceed from the assumption that objective conditions determine behavior not mechanically but via the subjective (and culturally shared) interpretations and definitions of the situation on the part of the actors. Such a two-pronged approach will avoid some of the shortcomings of both objectivist and subjectivist orientations. It will allow us to examine the rationales of peasants acting in their concrete existential situations.

CONCEPTUAL PROBLEMS

Peasants have been defined as small-scale "agricultural producers in effective control of land who carry on agriculture as a means of livelihood, not as a business for profit" (Eric Wolf, cited in Wagley, 1964: 21). While this definition makes no reference to the peasantry as a class, various authors (Wolf, 1969: 2–4; Foster, 1967c:6) have suggested that to be differentiated from "primitive" agricultural producers peasants have to be defined in terms of their distinctive interrelationships with other societal sectors. Characteristically, they produce some surplus beyond their subsistence needs, which is absorbed by nonagricultural (urban) groups who dominate the peasants politically, economically, and culturally (Sjoberg, 1955). This exploitative relation with the dominant sectors of societies determines the structural parameters of peasant life. Wolf (1966a: 3–4) describes peasants as "rural cultivators whose surpluses are transferred to a dominant group of rulers that uses the surpluses both to underwrite its own standard of living and to distribute the remainder to groups in society that do not farm but must be fed for their specific goods and services in turn." It might be argued that this is not only a definition but also an assertion about the nature of the peasants' position within the larger society and precludes designating as a "peasant" an agricultural producer who simply produces for his own subsistence above the level of what is considered primitive technology.

In Latin America there are a variety of different types of peasants. Some live in indigenous communities under communal landownership, others are independent small-scale producers who earn part of their means of subsistence by working on large estates (haciendas, *fazendas*), and still others live as *colonos* on the property of a larger landholder who provides them with food, housing, some land, and perhaps a small cash remuneration in return for domestic and field labor as well as a variety of other obligations (R.N. Adams, 1964:49). While agricultural wage laborers are usually not defined as peasants, in the particular case of Latin America it is actually difficult to distinguish rural wage earners and peasants as two separate populations, since part-time and seasonal wage labor are becoming increasingly prevalent among the rural lower sectors. For this reason, it may be more meaningful to use the more generic term *campesino* (R. N. Adams, 1967a: 91–93), which is widely used in Latin America. This term includes peasants as defined more narrowly above, but it also refers to

almost all poor rural dwellers; it includes peasants who own their land and rural laborers who may never have imagined owning land. The *campesino. . .* may be found in the ever-growing group of peasants who spend part of their time in wage labor or among laborers who keep a small plot under cultivation; he lives in tropical forest clearings, in coastal fishing villages, in highland haciendas, in lowland sugar planations, in independent towns. (R. N. Adams, 1967a: 91)

In this study I shall be dealing with those campesinos who interact directly with large landowners as renters, sharecroppers, or *colonos,* who have to exchange their privileges of land use for subordination and exploitation.

All of these groups are involved in a more or less exploitative exchange relationship with an upper-class patron, although the structures of these relationships clearly vary and may have different implications for mobilization (Stinchcombe, 1961; Paige, 1975; Galjart, 1972). I shall assume that the theoretical model explored in this book has a generic character that can handle the divergent historical situations of *colonos,* sharecroppers, and renters. Consequently, evidence for the general propositions will be drawn from all of these situations without an attempt to differentiate the historically unique characteristics of each type.

The term *peasant movement* will be defined with Landsberger (1969a: 8) as "any collective reaction by rural cultivators to their low status." The peasant movement is thus broadly conceived and can occur in a variety of manifestations ranging from retreatist and escapist attempts to cope with misery to organized and conscious political activity and warfare (Landsberger, 1969a: 8–14). The term will be used as a generic concept that leaves the differentiation in terms of goals, means, and consequences for later classification.

The term *traditional* will be used frequently in a strictly nonnormative way to describe interaction patterns. When using this term, no reference is made to the cultural and structural content of social patterns—this will be a matter of empirical specification. *Traditional* will simply denote ideal-typical forms that have prevailed in the past, whatever their nature may have been.

Throughout this study reference will be made to Latin America as a whole, although the evidence presented must necessarily come from individual countries. I am writing this book under the assumption that, regional and national variations notwithstanding, there is a sufficient historical continuity and unity on the continent with regard to cultural and sociostructural patterns to warrant an ideal-typical generic interpretation under which regional and national variations can be subsumed. This interpretation will be constructed not in terms of a static model but by reference to the major generic variables that appear to affect the development of campesino movements in different constellations.

SUMMARY

The theses outlined above will be explored more specifically by reference to the objective conditions that circumscribe the peasants' status as well as to the individual and culturally shared definitions peasants construct of their social world. While the decision to explore an exchange-theory model was based on prior readings in the literature on Latin American peasant mobilization, for purposes of exposition I will begin this book by presenting in Part I an overview of the various theoretical approaches focusing on social exchanges (Chapter 2) and will specifically focus in Chapter 3 on problems of dependence, power, paternalism, and solidarity. In Part II, the use of this model will be justified in terms of the historical contingencies involved in the traditional exchanges of Latin American peasants; the traditional parameters of horizontal and vertical solidarities for the peasants will be examined by analyzing the social, economic, political, and psychocultural factors that have affected the peasants' exchange relationships among each other and with their landlords. The basic thesis emerging from that analysis is that all these factors have tended to mitigate the development of peasant solidarity and to encourage the solidarization of individual peasants with their landlords. An ideal-typical traditional model of lord-peasant and peasant-peasant interaction can be constructed from this discussion, but it should be stressed from the beginning that we will be dealing with *variables* that had different influences under different historical conditions. The construction of such a heuristic model does, however, permit us to consider any given status quo in rural class relations and predict cognitive and/or behavioral changes when specified variables have changed. The propositions to be established can, therefore, be tested in longitudinal studies in which concomitant changes in objective conditions and subjective definitions on the one hand, and behavioral responses on the other, can be predicted. While the theory is concerned with why humans interact as they do, it will then be tested through hypotheses predicting conditions under which they will no longer act as they used to. That endeavor will be undertaken in Part III, which will be addressed to imbalances brought about through changes in the objective and subjective conditions discussed in Part II. The development of peasant movements in Latin America will be analyzed as a response to these imbalances.

A final chapter will be addressed to the issue of peasant emancipation through mobilization. While peasants in Mexico and Peru have been crucial participants in revolutions, and while traditional rural structures have been reformed to different degrees in virtually every Latin American nation, the question remains whether the overall outcomes of such changes have promoted the emancipation of peasantries as a subordinate class or perhaps only modernized traditional mechanisms of domination. The issue will be examined within the context of the theoretical approach based on patterns of solidarity in horizontal and vertical exchanges.

The evidence presented in this study will be gathered from the published literature; the effort is thus conceived as a historical analysis within the framework of exchange theory. The purpose of this study is to take stock of our current knowledge about some of the major peasant movements that have emerged in Latin America during the twentieth century and to explore the possibility of integrating this knowledge within an organized body of theory. An attempt will be made to assess the usefulness of the theory for organizing current knowledge as well as to assess the plausibility of the derived hypotheses. Stated in another form, our question will be: could the existing empirical generalizations about Latin American peasant movements have been deduced from the propositions developed in this study?

CHAPTER 2

Major Dimensions of Exchange Theory

REINFORCEMENT AND ELEMENTARY EXCHANGE

Although the problem of exchange in social relations had already been stated in the nineteenth century by Albert Chavannes (Knox, 1963), by classical anthropologists such as Marcel Maus, Malinowski, and Lévi-Strauss, as well as in Gouldner's (1960) analysis of the "norms of reciprocity," the systematic formulation of exchange theory began mainly with Homans's (1958) essay "Social Behavior as Exchange." Of the various approaches toward exchange theory formulated subsequently, that of Homans (1961) can be considered the least complex, since it is addressed only to what Homans calls "elementary" behavior, in other words, behavior motivated and reinforced by observable prior events experienced as rewarding by the actor.[1] Acknowledging his intellectual debt to the behavioristic social pscyhology of B. F. Skinner, Homans argues that interaction is determined by the rewards received by the actors as well as limited by the costs they incur. When the costs of an act outweigh the reward for the actor, the interaction becomes unattractive for him. As it is unusual that the provision of inducements to Other is in itself rewarding for Person without involving any cost (an ideal, but utopian condition), and as the same holds for Other, exchanges manifest a delicate mutual balance of costs and rewards in which neither party can obtain "perfect" outcomes, outcomes that entail the highest possible rewards with minimal costs. "The open secret of human exchange," according to Homans (1961: 62), "is to give the other man behavior that is more valuble to you than it is costly to him."

Homans conceives of exchange in terms of this "elementary" behavior, which is reinforced by past rewards regardless of the actors' subjective intentions and cognitions (1961: 80). While this approach may go far toward explaining behaviors that are indeed at the elementary level or when cognitive and cultural factors can be "kept constant" or accounted for as "unexplained variation," it has to be recognized that much (if not most) human behavior is more complex and involves cognitions, intentions, values, and norms that may produce or perpetuate behaviors independent of environmental conditioning factors (Singelmann, 1972; 1973a). Criticizing Homans's theory, Abrahamson (1970: 283–84) points out that not an actor's experience as such, but his perception of it (which can be culturally and psychologically mediated) determines his responses. What does and what does not constitute a reward thus depends on the meanings attributed by actors to the objects of their perception relative to their definition of the situation and their goals. Homans recognizes this difficulty himself when he concedes that in distributive justice the proportionality of costs, rewards, and investments depends on the actor's assessments, and that these assessments are subjective "matters of taste" (1961: 247). Thus, there can be ultimately no just society, although a degree of consensus may be achieved "among people who in similar backgrounds have acquired similar values" (1961: 247). This introduces both a cognitive as well as a cultural dimension into the definition of *reward,* a fact that has also been recognized by Homans in his discussion of "institutional behavior": in which elementary exchanges ("subinstitutional behavior") in complex social structures are mediated by indirect reinforcements and social norms (1961: chap. 18).

A further limitation of Homans's approach to exchange theory is his emphasis on the *frequency* of reinforcement, as witnessed by his first postulate. This approach becomes unfeasible in the explanation of many aspects of institutional behavior where what matters is not the frequency of a reward but whether it is given at all, whether it is given regularly, or whether it is given when needed. Two simple examples from peasant-landlord exchanges in Latin America may clarify this point: while certain quantitative aspects concerning the amount of outcomes are very crucial indeed (the amount of land rented to a sharecropper or the amount of his produce the sharecropper has to give to the landlord), certain benefits are qualitative and can be either received or not received. The right of tenants to use the pasture of the landlord, gather firewood on his property, use his roads, their obligation to give him the manure from their cattle, to have their wives and daughters work as servants in his town residence—these are rewards and costs of a qualitative nature, and peasant-landlord conflicts usually involve the overall legitimacy of these duties relative to the received privileges as much as they involve the relative amounts of the services exchanged. Another example is the occasional or regular "favors" that landlords grant to their peasants. When landlords contribute to their peasants' annual fiestas, the frequency (although not the amount) of these contributions is fixed in terms of the seasonal cycle. When landlords contribute medical assistance to their sick peasants, they can make such contributions only as often as one of the peasants is ill. While it is true that in traditional paternalistic peasant-landlord relations virtually no landlord completely takes care of all cases of illness among his peasants, so that there is some room for a greater or lesser frequency, it is evident from ethnographic observation throughout Latin America that what is perceived (and what motivates peasant behavior) is not the relative frequency of a landlord's medical assistance, but the peasants' overall perception of whether or not their *patrón* takes care of them. There is a hypothetical line separating a "bad" *patrón* from a "good" *patrón* who provides nothing or so little that he is not considered as benevolent. What matters is thus not a frequency continuum but a culturally defined dichotomy separating benevolent from "bad" *patrones,* and this dichotomy is not defined in terms of one specialized service (medical assistance) but in terms of the general contributions, attitudes, and favors of the landlord in a variety of contexts. This type of problem will have to be dealt with in the application of exchange theory to the analysis of interaction in institutional contexts.

EXCHANGE IN SOCIAL ORGANIZATION

Although Gouldner published an important statement on the "norm of reciprocity" in 1960, the extension of exchange theory beyond the simpler forms of elementary behavior to behavior in complex institutional structures has been primarily achieved by Peter Blau. Among the contributions of his *Exchange and Power in Social Life* (1964a), three may be highlighted:

First, Blau emphasizes the cultural and institutional matrix in which exchanges take place. Accordingly, social norms and their enforcement affect the reward–cost ratio of self-interested behaviors and render exchanges indirect by substituting generic rewards such as social approval for some of the rewards that would normally be received from other interactants directly (1964a: 255–63; 1964b: 200; Homans, 1961: 380). Shared values and norms mediate social exchanges by extending the range of social interactions over time and space (Homans, 1961: 263–73) and determining what constitutes "fair" rewards for given services rendered (Blau, 1964a: 156; 1964b: 195–96, 205). Finally, Blau emphasizes that exchanges become institutionalized, in other words, they become perpetuated beyond the life span of the individuals with whom they originated through formalization and the socialization of new group members into the values and norms supporting the current behavior patterns (1964a: 273–82).

Blau's second major contribution to the development of exchange theory is his analysis of power. Power, the capacity to modify the behavior of others according to one's desires (1964a: 115), is founded on a person's ability to apply coercion to others or on his superior control over resources and rewards needed by others (1964a: 117). Exchange, in which "the benefits each supplies to the other are rewards that serve as inducements to continue to supply benefits" (Homans, 1961: 21), can thus be either *bilateral* (where the mutual rewards are equivalent) or *unilateral* (where a person needs something from another without having at his disposal equivalent rewards as inducements) (Blau, 1964a: 21–22). In unilateral exchanges, manifestations of gratitude may initially be a sufficient reward for the person with the superior resources to provide the benefits needed by the other; but in the long run, unilateral exchanges give rise to differentiation of power (1964a: 21–22, 115–42), unless Other is able to force Person to give him the benefits, to provide inducements, to obtain them elsewhere, or to do without them (1964a: 22, 118–25). In this case, Other will have to subordinate himself to Person; "willingness to comply with another's demands is a generic reward, since the power it gives him is a generalized means, parallel to money, which can be used to obtain a variety of ends" (1964a: 22).

One mechanism that consolidates power in social relations is *dependence*. A person's dependence on another is defined in terms of the degree to which Person's alternatives are restricted, in other words, the degree to which Other is the only one who can offer Person the things he needs or desires. Dependence, as exchanges, can be unilateral or bilateral. To the extent that Person's dependence on Other is unilateral, his bargaining position is the weaker one and he may have to reciprocate for benefits received with the generic reward of obedience.

Coercion is a limiting situation involving power relations and extremely unilateral exchanges characterized by dependence. Coercion may be applied to forcefully restrict the alternatives of subordinates and thus fortify dependence. Or it may be applied to force others into unfavorable exchanges in which they would not voluntarily remain (Thibaut and Kelley, 1967). Applications of coercion have characterized the traditional *patrón*-campesino relations in Latin America.

Both coercive and noncoercive forms of power can become

institutionalized; they can become routinized patterns of interaction without the continual application of punitive sanctions on the part of the powerholders. Institutionalization in this sense does not necessarily entail legitimation. When subordinates grant legitimacy to the demands of a powerholder, the power of the latter becomes *authority*. In authority relations the exercise of power is thus judged by the subordinates in terms of social norms of justness and fairness. The greater the powers of a person over his subordinates, the greater the likelihood that given demands he makes will be considered legitimate by his subordinates; stated in other terms, the greater his power, the less his need to "exploit" (make unlegitimate demands to) his subordinates. Exploitation is likely to occur either when legitimate demands do not bring the desired ends or when legitimation is not relevant for the powerholder. In that case, legitimation is likely to be withheld and opposition to the powerholder will develop (Blau, 1964a: 199–223; 1964b: 202–4). On the other hand, the institutionalization of power relations through formalization and the socialization of new subordinates, as well as the manipulation of power per se, can perpetuate these relations even when a powerholder no longer provides all the services to the subordinates that originally legitimated his authority, or when these services become obsolete.

A third major contribution of Blau is his dialectic approach to the analysis of social dynamics, in terms of which the very processes through which social organization originates contain the seeds of its destruction and modification. This general idea is reflected in two major postulates: (1) there is a strain toward reciprocity and balance in social interaction, but (2) the same forces that restore balance in some respects create imbalances in others and thus give rise to a perpetual process of disequilibrium and reequilibration (1964a: 7). Such dialectics have two types of sources. The first type rests within the context of given interactions and leads to internal dilemmas. For example, in exchange partners always have some common and some conflicting interests; the very outstanding qualities that make a person an attractive associate make him also a threat to the other's independence; the more gratification one gets, the less one needs; and the very cultural values that legitimate institutional structures can also legitimate opposition to them if they fail to satisfy idealized expectations (for a summary, see 1964a: 314–21). The second source of imbalance rests in the interdependences of given exchanges with macrostructural processes that differentially affect the needs, values, and bargaining positions of the interactants. Empirically there exist no closed interaction systems; as the external macrosocial environment does not remain constant, it renders any microsystemic processes inherently unstable (1964a: 283–311).

This kind of analysis makes it possible to take the microsocial exchanges of campesinos as a point of departure for assessing the effects of macrosocial variables on the emergence of class solidarity. Much of this study can thus be dedicated to the analysis of macrostructural changes as they differentially affect the bargaining positions of campesinos and landlords. It is within the context of these changes in relative bargaining positions that the breakup of traditional *patrón*-campesino relations and the formation of campesino movements can be understood.

COGNITIVE ELEMENTS OF EXCHANGE

While both Blau and Homans have occasionally referred to cognitive factors in exchange (expectations, interpretations, awareness of alternative courses of conduct), neither of them has made an attempt to systematically incorporate cognitions into his theoretical scheme. Homans even explicitly rejects the necessity of dealing with the problem of consciousness, since "conscious" and "unconscious" behavior come out of the same place (1961: 80). While this argument is valid in the sense that actors usually do not "correctly" understand the larger structural implications of individually motivated acts, it would be erroneous to pretend that acts are not subjectively meaningful for the actors and that the meanings of acts do not constitute part of the actors' motivations. Person may indeed not understand the exchange he is engaged in in the way Homans does. But, as Homans concedes (1961: 82), Person usually is aware that he needs Other's help and that he wants (and is expected) to express his gratitude through praise. His behavior is thus not only cognitive but also self-directed in the sense that he sees himself as someone who needs help and interprets Other's actions in relationship to his needs (Singelmann, 1972).

The most systematic exploration of cognitive elements in exchange is found in Thibaut and Kelley's (1967) social-psychological approach to exchange. Like game theorists, they begin by outlining a matrix of all possible interaction outcomes and combinations thereof. But unlike game theorists, they reject the notion that actors optimize outcomes for themselves in terms of this matrix of "objectively available outcomes" (1967: 25), a position they share with Homans (1961: 80–81) and Blau (1964a: 18–19). Rather, they argue, actual behavior is determined by a matrix that describes the subjective understandings and anticipations of the possible interactions and outcomes, however inadequately these may represent the actual universe of possibilities (1967: 25). The conceptualization of exchange as a cognitive process is reflected in Thibaut and Kelley's key notions of *comparison level* (CL) and *comparison level for alternatives* (CLalt). The CL is "a standard by which a person evaluates the rewards and costs of a given relationship in terms of what he feels he 'deserves.'" It is "the standard against which a member evaluates the 'attractiveness' of the relationship or how satisfactory it is" (1967: 21). The CLalt is "the lowest level of outcomes a member will accept in the light of available alternative opportunities," the "standard a member used in deciding whether to remain in or to leave the relationship" (1967: 21).

The cognitive components of exchange are crucially important in the actors' conception of distributive justice. Lack of distributive justice, or inequity, can be conceived in terms of cognitive inconsistencies (imbalance, dissonance). Blau (1964b: 194–95) wrote:

The implication of the rule of justice is that men compare themselves with each other in terms of their investments as well as in terms of the rewards they receive for their services and expect differences in the latter to correspond to differences in the former. Their satisfaction depends not only on the absolute amount of reward they receive for their services but also on the fact that the expectations raised by these comparisons are not disappointed.

This point has been taken up by Alexander and Simpson (1964), who formulate the concept of justice in terms of cognitive balance. Accordingly, lack of justice implies an imbalance between perceived and expected outcomes for at least one interactant who perceives his rewards to be incommensurate with his costs and investments relative to the outcomes of Other (1964: 187–89). A person tends to restore balance in exchange by changing parts of his behavior or parts of the cognitions involved in the interaction (1964:189–91). As Alexander and Simpson point out, this balance factor in exchange limits man's hedonistic striving for increasing rewards, since a person's conception of justice requires him to grant a fair outcome-investment ratio to others as well as to himself. Men not only resent undeserved punishment and low rewards, they also feel uncomfortable with unearned rewards (1964: 187). J. Stacey Adams (1965) offers a similar formulation of equity in terms of cognitive dissonance. Defining inequity (lack of distributive justice) as the existence of unequal outcome-input ratios as perceived by at least one interactant (1965: 273), he proposes that the resulting tension is resolved by such means as Person altering his inputs or outcomes, distorting his inputs or outcomes cognitively, leaving the field, acting on Other(s), or changing his reference sources (1965: 283–95).

In general, Thibaut and Kelley (1967) provide the most extensive treatment of exchange imbalances and cognitive inconsistencies, and their work is directly relevant for explaining peasant movements. This approach becomes especially significant in the treatment of responses to deprivation and low status. Actors feel relatively deprived when they do not obtain outcomes at their CL in a relationship. As Thibaut and Kelley show, actors respond to the resulting discontent by (1) lowering their CL or (2) finding means to achieve the unattained outcomes. Examples of these responses are the devaluation of alternative relationships, a decrease in the salience of the good outcomes of alternative relationships, self-definitions imputing powerlessness, a shortening of one's time perspective, and aggression against powerholders or against self (1967: 173–84). Similar processes operate when low-status persons rationalize their inferior position in terms of superior service of upper-status individuals (1967: 229–31).

NETWORK ANALYSIS

The most visible expansion of exchange theory has taken place in the growing, although externally controversial and internally contradictory, movement of network analysis.[2] This approach is based on the radical position that social relations begin with *individual* interests and decisions, which constitute the basis for *social* interactions in small groups, which in turn are extended through the same kind of process to form larger social networks. While concrete analyses within this perspective tend to focus on small and intermediate-sized groups, the approach is theoretically expandable to larger groups or whole societies through an expanded network analysis that becomes increasingly complex. Given the determination of social relations by combinations of subjectively intended individual activities, social relations are in continuous flux, change, and readjustment. There can, hence, not be a fixed social order (Boissevain, 1973; Wolfe, 1978). Within this basis of analyzing social relations, the fulfillment of individual interests depends in part on potential benefits that may be received from interaction with others, but have to be reciprocated in order to (1) motivate others to provide these benefits and, specifically (2) motivate others to sacrifice some of the resources or benefits available to them. Hence, the radical extreme of network analysis offers an approach that conceptualizes social relations in terms of individual interests and the principle of constant change and readjustments that defy an understanding on the basis of conventional sociological conceptions of "social order," which tend to emphasize systems that guide and control "typical" and "normatively approved" patterns of conduct.

While this general perspective is frequently stated in such a radical form, concrete analyses of social networks tend to suggest patterns of social relations (illustrated in drawn networks that do not get erased and, in this sense, entail assumptions about regularities that are inconsistent with the radical theoretical approach). Given the complexity of constantly changing and multidimensional networks, most of the theoretical analyses of empirical data have focused on small groups as a "starting point." But a number of attempts have also been made to expand the network approach to whole communities and even large-scale societies.[3]

One general approach focuses on small groups, frequently (but not necessarily) conducts experimental research, and generally attempts to utilize the relatively more limited complexity of small groups to develop a "starting point" of established knowledge, which can subsequently be extended to social analyses of increasing theoretical complexity. While this approach tends to be dominant in network analysis, a number of authors are specifically attempting to develop generic principles of social conduct (for example, Heckathorn, 1978; 1979; 1980) through critical refinement of previous propositions and development of basic generic principles.

While this concern with generic principles is shared by exchange theorists in general, another approach (formalized by Hingers and Willer, 1979; Willer, 1980a; 1980b) focuses on the application of network analysis to large-scale, macrosocial dimensions of social organization. In this approach the potential for developing a generic theory of social relations is equally explicit (Willer's [1980a] reformulation of Weberian and Marxian theories of social class with a joint abstract conceptualization).

If social conduct is, however, conceptualized in terms of common collective interests and behavior patterns under given conditions, it is not possible to maintain the extreme position of unpredictable, continuously shifting, and individually determined social relations. Hence, network theory in its interpretation of real social phenomena cannot (and, indeed, does not if read closely) avoid generalizations and, by the same token, cannot analyze social conditions that limit and promote given patterns of behavior under given cultural-structural conditions.

Radical psychologistic reductionism has, thus, to be rejected, as does sociologistic determinism (Hingers and Willer, 1979: 183–84).

It is with the recognition of the complexity and contradictions inherent in social organization (Hingers and Willer, 1979: 184) that the starting point of social science, be it subjectivist or objectivist, must entail a dialectical recognition of special change entailed precisely by elements of stability, reproduction, and structures (Willer, 1980a).

In a similar vein, the issue of normative control has been related to problems of social stability, rather than to unpredictable and permanent transformation, in the work on "normative control" in exchange theory (Blau, 1964a) and specifically in network analysis (Southard, 1980; the debate between J. C. Mitchell, 1973; Boissevain, 1974: 228–33; and Banck, 1973). Within this context, network analysis has not been able to avoid the debate over social processes related to behavioral convergence and social stability.

In the study of peasant societies, there has been little question about structural dimensions of a certain regularity involving religious activities, extended family networks, redistribution, as well as mechanisms of domination and the macrosocial context-shaping structures of domination or supporting movements of rebellion. These patterns of stability, behavioral regularity, and changing conditions encouraging or being promoted by peasant movements are, in fact, reflected in the work of network analysis (Blok, 1973; Carlos and Anderson, 1980; Boissevain, 1974: chap. 5). A distinction should, therefore, be made between (1) the understanding of social networks as basic dimensions of social contact with direct motivational impacts on actors constrained, and offered alternatives, by larger structural unities, and (2) the radical assumptions of network analysis about the permanent change and infinite variety of network alternatives, assumptions that would be incompatible with any generic statements related to explanation and prediction and that would stand in the way of developing a network theory.

It is within this potential for generalizing propositions that network analysis and related approaches (particularly in anthropology) have offered models of (small- and large-scale) social organization that are promising for the analysis of contradictory obligations and interests of peasants. Traditionally, peasants have been involved in "triadic" social relations (peasant–other peasant (s) versus peasant–landlord or peasant–alternative brokers) and have had to resolve problems of deciding for horizontal versus vertical solidarity, rather than horizontal and vertical solidarity. While these types of models have been applied to fieldwork on traditional social structures and the effects of modernization, industrialization, and political development, particularly in Latin

America (Bourque, 1971; Cotler, 1969; 1970b; Craig, 1969; Dandler, 1969; 1971; Singelmann, 1975b; 1976), attempts have been made to formalize harmonious versus conflicting triadic models in various works via network analysis.[4]

DIRECTIONS OF EXPANSION

While the works of Homans, Blau, and Thibaut and Kelley have laid the foundations of systematic social analyses in terms of exchange relations, their very differences in terms of their theoretical assumptions and conceptualizations suggest that social exchanges are significant phenomena, independent of specific theoretical approaches or paradigms dealing with such processes in the social sciences. This is reflected in the expansion and critical refinements of the behaviorist (Emerson, 1972; 1976), and anthropological (R. N. Adams, 1975:68–93) approaches, as well as the formulation of exchange analyses in game–theoretical approaches (see Meeker's formulation of alternative exchange routes, 1971), functionalist approaches (Mulkey, 1971), social psychology (Chadwick-Jones, 1976), symbolic interactionism (Singelmann, 1973a; 1974; Schafer, 1974), ethnomethodology (Mitchell, 1978) and general social theory (Ekeh, 1974). While I do not agree with a position that would postulate that all social conduct should be analyzed in terms of exchange patterns, the growing literature from a variety of theoretical perspectives suggests that exchange systems and alternatives constitute a crucial element in social organization and social change.

IMPLICATIONS

From the previous analysis, the following implications can be derived:

1. Exchanges entail more than quasi-mechanical behavioral responses to reinforcing stimuli. They are constructed, emerge from interaction, and involve complex cognitive activities such as "definitions of the situation," formations of values and goals, evaluations of means, expectations of outcomes, and assessments of fairness.

2. Cognitions are not only individually constructed but also socially shared. Cultural values and social norms legitimize interaction patterns and provide a matrix within which exchanges take place. They make possible complex interactions and some degree of consensus about appropriate behaviors and fair returns for services or benefits rendered. Internalized cultural values and socially shared interpretations of the world motivate actors to

maintain institutionalized behaviors over time. Cultural patterns can thus become autonomous processes that tend to underwrite existing power and exchange relations. This explains in part the conservatism or traditionalism of social groups in the face of environmental (social, political, economic, ecological) changes.

3. Values, norms, and interpretations of reality are transmitted from generation to generation through socialization. Institutional structures perpetuate given exchanges over time; they provide a framework of constraints and opportunities for individual actors whose behaviors are subject to social control.

4. Power is a basic factor in the perpetuation of social relations even when the exchanges with which they had originated are no longer salient for the interactants.

5. Exchanges are inherently unstable because of endogenous dialectical contradictions and because they exist within a macrostructural framework that differentially affects the bargaining positions, values, and needs of interactants. Inconsistencies and conflicts arise (a) when individual actors change their definitions, values, or needs so as to render current outcomes unsatisfactory for them, and (b) when individuals' outcomes change and thus require either cognitive adaptations or a change in their behavioral outcomes. Exchange theory, as any theory of human behavior, has to incorporate the problem of the interdependence of, and imbalances between, actors' subjective cognitions and objective conditions.

It should be emphasized that these are only guidelines for analysis; their application must be determined by the specific historical context of given campesino movements. It should also be emphasized that the present theoretical framework draws on a variety of different exchange theorists, selectively incorporating elements that seemed to be helpful for this particular study. It is not implied that all social behavior involves exchange, but most probably does—provided we do not conceive of exchange in narrowly economic terms. It is with these considerations that in the following sections an exchange theory conceptualization of processes such as solidarity, dependence, and paternalism will be formulated.

CHAPTER 3

Dependence, Solidarity, and Paternalism

In the light of our interest in peasants' interactions with landlords and fellow peasants, this chapter will more narrowly focus on the issue of power, dependence, and solidarity among actors. One of Homans's more debated propositions suggests that in exchange the frequency of interaction is positively correlated to the degree of liking among actors (1961: 181–86), but he later qualifies this argument by stating that continued interaction that is punishing for some members who are unable to leave the relationship is more likely to result in hostility (1961: 186–87). In power-dependence relations the inferior members usually have limited possibilities for alternative relationships and would thus be expected to resent those with higher outcomes, especially in forced exchanges. On the other hand, the low-status or low-power members may define the powerholder's investments and services as superior to theirs so that the exchanges appear just; in this case, hostility on the part of the lower-status members will not be expected. Furthermore, it is possible that members whose power over others is very high may provide certain benefits to the subordinates that they would not have to provide in view of their superior power. In such a case they create additional trust and obligations in the subordinates, which in extreme cases may lead to their unconditional loyalty and affection. It is this kind of situation in which so-called paternalistic relations develop between superiors and subordinates.

UNILATERAL DEPENDENCE AND PATERNALISM

Paternalistic relations rest on power differentials. An actor's power over others rests in his ability to control relevant reinforcement contingencies of their environment (R.N. Adams, 1967b), in other words, he is able to modify their reward-cost differentials (profits) (Thibaut and Kelley, 1967: 100–101). This power base has three components: first, it is determined by the nature of the

30

coercive means available to the participants; second, it is determined by the degree to which a powerholder controls the resources to obtain what he and his subordinates need; third, it depends on the alternative sources of supply available to the subordinates, in other words, on their dependence on the powerholders. Blau (1964a: 115–25) has suggested that under conditions of unilateral dependence there are five alternatives for the dependent actors: they can supply inducements to the powerholders to furnish needed benefits; they can seek to obtain the needed benefits elsewhere; they can take what they need by force; they can do without what the powerholder has to offer; and, last, if none of these alternatives is possible, they have to reciprocate with the generic reward of compliance to the powerholder's wishes whenever he chooses to invoke the obligations the dependents owe him. Thus, the greater a person's control over the resources needed by others (including his ability to restrict access to alternative sources of supply), the greater his capacity to control their behavior according to his wishes. Power relations are thus exchanges in which subordinates provide general obedience in return for benefits they need but cannot obtain at better terms elsewhere; in some forced exchanges, the only returns for the subordinates may be survival or subsistence.

It is reasonable to propose that men place prime value on their survival and subsistence (Lenski, 1966: 37) and that to obtain it they are willing to make efforts that are more self-sacrificing than those expended in the pursuit of any other goal. Powerholders who control their subordinates' means of subsistence can therefore extend their scope of control over all spheres of the subordinates' lives, a condition that has been typical for traditional *patrón-campesino* relations in Latin America.

Authority may be defined in Max Weber's sense as legitimate power, as a power relationship in which the subordinates accept the superior's demands as justified and fair. Authority relations thus entail exchanges that are unilateral but fair (Blau, 1964a: 151–60), in other words, they exhibit "distributive justice." It is thus important to note that objective imbalances in exchange per se do not generate change if the demands of the powerholders are conceived as just by the subordinates in relation to the benefits provided. Thus, exchanges that are perceived as fair do not preclude exploitation. Under conditions of extreme unilateral dependence, as are usually found in peasant societies, the powerholders (such as landlords) thus have the option of returning minimal benefits to the subordinates and maintaining their domination primarily by force and other means to perpetuate dependence, or they have the option of providing benefits perceived by the subordinates as adequate, with occasional bonuses in the form of favors, gifts, or some kind of assistance.

The greater the power discrepancy between superiors and subordinates, the more the superior may legitimately demand from the subordinates, and the less the subordinates expect to receive from the superior. A corollary of the principle of distributive justice is that people expect to be neither underrewarded nor overrewarded. If a powerholder voluntarily provides benefits to which he is not considered to be obliged, his subordinates experience a discrepancy between perceptions and evaluations of outcomes (Alexander and Simpson, 1964: 187). They will be grateful and at the same time be more obligated to him to deserve their improved outcomes. This makes their services appear more voluntary and legitimate (since they are more rewarded), regardless of the fact that they may be objectively extorted. We can summarize the argument thus far in a number of postulates and corollaries:

Postulate 1: The greater Person's dependence on Other, the greater the scope of the power Other can wield over Person.[1]

Postulate 2: The greater the degree to which Person controls Other's means of subsistence, the greater Other's dependence on Person.

Corollary 1: The greater the degree to which Person controls Other's means of subsistence, the greater Person's power over Other.

Postulate 3: The greater the extent of Person's power over Other, and the greater the extent of Other's dependence on Person, the less Other expects from Person in return for his own services.

Corollary 1: The greater Person's power over Other, the greater the probability that voluntary and unexpected services on the part of Person to Other will create in Other (a) incentives to improve Person's outcomes, (b) Incentives to increase his own costs and investments in furnishing benefits to Person, (c) a tendency to define his current investment-outcome ratios as just, and (d) sentiments of unspecified obligations, trust, and loyalty to Person (Blau, 1964a: 108–9).

These are then the conditions of what may be denoted as paternalism: The powerholder controls a significant part of his subordinates' means of subsistence; the scope of his control over the subordinates' actions is large; he occasionally provides bonus services to which he is not strictly obliged and thus shows his good faith and benevolence; the subordinates respond to such benevolence with obedience, loyalty, and occasionally even affection. Benevolent paternalism is thus a mechanism for legitimizing patterns of societal differentiation and inducing low-status persons to accept their position.

The degree to which paternalism is benevolent is empirically variable and depends both on the frequency and amount of services, including bonuses by the superior, and on the subordinates' definitions of these services. It is precisely when power discrepancies between superiors and subordinates are large that the former can maintain their domination by threat and coercion alone without providing services that adequately legitimate their demands to the subordinates or even providing bonuses beyond those expected. For this reason, R. N. Adams (1964: 68–69) in his discussion of rural labor relations in Latin America defines paternalism as a relationship in which the employer has rights against labor, but labor has only (unenforceable) privileges against the employer. Because of the relative unenforceability of their demands, rural laborers in paternalistic relationships will appreciate what little they do receive.

Nonbenevolent paternalism is founded on power alone, usually coercive power, whereas in benevolent paternalism superiors use their power sparsely and provide appropriate services to their subordinates, who, in turn, define the demands of the powerholder as legitimate. Scholars have long recognized an inverse relationship between force and legitimacy in social relations (Lenski, 1966: 50–54; Blau, 1964a: 200–205). Legitimacy means that according to the subjective perceptions of Others (1) Person rightfully receives what he receives, and (2) Others rightfully expend their efforts as they do to provide to Person what he ought to receive. A powerholder will choose his power strategies among those alternatives that require least costs and investments relative to the rewards obtained. If he can provide services to his subordinates that are sufficiently valuable to them to serve as incentives for submission, and if these services cost him less than the use of force would, the result will be (1) that his domination will be legitimated, and (2) that he will not need to maintain his domination by the use of force.

The difference between benevolent and nonbenevolent paternalism has obvious implications for social change. In both cases it may be expected that subordinates will display extensive manifestations of submissiveness and subordination if these are among the conditions for their receiving what little they get. But only under conditions of benevolent paternalism can the balance of power be expected to be underwritten by supporting sentiments and definitions on the part of the subordinates. In the case of nonbenevolent paternalism, manifestations of deference may mask deep underlying hostilities and frustrations. In such a situation, it may take little more than a decline in the superiors' command over force to make the subordinates leave the relationship or change it in a reforming or revolutionary manner. Ideological changes or the development of new alternatives is not likely to be conducive to resistance in this case, since the subordinates are already dissatisfied with their situations and remain in the submissive alternative only for lack of means of coercion. Under conditions of benevolent paternalism, it is precisely ideological changes or the opening of alternative sources for obtaining the means of subsistence that leads to dissatisfaction among subordinates, but not their relative increase in coercive powers. In the first case, the subordinates change their behavior in response to the decreased *costs* of alternatives (no longer fear of coercion, loss of subsistence, or killing), whereas in the latter case subordinates respond to either dissatisfaction with current rewards or the increased attractiveness of the rewards from alternative responses. This is consistent with Thibaut and Kelley's proposition that persons instigate their behaviors increasingly from the cost components of outcomes as their powers decline (1967: 89). Since costs have been defined as the forgone rewards from alternative responses, our argument also states that people in high power are more likely to instigate their behaviors from the (low) costs of current choices, whereas people with low power are more likely to instigate their behaviors from the (high) costs of alternative choices. In summary:

Postulate 4: In exchange, the greater a powerholder's reliance on coercion to enforce his demands, and the less valuable his services to the subordinates, (a) the greater the probability that an increase in the subordinates' relative coercive power will lead them to revolt against him or to leave the relationship, and (b) the less the probability that ideological changes on the part of the subordinates, or the emergence of new alternatives for them, per se will induce them to revolt against the powerholder or leave the relationship.

Corollary 1: In exchanges, the better the perceived services by the powerholder to the subordinates and the less his use of coercion, (a) the less the probability that an increase in the subordinates' relative coercive power per se will lead them to revolt or to leave the relationship, and (b) the greater the likelihood that ideological change on the part of the subordinates, or the emergence of new alternatives for them, will lead them to modify or leave the relationship.

It should be noted that this juxtaposition of coercive and benevolent power relations is ideal-typical and should be viewed within the context of general theory. The reality of rural-class relations in Latin America has generally been closer to the coercive pole of the continuum. For this reason the postulate will apply to more cases than the corollary.

THE INSTITUTIONALIZATION OF PATERNALISM AND
DEPENDENCE

Responses to powerlessness and dependence, as they have been identified in the literature (Thibaut and Kelley, 1967: 173–81; Blau,

1964a: 151–60), can be classified as either active (entailing an active assault on the barriers) or cognitive (generally entailing the resolution of certain cognitive imbalances or dissonance). Thibaut and Kelley have argued persuasively that active responses to powerlessness, dependence, and deprivation are most likely to be adapted when they are perceived to have relatively good chances for success (1967: 181), while conditions of extreme powerlessness are likely to render the costs and risks of active responses too high, so that cognitive adaptions are most likely to be forthcoming (1967: 180). Such cognitive responses are thus partly due to past experience and correspondingly realistic expectations for the future; in part they also constitute rationalizations for accepting outcomes below the comparison level. Lowering the comparison level (aspirations, expectations) and magnifying external constraints exemplify this kind of adaptation (Thibaut and Kelley, 1967: 174–76). It is worthy of mention, however, that these cognitive adjustments often merely explain to the subordinate his deprivation without necessarily justifying it. He may lower his expectations but not his aspirations; he may submit to what he perceives as superior power (fatalism) without legitimizing his deprivation. Cognitive adaptations thus may keep him going without satisfying him. As will be elaborated in Part II of this book, these have been the traditional conditions of Latin American campesinos.

Cognitive adaptations that explain and excuse low outcomes to subordinates, the "mentality of dependence," characteristically include realistic assessments of opportunities and constraints as well as assessments of behaviors appropriate to given situations. Inasmuch as actors in similar situations are likely to share and communicate common definitions of the world, the *mentality* of dependence arising from individual cognitive adaptations to inferior positions becomes socially shared and reinforced by what has been called the *culture of repression* (Huizer, 1970b; 1972). Two aspects of such a culture must be distinguished. The first is that it consists of shared "definitions of the situation" that pragmatically guide behavior as a response to overwhelming constraints. These definitions include also normative standards for the subordinates when interacting with one another. The second aspect concerns the relationships with the powerholder. Again, pragmatic blueprints for behavior prescribing deference and submissiveness may be a part of this aspect, presumably resulting from simple reinforcement and fear of deprivation. But in this context the problem of the legitimacy of the powerholder's demands is another important dimension. Paternalistic relations resting predominantly on force will be culturally reinforced only in the sense that the subordinates, out of pragmatic necessity, internalize definitions and the modes of conduct that guide their action but handicap their ability to correctly define situations and their potential to develop behavior patterns that could liberate them from their subordinate position. Paternalistic relations founded primarily on the services exchanged receive additional cultural reinforcement by the normative standards that legitimate domination and submission, although it has to be noted that legitimation can also be bestowed on forced dependence when subordinates construct consistency between their evaluations and perceptions of outcomes by evaluating (or reevaluating) their submission as justified.

Among the types of definitions characterizing the culture of repression, the following have been suggested (Huizer, 1972: 7–19; Rogers, 1969: chap. 2): (1) a general world view holding that individuals of the community are relatively powerless to meet their needs and determine their destiny, (2) a belief that the world outside the community is hostile but powerful in its control over the individual's destiny, (3) pessimism about chances for improving one's situation in the future, (4) a short-term perspective focusing on moment-to-moment decisions and outcomes, (5) a belief that the individual members of the community are unable to protect themselves against hostile forces of the outside world and must therefore seek protection from some source in the outside world itself, (6) a belief that loyalty and obedience to a protector are a requisite for continued protection, and (7) an inclination to look for alternative protectors to obtain those things the present one does not provide. The most obvious person to seek as a protector may be the powerholder who controls the subordinate's outcomes, as long as there are no alternative protectors who can be played against the first. The greater the extent to which a protector-superior controls the means of subsistence of his protégés-subordinates, the greater the number of activities in which the latter follow the former as a clientele and the more they identify their own selves in terms of the protector.

While the culture of repression entails subjective definitions, these must be viewed within the context of structural constraints related to domination which gives rise to these definitions. These definitions are thus not the original obstacles to the emancipation of the subordinates, even if their function rests in adjusting individuals to a hostile and powerful environment. However, the behaviors that the definitions entail are enforced not only through the encroachments of powerholders from outside the subordinates' community, but also from within that community through socialization and social controls. They may therefore remain in force even when the environment has become less powerful and less hostile. The issue will be taken up again in Chapter 8.

To summarize the preceeding argument, we state:

Postulate 5: Powerlessness and dependence tend to generate manifestations of the culture of repression in the subordinates, which in turn reinforces existing patterns of domination.

SCARCITY, DEPENDENCE, AND SOLIDARITY IN TRIADS

When the means of subsistence in a group are scarce, exchanges can take one of two forms. Either there will be an all-out competition for survival with the result that the stronger members of the community survive comfortably while the weaker ones die, or patterns of interaction will arise that provide a minimum of security to everyone and tend to level differences in wealth. Anthropological evidence (see Chapter 8) suggests that in general the degree of precariousness of a community's subsistence is directly related to the members' inclination to be concerned primarily with security and the guarantee of a minimal livelihood. Such security can be obtained through various redistributive mechanisms as well as through the establishment for each member of a network of relationships with people he can trust for mutual help in times of need. As will be shown below, both of these adaptations have played an important role in Latin American peasant communities.

While scarcity encourages the establishment of security-directed networks of exchange and thus a degree of solidarity among the participants, it tends to undermine this same solidarity to the extent that the members of the community are likely to view any gains made by others as detracting from their own goods, unless these gains are perceived to come from sources outside the community. Thus arises the paradox that the members of the community must display a degree of solidarity in order to survive, while at the same time it is likely that there will be underlying tensions arising from fear, mistrust, and envy.

When under conditions of scarcity the members of a community are all more or less equally dependent on a powerholder outside the community who wields power over their means of subsistence, the relationships among them will depend upon the degree of generosity of the powerholder. If the powerholder regularly and amply provides all subordinates with what they need, the relationships between the latter may be relatively harmonious. But if, as scarcity implies, the powerholder dispenses his rewards only sparsely and unevenly, his services in themselves will be viewed by the subordinates as limited in supply, and each subordinate will seek to place himself in a favorable "survival-position" by attempting to get a maximal share of the superior's services (Homans, 1961: 132–38). The situation can be conceptualized as a triadic exchange, where each subordinate is involved in exchanges with both a powerholder and the other subordinates. Cooperation and solidarity are likely to develop among the subordinates when the rewards they receive from the interaction are greater than the rewards they would obtain from acting alone (Homans, 1961: 131), but in triadic exchanges, the relationship "is viable only to the degree that each member is above his CLalt; each member is thus dependent on only one of the others, a dyadic subgroup becomes an increasingly attractive alternative relationship, thus reducing the dependence on the triad" (Thibaut and Kelley, 1967: 220). In triadic relationships where two participants are both dependent on the third, solidarities between the two subordinates will develop only to the extent that they can provide mutual services to one another not provided by the third. But for each of the two subordinates, the relationships with the powerholder will override those with the other subordinate as long as the perceived conditions of power and dependence remain unchanged.

In triadic exchanges with unilateral dependence, subordinates and powerholders have different power strategies. For the powerholder who can keep the subordinates' resources scarce, it is relatively simple to play one subordinate against another by giving a limited amount of favors and privileges to those who display the greatest loyalty to him. The subordinates must thus compete for the powerholder's favors by acting in manners that further their own interests and especially those of the powerholders at the expense of those of their fellow subordinates. The maintenance of a relatively privileged position for a subordinate is thus contingent upon behaviors that interfere with the goal attainment of his fellows; the result will be mistrust and envy among the subordinates.

For the subordinate, the most obvious strategy is to seek alternative providers for things he does not obtain from the powerholder. In this situation, limited exchanges with members of his community may provide a few additional benefits, but if the basic necessities for subsistence cannot be obtained from within the community, a subordinate must seek sources outside the community for supply and protection. He may try to obtain privileges from the powerholder controlling the resources of the community; he may find additional protectors and providers outside the community whose services complement those of the local powerholder; or he may seek the assistance of an alternative protector whose interests conflict with those of the local powerholder and who can thus be played against the latter. However, the subordinates may not gain any increased autonomy from this latter strategy since the alternative protector may manipulate them for his own interests without providing significantly improved services. Subordinates can thus improve their position with this strategy only when their interests are complementary to those of the new protectors. We can summarize this argument in two postulates:

Postulate 6: In triadic exchanges with unilateral dependence of two subordinates on one powerholder, the more exclusively the powerholder controls the subordinates' subsistence needs, (a) the less each subordinate perceives gains from interaction with other subordinates, (b) the less each subordinate will interact with other subordinates, (c) the more interaction each subordinate will seek with the powerholder.

Postulate 7: Under conditions of scarcity in unilateral triadic exchanges, a limited amount of extra favors granted by the powerholder to some subordinates (a) motivates each subordinate to provide maximal services to the powerholder in order to obtain these favors, (b) motivates those subordinates who enjoy special privileges to maintain them by placing loyalty to the powerholder over loyalty to their fellow subordinates, (c) encourages in the subordinates the perception that their neighbor's gain is their own loss, (d) results in competition among the subordinates for the extra privileges, and (e) creates fear, distrust, and hostility among the subordinates.

In the following chapters we shall examine the utility of this theoretical framework for analyzing traditional Latin American peasant communities and their relationships with powerholders.

PART II

Horizontal and Vertical Solidarities
in Latin America: Traditional Parameters

CHAPTER 4

Traditional Rural-Class Relations and Economic Mechanisms of Domination

TRADITIONAL RURAL-CLASS RELATIONS IN LATIN AMERICA: SOME HISTORICAL PERSPECTIVES

Latin American rural-class relations had their historical origins in the Spanish and Portuguese colonization patterns during the sixteenth and seventeenth centuries.[1] In both Spain and Portugal the crown needed the services of European colonists as well as of Indian laborers to exploit the rich natural resources of the New World. In the Spanish colonies the colonists were compensated for their services through land grants (*mercedes reales* or *mercedes de tierra*) and the right to extract specified tributes and labor services from the indigenous population. Direct slavery was quite common, although there were various attempts on the part of the crown and of humanitarian elements in the New and Old World to limit and later prohibit it. Apart from slavery, the crown granted what was known as the *repartimiento,* which allowed the colonists to use circumscribed forms of forced Indian labor in their households, fields, and mines. The *ecomienda* granted the colonists the right to exact specified tributes in kind and often personal services from neighboring Indians. Both the *repartimiento* and the *ecomienda,* while often abused by the settlers, could function only because the Indians were expelled from their lands and forcefully resettled in corporate communities on lands granted to them by the crown (Wolf, 1957). In the case of the *encomienda,* the Indians, while living in their own communities, came to be legally bound to serve given landed estates and would remain in these services even when the owner changed. The corporate Indian communities were under the direct jurisdiction of the royal colonial administration and thus enjoyed some protection against the encroachments of trespassing *encomenderos,* although the latter expanded their lands and powers continually throughout the colonial period and thus weakened the effective power of the crown. Although the corporate Indian

43

communities governed themselves autonomously under their own *caciques* and enjoyed some protection from the royal bureaucracy, the evident policy of the crown was to keep their lands to a minimum so that they would be impelled to offer their labor services to the colonists in order to meet their subsistence and ceremonial needs (Wolf, 1957).

After the colonies achieved independence, the owners of the large estates (haciendas, *fazendas*) no longer faced the opposition of the royal administration in their expansion at the expense of the Indian communities. Subsequently many Indian villages lost their lands, but it has been pointed out that there were inherent limits to the growth potential of a hacienda due to its lack of capital, the traditional technology of its labor force, and the limited demand structure of the colonies (Wolf, 1965: 90–91). When the expansion of the hacienda had reached the limit of its potential, it could offer to the Indians not only opportunities for supplementing their ceremonial and subsistence funds but even a measure of protection against newly strengthened groups outside the community who were trying to convert the communal lands into marketable commodities (Wolf, 1965: 91–92). Indians and landholders thus forged a "hostile symbiosis" (Wolf, 1965) that allowed each group to draw on the services provided by the other, with the superior power clearly resting in the hands of the large landholders.

The development of the hacienda as a relatively self-sufficient community with direct control over the resident labor force was not an original consequence of the conquest. The *encomienda* involved temporary privileges to tributes and services from Indians in a specified community, but it did not grant legal titles to landed property (Wolf, 1965: 90; Konetzke, 1965: 52). The *mercedes de tierra* did grant such titles but did not include the automatic privilege to settle one's own labor force on the estate, and there were set legal limits as to the amount of land that could be granted. Furthermore, it was a principle of the Spanish policies that land grants to colonists should not restrict the property rights of the Indian communes. Such policies favored the development of medium-sized estates, but the more enterprising and ruthless settlers were gradually able to buy additional lands under various legal and semilegal circumventions of the crown's policy, thus building up the large *latifundia* that came to dominate the political life of the New World.

In the Spanish colonies the haciendas not only utilized the Indian part-time labor granted through the *repartimiento* and *encomienda,* but could also bind full-time labor to the estates through the institutions of *naboria* (Caribbean, Mexico) and *yanacona*

(Peru). These institutions provided personal and domestic servants to the *hacendados*. While in fiction these servants entered into a free contract with the landlord that could be dissolved, in reality they quickly turned into hereditary serfs not unlike the Roman *coloni* who were personally free but hereditarily tied to the soil. Apart from those who were more or less forcefully pressed into this service, many Indians who had lost their lands, were misfits in their own communities, or had fled their villages to escape forced labor in the mines, voluntarily turned to the haciendas for food, work, and protection. By settling within the domain of the estates, these Indians "abdicated much personal autonomy in exchange for heightened social security" (Wolf, 1965: 90). Thus developed the *colono*, a peasant who entirely depended on the landlord for his subsistence. He received a plot of land to produce part or all of his livelihood, in return for which he had to provide part of his crops, animals, labor, and a variety of other services to the *hacendado* (R. N. Adams, 1967a: 98; S. Schulman, 1955). Some of the poorest peasants in Latin America belonged in this category. Sharecroppers were in a similar position to the *colonos*, but their relations with the landlords were more contractual. They rented a given amount of land for which they paid with a certain percentage of their produce. They thus had as little control over the land they worked as the *colonos*, but they were more mobile (R. N. Adams, 1964: 60).

The hacienda in Spanish America may originally have been commercially oriented to provide subsistence necessities for the mining centers (Frank, 1969: 235–39), but the economic development in the colonies became increasingly differentiated (although within inherent limitations) and moved in different directions. On the one hand, with declines in the initially booming mining industries, the hacienda turned inward into a community with strong economic, juridical and political autonomy under the patriarchic domination of the landlord. As such, it operated largely outside the money economy and tended to remunerate its laborers in kind or with token coins that could be exchanged in the hacienda store (*tienda de raya*) for subsistence necessities. As a result, debt peonage was common among the labor force, which thus became legally tied to the estate and could be bought and sold with it (Tannenbaum, 1960: 77–94). The Brazilian *fazenda* developed into a similarly autonomous and patriarchically ruled community; the situation in Brazil differed from that in the Spanish colonies mainly in the relatively greater weakness of the royal colonial administration and the correspondingly larger degree of local autonomy of the *fazendeiros*, many of whom were impoverished aristocrats who brought their followers with them to their huge estates and preserved many feudal traditions (Konetzke, 1965: 57–58; for a fuller account of the Brazilian variant, see Vianna, 1949, vol. 1; Passos Guimarães, 1964).

On the other hand, new mining sectors and related activities developed to meet different demands in industrializing Europe; within the same context, the large-scale production of agricultural surpluses to meet increasing demands for cheap food in industrializing Europe increased the importance of surplus food produced for exportation to the industrializing areas. Such commercial production, however, did not necessarily lead to increasing monetary remuneration for labor. Given the extent of domination and the large areas of land in possession of the hacienda but usable for the rural labor force to produce its own means of reproduction as "peasants," even haciendas producing for monetary profit within the export sector were to a large extent able to remunerate their labor in kind, and at minimal cost, rather than with money. Toward the nineteenth century, this type of structure became increasingly important for subsidizing labor and certain capital costs in the European core areas of industrialization, while at the same time shaping the limitations of peripheral capitalist development in Latin America.

TRADITIONAL RURAL-CLASS RELATIONS

Rural-class relations during the colonial and postcolonial periods have varied a great deal in terms of socioeconomic structures (class relations, mechanisms of domination), specific historical variations, and degrees of stability (in terms of structural continuity as well as in terms of political-military stability within given time periods). But certain basic structural elements of class relations tended to persist and be shared across different colonial (or neocolonial) subsystems such as slavery, haciendas, plantations, sharecropping, and other arrangements structured around landlords' surpluses and the minimization of their monetary costs of production.[2] The large landowners, in Europe (Postan, 1972; Kula, 1976; Wallerstein, 1976) as well as under the different conditions in Latin America, have had the flexibility to remunerate their labor forces either in kind (means of subsistence), with land use (enabling them to produce their own means of reproduction or commodities sold at prices ensuring the purchasing of their means of subsistence), or with salaries, according to the historically variant larger economic constraints and opportunities. By the same token, their labor forces moved from one category of the lower class to another. The crucial issue is not so much such shifting, whether or not in tendentially permanent directions, of these mechanisms of exploitation, but (1) whether or not these shifts tended in given cases to result in instabilities by unbalancing previously balanced (but not equal) relations between landlords and peasants-laborers, and (2) whether or not imablances unfavorable to the peasants-laborers led to rebellions entailing either a rebalance of this structure (repression, upper-class compromises) or revolutionary changes. It should be emphasized, however, that these generic conceptualizations of the traditional rural lower class are not intended to deny that the concrete social conditions, and corresponding alternatives of the traditional rural lower classes, significantly vary between different types of domination and exploitation. Thus, the concrete conditions for social movements also vary accordingly (Moore, 1966; Wolf, 1969; Paige, 1975). What is argued is simply that within this conceptualization of alternative structural patterns, analyses of given patterns of domination and change can all be predicted within a generic theoretical perspective linking balances and imbalances of social exchanges to patterns of submission and resistance to class domination.

While it is always an ideal-typical simplification to begin with such alternative models of stability versus change, I would argue that for the purpose of this study it is historically defensible and theoretically useful to begin the analysis with a model of traditional peasant-class domination in terms of the processes that tended to contribute toward stability and rebalancing, although always under serious challenge by peasant resistance and class struggles, with historically variant degrees of successful resistance, and without suggesting that the inherent contradictions of class relations at hand were resolved.[3] What is taken as a point of departure is, however, a conceptualization in terms of which the notion and process of social inequality and exploitation are not equivalent to assuming that the subordinate classes always tend to seek radical change beyond rebalancing social relations toward acceptable outcomes and perhaps seeking to increase the chances to improve the social position within the given structures of class relations.

In traditional rural-class relations, land and labor were the initial dimensions on which colonial class structures were primarily founded. There was always, however, a greater degree of complexity than a conceptual focus on land and labor may suggest. The lower classes always had multiple resources for survival, with variations over time in terms of shifting emphases. Within the structure of constraints placed by the dominant class of landowners, the alternatives available to peasants for insuring their subsistence included land use for their own production, wages, small-scale commercial ventures to supplement subsistence and/or surpluses transferred to the ruling class, and a variety of other activities. Crucial in this kind of pattern are the opportunities the peasants have for at least maintaining their means of subsistence. While peasant societies in general include producers with potentials to accumulate part of their surpluses, rather than being maintained at their given levels of subsistence, it may be argued that a crucial dimension is the general tendency of peasants to be maintained at given levels of subsistence without capital accumulation, regardless of how much labor they provide and what amount of surplus they produce. Hence, the persistence of peasantries in surplus-producing economies is not founded on inherent economic mechanisms but rather mediated by patterns of power relations that enforce exploitative economic relations, or possibly on redistributive horizontal mechanisms of exchange entailing equalization within the peasant community and ceremonial uses of surpluses. It is these two processes of vertical exploitation and horizontal processes or redistribution that tend to maintain rural societies as peasant societies, but with opposite implications for the peasants' motivations toward maintaining a given social order. In the case of landlord domination, it is generally the process of dependence and domination that submits the peasantries to unequal exchange systems, regardless of the specific context (hacienda, plantation, peasant household, or additional sources of reproductive requirements) within which production operates.

Given the colonial domination based on conquest, rather than on socially evolved patterns of legitimate authority and domination, the landlords' access to cheap labor was based on an almost total disregard for formally existing native rights. Hence, levels of exploitation, over imported slaves or native Indians, tended to be limited only by potential losses and nonreplaceability of the labor force required by the colonists, or to the extent that native resistance became too costly for the dominant class. Under these conditions, increases in production under increasing (European) market demands tended to be based less on capital investment than on expanded use of land and increases in the labor force (given the availability of, and control over, both). There was, under these conditions, little stimulation for the landlords to increase their production by raising productivity through capital investment (Amin, 1974; 1975; Singelmann, 1978). In this manner, the dualism in the colonial economies entailed a separation of two interdependent social classes, not within a given mode of production, but in a social formation that integrated capitalist development in northwest Europe with the growth of local upper classes at the "periphery," whose enterprises tended to limit their capital development and instead depended on a rural labor force whose low cost was based on its continual involvement in precapitalist economic subsystems (Amin, 1974; Bartra, 1974; Bennholdt-Thomsen, 1976; Marini, 1973; Schirmer, 1976; Wolpe, 1975; Senghaas, 1974; Singelmann, 1978).

This economic system entailed inherent contradictions. Given its dependent incorporation within a forming world economy, and its dependence on the international market of a few specialized products in agriculture and mining, changing market demands and falling prices constantly threatened the persistence of given subeconomies within the colonies. In contrast to classical capitalist processes, colonial (and postcolonial) enterprises tended to respond to lowered demands and prices for their export products by increasing either their production or the rates of exploitation in order to compensate for the price declines. In either case, within this process the contradictions in the colonial economies were exacerbated. Over time, such problems may have been resolved for a while due to rebalances in the market process, in other cases they have led to more gradual long-term declines of profitability, and in many cases they led to spectacular rises and downfalls such as the Brazilian rubber plantations around the turn of the twentieth century. Under these conditions, colonial and neocolonial economies within the international capitalist system have constantly moved from specialized crops and mines to other areas under market booms that emerged for a given time.

It is the recognition of this pattern of contradictions, cycles, attempted adjustments by the upper classes, and peasant resistance to worsening conditions that we can add to the understanding of Latin American peasant movements. Within class structures, the differentiation in terms of power and exploitation can be analyzed in terms of the unequal exchanges they entail and the corresponding mechanisms of dependence, exploitation, and resistance. In the following section, some of the specific effects of such an economic basis on patterns of social control are discussed.

TRADITIONAL PATRÓN-CAMPESINO RELATIONSHIPS IN LATIN AMERICA

The differentiation of power between landlords and campesinos that originated in the conquest and subsequent forceful colonization of the continent still finds its present-day manifestation in the concentration of land in the hands of relatively few large landholders, while the mass of the campesinos owns only a minute fraction of the areas under cultivation. This coexistence of few

TABLE I *Relative Number and Area of Farm Units by Size Groups in ICAD Study Countries*
(Percentage of country total in each size class)

Country	Sub-family	Family	Multi-family Medium	Multi-family Large	Total
Argentina					
Number of farm units	43.2	48.7	7.3	0.8	100.0
Percentage of farm area	3.4	44.7	15.0	36.9	100.0
Brazil					
Number of farm units	22.5	39.1	33.7	4.7	100.0
Percentage of farm area	0.5	6.0	34.0	59.5	100.0
Chile					
Number of farm units	36.9	40.0	16.2	6.9	100.0
Percentage of farm area	0.2	7.1	11.4	81.3	100.0
Colombia					
Number of farm units	64.0	30.2	4.5	1.3	100.0
Percentage of farm area	4.9	22.3	23.3	49.5	100.0
Ecuador					
Number of farm units	89.9	8.0	1.7	0.4	100.0
Percentage of farm area	16.6	19.0	19.3	45.1	100.0
Guatemala					
Number of farm units	88.4	9.5	2.0	0.1	100.0
Percentage of farm area	14.3	13.4	31.5	40.8	100.0
Peru					
Number of farm units	88.0	8.5	2.4	1.1	100.0
Percentage of farm area	7.4	4.5	5.7	82.4	100.0

Subfamily: Farms large enough to provide employment for less than 2 people with the typical incomes, markets, and levels of technology and capital now prevailing in each region.
Family: Farms large enough to provide employment for 2 to 3.9 people on the assumption that most of the farm work is being carried out by the members of the farm family.
Multifamily Medium: Farms large enough to provide employment for 4 to 12 people.
Multifamily Large: Farms large enough to provide employment for over 12 people.
Source: Barraclough and Domike, 1970: 48.

large estates (*latifundia*) with a large number of subsistence-size plots (*minifundia*) has been documented in recent surveys of Latin American countries, as shown in Table 1.

Due to limitations in measurement techniques this table actually underestimates the extent of land concentration (Barraclough and Domike, 1970: 49–50; CIDA, 1966a: 106), but it reflects the degree to which the resources on which Latin America's rural population depends for its subsistence are monopolized by a relatively small landed elite.[4] Since in most Latin American societies the population actively engaged in agriculture varies between 51 and 83 percent of the total population (CIDA, 1963: 53), there exist throughout the continent a large number of campesinos with insufficient or no lands who depend heavily on larger landholders to provide for their livelihood (Feder, 1967: 99–102) and have to accept whatever terms are set by the latter for providing land and employment. While the tenure and labor arrangements vary regionally, we may consider Martínez's (1963b: 40–42) account of the labor relations of a contemporary (1960) hacienda in the Peruvian highlands as an example of the type of unilateral exchange associated with power imbalances between campesinos and *hacendados*. The service-tenants (*yanaconas*) had the following obligations: (1) One hundred sixty workdays for the estate as service-rent for the use of a plot of estate land; (2) additional services without payment when required, such as to watch over the estate's crops, look after harness and harness room, supervise field labor, domestic service in the owner's home, various backyard tasks; compensation consisted of a meal when the work period included a mealtime, and a ration of coca; (3) to pay for pastorage by the delivery of part of the annual increase, provision of beasts of burden, and use of the *yanacona*'s cattle to manure the fields; (4) a variety of petty obligations such as fines when something prejudicial happened to the landlord during the tenant's work period. In return for these duties, the *yanacona* had the right (1) to cultivate his allotted plot as he wished; (2) to plant corn or potatoes on special lands set aside for this purpose for payment of additional rent; (3) to pasture his cattle on the above terms and benefit from the manure of the owner's cattle when they grazed his field after the harvest; (4) to one lamb per year from the owner's flock; (5) to receive fifty centavos and a ration of coca or corn beer as payment for the obligations fulfilled each week.

Similar labor and tenancy arrangements have been reported throughout most of Latin America.[5] An extreme case of this sort is the *cambão* in Brazil. As Correia de Andrade has described it (1963: 200),

This means that the tenant is obliged to give the owner one day per week to work free of charge. . . . It is a personal obligation as a "homage" to the owner which implies that in some areas it is not allowed that the tenant pay someone else to undertake this task. (translation from CIDA, 1966a: 227)

Such tenancy patterns involve campesinos who reside on the property of the haciendas, but it should be noted that the domination of the landowners also reaches independent smallholders and members of indigenous communities. These may have to fulfill some obligations to the landholder in return for the privilege of passing across estate lands to reach roads, of using water from a brook that passes through the estate (CIDA, 1966a: 174), of marketing their produce through the aid of the landholder (Hobsbawm,

1969: 43), and of augmenting their livelihood through part-time labor (R. N. Adams, 1964: 59).[6]

As a result of the differential control over land, the power of the landholders over the campesinos in their domain was almost total during the colonial period and has by no means been destroyed today in many parts of Latin America. The concrete practice of this domination is indicated by Barraclough and Domike's summary description for traditional rural Latin America:

Tenants and workers on the large estates depend on the *patrón* for employment—there being no alternatives—and for a place to live. Wage and rental agreements can be adjusted to suit the landowner's convenience so that all productivity increases and windfall gains accrue to him. Permanent improvements such as buildings or fruit trees belong to the estate even when all the costs are borne by the tenant. On many large plantations residents are strictly forbidden to make improvements without permission for fear they would acquire vested interests in the land or take resources away from the production of the cash plantation crop. Residents of the large estates can be expelled at will in traditional areas where there is neither a strong central government nor a labor union to defend them. The ICAD researchers found haciendas in certain Andean regions which required that people of the neighboring communities work without pay in order to have the right to use the paths and bridges on the property. In some cases the administration's consent is required even to receive visitors from outside or to make visits off the property. Even though it was prohibited as long ago as the seventeenth century, the practice of "renting out" workers still persists. And corporal punishment is still occasionally encountered on some of the most traditional plantations and haciendas. Tenants depend on the *patrón* for credit, for marketing their products, and even for medical aid in emergencies. Food and clothing are frequently obtained through the estate's commissary and charged against wages or crops. (1970: 53–54)

These power relations were maintained through a variety of institutional mechanisms in the economic, social, political, and cultural-psychological spheres. They will be examined in the following chapters.

ECONOMIC MECHANISMS OF DOMINATION

The general economic context of the campesinos' dependence in Latin America has been extensively documented and well synthesized by Feder (1971; see also Smith, 1969). Perhaps the most basic problem is the ever-increasing concentration of land in the hands of *latifundistas* with the concomitant crowding of the vast majority of the rural population in *minifundias*. Underutilization of labor and capital and inefficient management of the large estates have generally combined to produce not only unemployment or underemployment in the agricultural labor sector but also a striking underperformance in agricultural production (Griffin, 1969: 75–

80). According to Feder (1971), a major reason for this condition is the general orientation of most large landholders toward maintaining traditional rural dependency relations rather than toward maximizing productivity.[7]

The coercive control of the large landholders over the campesinos' means of subsistence has provided the primary institutional mechanisms for the perpetuation of exploitative class relationships in rural Latin America, as it enabled the landholders to impose highly arbitrary and unfavorable labor and tenancy conditions on their dependents. It is generally a strategy of the landholders to provide minimal benefits to their workers so as to maximize their own gain and avoid establishing a precedent for future claims by the workers. Conversely, any claims by workers against the landholders are perceived by the latter to constitute bona fide violations of the work contract or customary obligation and are answered with repression or dismissal of the claimants. A description of tenure relations in a Brazilian rural community by J. Ferreira de Alencar (cited in CIDA, 1966a: 573–74) is illuminating. Referring to a simple matter such as a sharecropper's desire to use his own seed rather than that supplied by the landlord, Ferreira explains:

If one makes the assumption that the sharecropper would insist on planting his own seed, given the existing values, nothing would be more logical for the owner of the enterprise or his agent to conclude that this sharecropper wishes to obtain in the future some additional right beyond those commonly established by the contract of sharecropping. If such a proposal would come from a worker not yet admitted to the farm, but candidate to a parcel, it would be only with difficulty that he would become a sharecropper. If he is already a sharecropper on halves of the enterprise, he would not receive another parcel to begin his plantings. If he were to insist, he would be dismissed from the farm for breach of the original contract and without receiving any indemnification. . . . in the words of the owner "since he left of his own will, that is he created the situation to leave." This problem can only arise in the realm of hypothesis since the producer who is well integrated in the social organization of the community. . . . makes a careful selection before admitting any workers with a view to avoiding conflicts and tensions on his property.

Such economic constraints founded on social dimensions of powerlessness and dependence have historically led to social relations in which peasants tended to be totally dependent on their *hacendadas* for their access to economic resources within the larger economic structure. In this context, Pearse's (1975; 130) observations on prerevolutionary Bolivia apply to conditions that have been common throughout the continent: "The *haciendas* represented a multi-cellular container in which the peasant could be put to work in permanent dispersion and isolation, prevented from aggregating into a social force with common aims and symbols and appropriate internal structuring.'' It is worth examining some of the mechanisms whereby landholders have traditionally been able to fortify their position by increasing the poverty and debts of their tenant-laborers.

POWER MONOPOLIES AND RURAL POVERTY

As a result of several combined factors, the level of living of a large number of campesinos tends to remain at or below the subsistence level.[8] Apart from the ecological aspects (underemployment, underutilization of land, population pressures [Feder, 1969a: 416–23; Barraclough and Domike, 1970: 44, 55–63], wages are notoriously low in areas where labor is abundant and minimum-wage laws are unenforced (CIDA, 1966a: 194–297; Julião, 1962: 54–56, 62; Foland, 1968, no. 23: 2–3), so the campesinos have to struggle continuously on the margins of existence. The salaries of the Ecuadorian *huasipunegeros* ''correspond more to a fiction than a reality'' (CIDA, 1965b: 144). In Brazil it has been observed that the cash expenditures of rural workers and small farmers continually exceed their cash receipts as a result of rising food prices (CIDA, 1966a: 266, 283) and ''the systematic undermining of opportunities for accumulating savings on the part of the employers and landlords'' (CIDA, 1966a: 566). Factors contributing to such a precarious financial situation are various. Wages are kept as low as possible, frequently by circumvention of minimum-wage laws (Feder, 1969: 424). Landholders may switch back and forth between different wage schedules and tenancy forms in ways that keep the wages constantly low while maximizing their own profits (CIDA, 1966a: 237). Rents are raised and lowered according to the renter's productivity to siphon off any surplus, or the work load of laborers may be expanded or intensified in ways that wipe out wage increases (CIDA, 1966a: 272; A. Leeds, 1957: 457). Then there are a variety of monopolies and restrictions imposed on renters and laborers that function to prevent the accumulation of savings. Landholders order their tenants to plant certain crops and prohibit the planting of others, especially of cash crops; such restrictions have been reported in Brazil (CIDA, 1966a: 239), Colombia (Gilhodès, 1970: 412; Hirschman, 1965: 141–42), and Peru (Craig, 1969: 284, 285; CIDA, 1966c: 277–83). Frequently workers are forbidden to plant permanent types of crops or to make improvements on the plots (such as building or mending a house), since this would give them rights to the plot or would require the landlord to pay an indemnity upon dismissal of the worker-tenant (Craig, 1967: 21; Feder, 1969a: 428–29; CIDA, 1966a: 230–31).

The traditionally monopolistic position of the landholders has adversely affected the campesinos' position in the market:

1. Frequently campesinos, especially those who utilize estate land under various tenancy arrangements, are forced to rent their equipment and buy their foodstuffs, seeds, and tools from the landlord at exorbitant prices, which are charged against their wages and other remunerations. The company store, traditional on the large estates (Tannenbaum, 1960: 84; White, 1969: 106), is still surviving by virtue of the landholders' power to dictate the terms of employment and tenancy, and because of the prohibitive remoteness of many estates from the market towns (CIDA, 1966a: 238). Informants from large estates in northeast Brazil still remember the days (before 1929) when the *fazendas* were truly closed worlds where the workers never received any cash and small merchants could enter the estates only at the express order of the owner or clandestinely at night (CIDA, 1966a: 291).

2. Campesinos are not only restricted in their buying power, but they are also frequently forced to sell their own produce below the market price to the *hacendados* (CIDA, 1965b: 254–55; 1966b: 192–97; Wilkie, 1964: 5). In part this dependence is due to the isolation of the estates, which makes market centers almost inaccessible to the campesinos residing on estates, and in part the general power of the landholders is sufficient to enforce unfavorable prices on the peasants; these arrangements may be considered a modified form of sharecropping where rent payments in produce are lowered a little by a small cash compensation (CIDA, 1966a: 200–209).

3. The frequent de facto monopoly of large landholders over credit facilities provides another source of dependence for the campesinos (Feder, 1969a: 417; Smith, 1969). If landholders refuse to cosign loans of their campesinos at established banks, they are able to lend them money themselves at usury rates; a Brazilian farmworker reported the annual interest rate of a loan received from the landholder at 100 percent (CIDA, 1966a: 239). As a result of the campesino's lack of cash, he is in danger of continuous indebtedness that leaves him at the mercy of his creditors. Debt peonage has been a traditional mechanism on large estates in Latin America for retaining a subservient and powerless labor force. This pattern has been aided by the relative self-sufficiency of the classical hacienda (Tannenbaum, 1960: 84), which made it possible to minimize monetary operations in the sustenance of the estate.

Labor was preferably remunerated in kind, and residents of the estate had to buy their necessities in the hacienda store, which kept an account for the debts of the buyers. These debts could be paid off in principle, usually through labor, but the campesinos were rarely able to accumulate enough credits to cancel their constantly rising debts. Without payment of these debts, they were not allowed to leave the estate. Labor over and above the traditional obligations was generally remunerated in token coins that could only be exchanged in the hacienda store and sometimes bore imprints such as *vale un dia de trabajo* (worth one workday) (Tannenbaum, 1960: 84). One consequence of this system, which systematically deprived the campesinos of cash, was to maintain a pattern of particularistic obligations and dependencies that restricted the alternatives and choices of the peasants.[9]

DEBT PEONAGE

Debt peonage represented one of the mechanisms whereby the control of landlords over the rural labor force shifted from its formal restrictions via the colonial administration to the unlimited domination of the *patrones* over the campesinos (Pearse, 1975: 35–36).

Debt peonage existed in Mexico until the revolution of 1910 (White, 1969: 106) and is still operating in some countries. In Ecuador the salaries of the *huasipungueros* are rarely high enough to enable them to pay off their previous accumulated debts, since they are paid irregularly and mainly in kind; with these means the owners systematically bind their labor to the estates (CIDA, 1965b: 143–46). In large parts of Brazil rural workers receive cash incomes that do not cover their basic subsistence needs, so they remain in constant debt (CIDA, 1966a: 255); CIDA (1966c: 144) reports similar conditions in Peru. In Amazonia, the *seringueiros* (rubber collectors) are constantly indebted to the rubber buyer who sells them food and other items in return for the rubber (CIDA, 1966a: 141); in the Brazilian state of Espíritu Santo coffee sharecroppers must finance the care and harvest of their product through the landowner who also has a preferential right to purchase the croppers' shares; at the end of the year the croppers do not take in enough cash to pay their debts so they must remain "prisoners" on the estate for another year (CIDA, 1966a: 214–15). The extremes to which such servitude could go in the 1960s can be seen from Correia de Andrade's (1963: 116–17) description of the *compra do trabalhador,* the "purchase of the worker":

This consists in the owners facilitating the workers small loans. Since the worker earns little and has a numerous family and buys in the owner's store which always charges high prices, he makes new loans every week and new debts. When the debt has reached 4 or 5000 cruzeiros, the owner refuses to grant new loans, claiming that the account is large. . . . The worker in despair attempts to go to another property, but the first does not authorize his leaving without first settling the account. Then he requests a loan, equivalent to his debt, from the new owner where he is going, pays his creditor and moves; he is not free however since he "sold himself to the new owner" and can leave the farm only when he pays off. It is incredible that when the worker does not find anyone who will "purchase him" and "leaves at night, a fugitive"—this is the expression normally used—it is common for the owner to seek the assistance of the authorities and to return the fugitive so that he will work for the creditor until his debt is paid off. At times a worker who fled remains in the property of the creditor during the day and remains prisoner at night in quarters under surveillance of guards in truly private prisons. Such facts occur these very days in the zone of the litoral, north of Recife, in Pernambuco. (Translation from CIDA, 1966a: 243)

While the preceding discussion has centered around what were termed economic mechanisms of domination, it is apparent that the economic powers of the landholders are intimately tied to their simultaneous control over legal, political, and military resources. The general effect of these combined factors for the campesino is an extraordinary precariousness in his sustenance resources (Feder, 1969a: 433–39). A large proportion of the rural population in Latin America truly has to struggle for survival by seeking out an economic niche for itself. The term *precaristas* is characteristically used in Brazil for those who work the land under precarious, unstable, marginal arrangements of land tenure that deny them social and economic security (Moraes, 1970: 467, fn.). Under such conditions of uncertainty, any natural catastrophe—a bad crop or a drop in the market price for the product—can lead to indebtedness, loss of land, or starvation. Frequently, insecurity is increased by the legal ambivalence of land titles (Tullis, 1970: chap. 6; CIDA, 1966a: 113) or by fear of land grabs by the landholders. Vague oral (and even written) contracts (Feder, 1969a: 436–38), fear of arbitrary dismissal (Cotler, 1970a: 551; CIDA, 1966a: 284), fluctuating wages according to arbitrary decisions by the landowners (CIDA, 1966a: 289), and in many areas an oversupply of docile labor—all these conditions are combined with the campesinos' general poverty and their intimidation by police and private strongmen to not only create a climate of insecurity that leaves little room for self-confidence and courage to resist the owners, but also make acquiescence on the part of the campesinos appear to be a realistic response to powerlessness and deprivation—for the time being.

CHAPTER 5

Social Mechanisms of Domination

ISOLATION

Social relations in traditional rural Latin America have been dominated by the organization of the large estates. Internally the traditional hacienda has been not just an economic enterprise, but "an
entire social system" that "governs the life of those attached to it
from the cradle to the grave" (Tannenbaum, 1960: 80):

> It embraced all of government. In its lordly lands it sanctioned and executed
> the law, administered justice, exercised the civil power, exacted contribu-
> tions and imposed fines, kept its own jails and stocks, punished the recalci-
> trant, monopolized commerce, and prohibited the exercise of any industry
> other than that on the plantation. (Tannenbaum, 1960: 76)

Although commercially oriented from its very beginning,[1] the
hacienda has traditionally tended toward relative self-sufficiency;
income from commercial activities was used mainly to underwrite
the aristocratic life-style of the owners with minimal capitaliza-
tion, while the subsistence of the estate was largely internally
produced (Tannenbaum, 1960: 80–86). As a result of the closed
nature of the hacienda's social organization and the frequently
huge size of the estates,[2] the resident campesinos had very little
access to, and contact with, the outside world. They belonged to
the estate together with the houses and livestock[3] and were linked
to the larger society only through such "cultural brokers" (Eric
Wolf) as their *patrón* or the priest. Still today the social life of many
campesinos is confined by the boundaries of the estate on which
they live. Witness Celso Furtado's comment on the status of the
moradores[4] on a Brazilian *usina* (sugar plantation with factory):

> The status of the morador is almost imcompatible with that of the citizen.
> The urban worker who leaves the factory for his home is aware that the
> norms which govern the life of the citizen are different from those which
> govern work, which enables him to observe the work relations critically. On
> the large plantation, the man who leaves or enters his house is leaving and

58

entering a part of the estate. Thus no aspect of his life escapes the system of norms which discipline his life as a worker. In this manner, his practical life experience does not allow him to become a citizen and develop a sense of responsibility with regard to his proper destiny. All acts of his life are the acts of a "retainer," an element whose existence in all respects integrates that great socio-economic unity which the sugar plantation is. (Furtado, 1964: 147–48. My translation)

The isolation of traditional campesinos from the larger society was marked not only for the large estates but also for independent corporate villages or smallholders' communities. Still in the mid-nineteenth century the *minifundia* communities "are generally dependent for their contacts with the outside world upon a small group of town-dwelling politicians, landowners, merchants, secular and ecclesiastical officials" (Barraclough and Domike, 1970: 54). As a result of their "brokerage" function, these people wield considerable power over the campesinos, who need them to obtain loans, sell their goods, or transact official and legal business (Cotler, 1970b: 418–19). These characteristics were critical dimensions of the "inward-faced" (Pearse, 1975: 69) or "inward-shielded" (Migdal, 1974: chaps. 2, 3, 4) structure of agrarian enterprises whose owners or managers attempted their position of political and economic monopolies in order to minimize the monetary cost of agrarian production and to strive for self-sufficiency (Pearse, 1974: 80–81; for Fowler on the Mexican case before 1910, see 1978: xiii–xiv, xvii–xviii). It is interesting to note in this context that the traditional brokers (landholder, priest, local merchant, or political boss) used their powers to strengthen their elitist position over the campesinos. Today, new brokers (schoolteachers, labor leaders, sympathetic politicians, and professionals) have greater access to formerly isolated and tightly controlled regions (Wagley, 1964: 45–48), which increases the campesinos' opportunities for political participation and liberation from traditional repression.

ORGANIZATION OF THE LARGE ESTATES

While the traditional hacienda secluded the resident campesinos almost totally from the outside world, it was internally structured in a partriarchal and strictly hierarchical manner. All authority was vested in the *hacendado,* who was treated by his subordinates with greatest humility and deference (Tannenbaum, 1960: 90; CIDA, 1965b: 86). What the CIDA investigators reported about the Brazilian *latifundista's* powers can be extrapolated to include all the traditional rural areas of Latin America:

What makes this power distinctive is its near absoluteness and vastness. An estate owner's decisions are orders. In this respect the organization of the *latifundio* is not unlike that of any organization in which the top command retains the exclusive privilege of making decisions on all matters concerning the subordinate's activities and where the delegation of power exists only within certain narrow limits—qualified always by the right to intervene. Decisions on minor issues made by subordinates of the *latifundista* to whom some power of decision-making is granted, are always subject to explicit or implicit sanctions by the "top command." (CIDA, 1966a: 137)

There are variations in the formal organization of the traditional hacienda or plantation, but it generally follows a pattern in which the proprietor has the final authority; often he has an administrator or manager, who may either have little discretion or actually run the whole enterprise (CIDA, 1966c: 3a); below him are the foremen and overseers, who occupy several different ranks; at the bottom are the ordinary workers, *colonos,* and other operators; apart from the regular chain of command there may be other positions for veterinarians, migratory labor contractors during harvest periods, and other services.[5] Very frequently the administrators have very little discretion, with only the responsibility of supervising the routines and seeing to it that the owner's orders are carried out; they often have very limited knowledge of farming and marketing except for their practical experience with the job and their intimate knowledge of the workers' customs (Feder, 1969a: 405; CIDA, 1966a: 150–52, 154, 157; 1966b: 169). On the other hand, there are cases where the actual owners take only a minimal interest in the operation of their estates, especially those who do not reside on the land. In such cases the manager or administrator may take effective control over the estate. Many landowners thus come to depend on their administrators, even though they may be afraid of being cheated. H. W. Hutchinson, for example, found on a Brazilian plantation that

in order to keep the plantation running properly all year long it was necessary for someone with knowledge and authority to be present all the time; so the former *feitor mor* become known as the overseer, with a house better and larger than that of anyone else on the plantation except the owner. As time went on, the overseer gathered more and more rights and privileges unto himself, until today he is the veritable owner of the plantation in all but the legal sense. He has the confidence and loyalty of the workmen, without which he would be a failure. (H. W. Hutchinson, 1957:57)

Rates of absentee ownership are generally high in Latin America (Feder, 1971: 85–86). In Colombia it is estimated that at least 42 percent of all agricultural lands are neither cultivated nor managed directly by their owners (CIDA, 1966b: 169). In eleven *municípios* surveyed in Brazil the rate of absenteeism averaged 50 percent for the *latifundia* (ranging from 40 to 86 percent), 35 percent for medium-sized farms, and 14 percent for *minifundia* (CIDA, 1966a:

160). While such statistics do not give any indication about the proportion of cases where administrators have taken effective control of the operation, they do suggest that the administrator on many estates is the man who deals with the labor force and has to settle conflicts that might arise. As he often has very little discretion about policy decisions, he may have no authority to bargain with workers who demand higher wages or better tenancy and rental conditions. The inflexibility of such arrangements functions to obstruct institutionalized conflict resolution and to aggravate existing tensions (Feder, 1969a: 408). Frequently workers see very little of the landlord, since he gives all orders through his administrators and foremen (CIDA, 1966a: 157–58); when tensions arise under these conditions the administrator becomes the first object of resentment and thus may deflect the workers' hostility from the actual owners. In this manner they may have a stabilizing function for the existing power structure (Feder, 1969a: 406–8; 1971: 125–28).

SPECIAL FAVORS

Administrators and especially foremen are frequently ordinary tenants and workers (H. W. Hutchinson, 1957: 50–51, 107; CIDA, 1965b: 224; 1966b: 169) who have gotten promoted for their loyalty and experience. Such promotions entail increased privileges and a possibility of gaining additional security or even accumulating some savings. Evidence from several countries indicates that even small and temporary promotions are very rewarding in view of the generally precarious economic status of the workers and are much sought after (Cotler, 1970a: 543–44; Heath, Erasmus, and Buechler, 1969: 99–102; CIDA, 1966a: 150; 1966b: 120–21). For example, Vázquez (1963) found on a hacienda in the Peruvian highlands five levels of formal authority from the *patrón* down to the peons; in addition there were men assigned as *varayos* who acted as enforcers when a peon was punished by what may be called a "fine in kind." These jobs were open to the ordinary peons and were considered highly attractive as a source of prestige, power, and respect. Promotions of this kind were generally given to people who had proved themselves to be trustworthy and loyal to their *patrón*, and campesinos clearly recognized that to get such extra rewards they must win the confidence of the landlord. Brazilian workers expressed their expectations in this regard with statements such as: "In order to improve the situation, one has only to show that one is worthy of the trust of the landowner," and "To improve one's condition, one depends on the recognition of the employer. In due time if the employer has confidence, one can be promoted to administrator of his farms'' (C. A. de Medina, cited in CIDA, 1966a: 292). Other cases of special favors given to workers have been reported in Ecuador where one member of an indigenous community with some elementary education was promoted to veterinarian because of his practical skills (CIDA, 1965b: 224). Reports about corresponding practices in Brazil indicate that people may get terms of rent or employment that are more favorable than those of their fellows, which enables them to survive more comfortably (Feder, 1969a: 415). Feder comments on such practices:

The selection of "pets" is no doubt often made carefully by the landlords in an attempt to raise in the other peasants greater hopes in the possibilities of advancement—a useful maneuver in the face of the stark reality which affords farm people practically no outlook for betterment. (1969a: 415)

People who receive preferential treatment from the landlord tend to be his men, in other words, they place loyalty to him higher than solidarity with their fellow campesinos (Heath, Erasmus, and Buechler, 1969: 100–101; Ford, 1962: 115–16). When the landlord orders it, they willingly administer punishment to their peers and inform the landlord about their activities. In Peru such informers (*soplones*—squealers) keep the landholders up to date about gossip, complaints, and potentially subversive activities in the villages so that the latter can in time dispense benefits or sanctions as they see fit (Tullis, 1970: 93, 113). It has also been noted that the existence of such informants stifles the development of class solidarity among peasants by creating general distrust (Tullis, 1970: 113). In general, landlords like to select their administrators and foremen from their peons precisely because in this manner they not only ensure themselves of the most reliable overseers but also render the self-interest of the individual campesinos incompatible with their class interest (Ford, 1962: 114–15; Tullis, 1970: 99; Feder, 1969a: 402; 1971: 124–28).

PATERNALISM

The granting of special favors to selected subordinates is a significant aspect of the paternalism that characterizes traditional *patrón*-campesino relationships. Paternalism arose from the secludedness of the landed estates and the absolute power of their owners over the resident labor force in the colonial period. After the conquest, the native Indians were legally defined as minors who were under the special protection of the Spanish crown and under the delegated tutelage of the colonists or missionaries. Later the large haciendas and *fazendas* became entire communities in which the owners and their workers formed one big family, as has been so vividly described in Gilberto Freyre's *The Masters and the Slaves* (1946). This familial conception of employer-worker relations is still reflected in Bolivian ex-*hacendados* who were displaced from their estates after the revolution of 1952. They still consider the campesinos irresponsible and incapable of managing their own affairs and nostalgically remember the days when their Indian peons were *como niños de las casa* (like children of the house) and had *cariño al trabajo y al patrón* (love for work and *patrón)* (Heath, Erasmus, and Buechler, 1969: 133–34). Paternalism has not only characterized the relationships between *hacendados* and workers but also pervaded most interpersonal relationships campesinos have had with members of the upper sectors (Eisenstadt and Roniger, 1980). Paternalistic relationships involve sentiments of loyalty and responsibility as well as a degree of affection between a *patrón* and a dependent. In Latin American rural-class relations, paternalism can be conceived as an exchange in which the campesinos receive land, security, occasional gifts, and sometimes assistance in times of need in return for their servitude. This system is still widely prevalent in the more traditionalistic parts of Latin America (Wagley, 1960: 183–86; H. W. Hutchinson, 1957: 7–8, 61–62, 70–71; Tullis, 1970: 90–91; CIDA, 1965b: 86) and may be summarized in the words of John Gillin (1960: 36):

The *patrón* relationship was originally a reciprocal arrangement tying members of varying social strata together, not in terms of social or economic equality but of reciprocal obligations of an unequal sort. On a typical hacienda . . . the owner was, and usually still is, *patrón* to his tenants. They owe him a certain amount of work, variously calculated, in return for his supplying them with housing tools, and perhaps individual plots of land. They owe him also a certain loyalty in disputes and in other difficulties. In return he acts as their "protector" in brushes with the law and with higher authority. The custom by which *patrones* serve as godfathers to the children of their more faithful retainers sets up a solemn time of ceremonial kinship, which in a way defines the whole enterprise as "one big family," although social equality is by no means implied. The *patrón*, nonetheless, is expected to take a personal interest in the welfare of his workers or tenants and their families. He knows them by their first names, attends them or sends them aid when they are ill, and contributes to their *fiestas*.

A word of caution is in order, however. The image of the benevolent *patrón* is often a mere fiction of the landholding classes that, intentionally or not, serves as a rationalization for the oppression of the tenant-laborers. In other cases, landholders do not even bother to play the benevolent protector. In all cases, paternalism involves highly exploitative class relations that are legitimated to the campesinos precisely by the generous gestures of a good *patrón* (Huizer, 1972: 13–19). The implications of this are spelled out clearly by Huizer:

Since the peasant is heavily dependent on the relationship with his patrón and on the degree of favor he enjoys in this relationship, the horizontal solidarity among the peasants tends to be weak. It is clear that in order to create viable and representative peasant organizations, the link with the patrón has to be changed drastically, if not broken. (1972: 18–19)

COMPADRAZGO

An interesting aspect of paternalism is the establishment of godparent relationships (*compadrazgo*) along vertical lines. Heath (1969: 202) found in Bolivia that even after the revolution of 1952 many campesinos retained relationships with their former landlord that were strikingly paternalistic and included the continued establishment of the *compadrazgo*. Harris (1956: 131–55) found that in the Brazilian community of Minas Velhas upper-class individuals were much sought after as godparents and had an average of 33.6 foster children, as compared with averages of 5.2 for the middle classes and 0.7 for the lowest class. People in the community felt that godparents could be useful for their children and perhaps themselves and indicated that they preferred a powerful but disinterested *compadre* to one who was weak but interested. Harris concluded that in this community the establishment of godparent relations was but another reflection of the ubiquitous search for the boss (1956: 155). Similar observations have been made in Peru (Martínez, 1963b), Guatemala (Tumin, 1952: 76), and Puerto Rico (Landy, 1959: 52–53).

The thesis that the *compadrazgo* is used by lower-class persons in Latin America to obligate a protector is corroborated by the observation that the type of person sought out as godfather frequently changes as power relations change over time. Bolivian peasants who no longer depend on their landlords for marketing their products now depend on town-dwelling middlemen and merchants (many of whom are, in fact, former landlords). With these merchants the campesinos have established personal relations as with their former landlords, and many of the merchants serve also as *compadres* for their clients (Heath, 1969: 205). The previously described foreman of the Brazilian plantation who acted as the de facto owner became related to most of the workers through a godparent relationship and was actually more sought after for this purpose than the owner himself (H.W. Hutchinson, 1957: 57).

The godparent relationship is, of course, established in Latin America not only between a *patrón* and a dependent, but also between equals both in the upper and lower sectors. In a broader comparative and historical perspective, Mintz and Wolf (1967) have suggested that the establishment of horizontal godparent relationships in the lower sectors tends to undermine vertical solidarities between members of the upper and lower sectors. In examining historical developments in medieval Europe, for example, they found that vertical godparent relationships between barons and peasants developed along with feudalism; but "with the breakdown of feudal land tenures and the increased peasant rights, such ritual ties were again rephrased horizontally to unite the peasant neighborhoods in their struggle against feudal dues" (1950: 196). The direction of godparent relationships can thus be considered as an important indicator of the nature of class relationships. In societies with a highly differentiated and relatively rigid class structure, peasants are likely to gain from vertical ties of godparenthood, which thus function as a stabilizing mechanism for interclass integration (Mintz and Wolf, 1967: 190; see also Martínez, 1963b). Similar observations have been made by B. Hutchinson (1966) in Brazil where, he suggests, the current movement is away from horizontal relationships toward vertical ones with "an expectation of exceptional advantage for the godchild, who will be provided with benefits promoting his interests *at the expense of others*" (1966: 14; my italics). Cotler (1970b: 416) has put the problem succinctly. Referring to the Peruvian Indian's perception of the *patrón* as an all-powerful source whose good graces he must maintain, he suggests that the Indian must seek to establish paternalistic ties with the boss and other authority figures

so as to commit them to a situation *which might place him into preferential status with respect to the other tenants.* If he gets the boss to be godfather to one of his children, he may have fewer duties to perform, and there may be a chance that he obtain a certain degree of indulgence in case of nonfulfillment of his duties or, at best, he might even be taken as the boss's man. The landlord, for his own part, uses this paternalistic relationship to strengthen the tenant's ties of personal loyalty—highlighting the latter's exceptional status and thereby constituting himself as the single source of identification of his tenant-farmers—*thus avoiding the formation of class identifications.* (My italics)

CONCLUSION

Patron-client relations entail exchanges based on social inequality within an integrated, but inherently contradictory, pattern of interrelations between micro- and macrosocial relations.[6] These are associated with powerlessness on the part of dependent campesinos. In this situation, the search for a protector who can supply scarce benefits and a degree of security is a rational response

(Foster, 1967a: 222–30). The more precarious a campesino's situation, the greater his need for a protector. However, as has been observed in Brazil (B. Hutchinson, 1966: 18), Chile (Petras and Zeitlin, 1970: 522), and Peru (Cotler, 1970b: 416–17), patron-client ties with the landholders and other protectors may lead the campesino to identify himself totally as an emanation from his *patrón* in a manner that diverts his attention from his class interests. Moreover, since the favors from the *patrones* are scarce, the campesino has to devise strategies that maximize his position of favor with the landlord. Such strategies are not only developed in competition with his peers, but may even force him to act in manners detrimental to the interest of his class as a whole.

Due to the unilateral dependence involved in paternalistic relations, the bargaining power of campesinos is generally low; they frequently have to settle for whatever privileges the landlord is willing to concede to them—which is largely a matter of discretion. Their welfare depends, therefore, not only on whether they obtain enough favors from the landlord, but also on whether the latter is a good or bad *patrón* (Pearse, 1970: 27). It may be argued that a conception of *patrones* as good or bad (Heath, 1969: 183) makes it possible for the peasants to explain the action of a harsh landlord by stating that he is a bad landlord. In this manner the relationships become particularized and the campesinos' focus of observation is deflected from the class aspect of their interactions with the landlords. Instead of seeking to change the institutional and economic structure that renders them dependent, peasants may simply seek alternative *patrones* who are good and provide them with better benefits. But, as Feder points out (1969a: 401), "the crucial point is not whether the landlords are villains or not, but that a 'decent' landlord can reverse his attitude and become a 'villain' without incurring risks of punishment or damage to his status." Alternative *patrones* may indeed provide better terms of employment; involved and progressive leaders may take a genuine interest in bettering conditions for the campesinos. But it is equally likely that alternative *patrones* will be just that—*patrones* who manipulate the peasantry for their own ends and establish new dependencies.

CHAPTER 6

Political Mechanisms of Domination

THE PERVASIVENESS OF COERCION

Ever since the conquest of Latin America, force has been the ultimate source of the landholders' control over the campesinos (Pearse, 1975: 36; Galjart, 1972: 5). Uprisings by Indians, slaves, and other campesinos have been numerous throughout the colonial and republican periods in the Andean countries, Mexico, and Brazil (Vianna, 1949, vol. 1: 198–99; Cunha, 1944; Silva-Herzog, 1959: 105–7; Villanueva, 1967: 58; Gilhodes, 1970: 408–10; Cornblit, 1970), but they have been generally put down by the army and the police.

The rule of force is still marked in contemporary Latin America. In Ecuador, striking campesinos have been intimidated by armed police and their leaders have been thrown in jail (CIDA, 1965b: 95–96, 163). In 1922, the resistance of Indian campesinos against the encroachments of landholders in Peru's La Mar province was broken by a pacification program in which, according to official statistics, 430 Indians were killed, 1,400 homes burned, and incalculable amounts of produce destroyed (Béjar, 1969: 89–91). Brazilian landholders were still in 1966 reported to grab lands from smallholders by means of fraud and arms (CIDA, 1966a: 16, 113), and they violently resisted the peasant leagues and syndicates that began to emerge in the 1950s by beating up their members (CIDA, 1966a: 316) and receiving the organizers with gunfire (CIDA, 1966a: 316).

The climate of intimidation created by such reaction was described by an informant:

The political situation here is very tense. Whoever speaks in favor of the liga can expect to be shot at any moment. None of us who are here in this shed are safe. A shot can come out of the dark, from one of the capangas who must be watching us now (CIDA, 1966a: 314–15).

Not only has force of arms upheld the general regime of the large estate owners since colonial times, but also within the domains of individual estates the owner has had almost unlimited power over the life and death of his subordinates. Before the revolution of 1952, Bolivian landlords could lock up their runaway *arrienderos* in private jails (Heath, Erasmus, and Buechler, 1969: 125). Ecuadorian campesinos have filed long lists of complaints against the physical abuses of *hacendados* or their administrators (CIDA, 1965b: 85). From Peru there are reports of landholders who whip, incarcerate, and in some cases even behead their workers and molest their wives sexually (CIDA, 1966c: 113–14; Villanueva, 1967: 28; Béjar, 1969: 92–95). Similar incidents have been reported in Bolivia before 1952 (Heath, Erasmus, and Buechler, 1969: 99–100). A visitor to a traditional Brazilian *engenho* (sugar plantation) was shown a veritable arsenal of firearms, including hand grenades, by the owner and observed that the latter never left his house unarmed or without a *capanga*. *Capangas* are hired gunmen, bodyguards, and the private police of the Brazilian *fazendeiros*. They have traditionally been used by the landholders in their fights with political rivals and to uphold orders on their estates; today they still maintain order for many *fazendeiros* by evicting and killing resident laborers, inflicting punishment, and in general making them toe the line through terror and intimidation (CIDA, 1966a: 140, 142–44, 231–32; see also Feder, 1969a: 440–42).

The brutalities of landholders could persist in the past because the landholders had an effective monopoly in their domain over institutionalized means of coercion, without interference from the government. As will be seen in later chapters, campesino mobilization in the twentieth century has occurred when and where this monopoly over means of coercion broke down. Today governments have asserted an increasing control over coercive resources, which enables them to provide campesinos with some protection from the violence of the landholders if they choose to do so. However, in the 1970s most governments have not made such a choice. On the contrary, they mostly use their resources to constrain and repress campesino movements. In Paraguay, peasant organizers are kidnapped, arbitrarily arrested, and tortured (USLA, 1973c). In Mexico, only the official peasant organization CNC can operate freely because it respects the limits of acceptable mobilization set by the PRI leaders. Organizers of independent peasant movements may be assassinated by army commandos (for example, Ruben Jaramillo with his pregnant wife and five children) or incarcerated by the civil authorities (such as currently a number of CCI leaders) (Katzin, 1973–1974a; 1973–1974b). In Brazil landowners can count on the police and the military to crush any independent peasant organization. A case in point is the movement led by Manoel da Conceição in the 1960s against landowners harassing their community in the state of Maranhão.[1] Arrested in 1968 and again in 1972, da Conceição was subjected to sadistic tortures in several military and civilian prisons. In a letter of November 1972 from the prison he relates some of his experiences:

For four months I was severely tortured by the army in Rio de Janeiro and then in the Navy Information Center (CENIMAR). For the sixth time, I was taken, practically lifeless, to the hospital. So harsh was the beating that my body became one huge hematoma. The blood coagulated on my skin and all the hair on my body fell off.

They tore out all my fingernails. They stuck a needle all the way through my sexual organs and dragged me out onto the balcony by a rope tied around my testicles. Immediately after this they hung me up by my heels.

Then they hung me from a bar with my wrists handcuffed together, tore off my artificial leg, and tied my penis so I could not urinate. They left me standing for three days on my one leg with no food or drink and gave me so many drugs that I have lost my hearing and I am impotent. They nailed my penis to a table top for 24 hours. They dragged me to a tub, tied like a pig, and I nearly drowned.

They put me in a cell that was in complete darkness. For thirty days I was kept in this cell, urinating and defecating in the same place where I slept. All they gave me was bread soaked in water. They put me in a rubber box and turned on a horn, and for three days I did not eat or sleep. I almost went crazy.

They injected a "truth serum" into my blood. I was in an insane state and completely unaware of the situation I was in when they interrogated me. They laid me down on a floor and threatened to get confessions out of me by putting a three-pointed iron tool, with three rows of teeth like those of a wood saw, into my anus.[2]

Other forms of terrorism sanctioned by the governments are represented by conservative vigilante groups that assassinate communist political organizers. Prominent groups of this type are *Ojo por Ojo* and *Mano Blanca* in Guatemala as well as the death squads in Brazil and Uruguay. The latter are generally acknowledged to be composed of off-duty police and military officers operating with the tacit approval of the governments. The regimes tolerate if not sponsor these repressions, and other forms of repression generally receive strong assistance from the United States in the form of loans, arms, and counterinsurgency training.[3] In at least one case (that of the Uruguayan death squads) it has been possible to prove the direct involvement of U.S. advisers in vigilante terrorism (Klare and Stein, 1974: 21).

The brutality inherent in traditional *patrón*-campesino relations has its counterpart in the macropolitical structures of *caudillismo* on which the powers of the landholders rested and which still exist today in many parts of the continent in only slightly modified forms.

REGIONALISM AND CAUDILLISMO

In the Spanish colonies the crown wielded absolute authority. The royal bureaucracy administered the colonies centrally, and self-government existed for the colonists only on the local level of the *cabildos*. After the colonies had achieved independence from Spain, the legitimate authority that held the vast region together vanished, and there was no substitute available that could assume this function. As a result, the Spanish empire not only disintegrated into several rivaling states, but also within each of these emerging states political power was localized in the hands of regional strongmen, *caudillos*. The geographical isolation and relative inaccessibility of the regions encouraged the political system of *caudillismo* (also called *gamonalismo*), a system in which all effective power resided in the local *caudillos* or *gamonales* and in which power at the national level was weak, dependent on the support of local powerholders, and usurped by whoever was strong enough to grab it.[4] Within the context of this "norm of illegitimacy" (Horowitz, 1969), the men who traditionally commanded the most important power resources were the *hacendados;* they came to dominate the provinces as though they were their private domains, without any more checks and controls over their treatment of the Indian laborers. In the 1934 words of the Peruvian writer José Carlos Mariátegui:

> *Gamonalismo* inevitably invalidates any law or ordinace for the protection of the Indians. Written law is impotent against the authority of the *hacendado* or *latifundista,* which is sustained by environment and habit. Unpaid labor is prohibited by law; nonetheless, unpaid labor, and even forced labor, survive on the *latifundio*. The judge, the subprefecto, the commissar, the teacher, the tax collector, are all vassals of the *latifundium*. The law cannot win against the *gamonales*. Any functionary who might try to impose would be abandoned and sacrificed by the central authorities, over whom the influence of *gamonalismo* is always omnipotent, for it acts directly or through parliament with equal efficiency. (Translated in Frank, 1969: 266)

That *caudillismo* or its Brazilian variant, *coronelismo,* is still a twentieth-century phenomenon in many parts of Latin America has been well documented (Nuñes Leal, 1948; Blondel, 1957; Cotler, 1970b: 423–25; Fals Borda, 1955: 241–44; Paré, 1973; also Frank, 1969: 265–66). Some of its legal and political ramifications shall be discussed briefly in the following sections.

CORONELISMO AND POLITICAL MACROSTRUCTURES: AN EXCURSUS ON THE BRAZILIAN VARIANT

The political role of campesinos in traditional Latin America cannot be assessed without reference to their dependence on the local *caudillo* and the place the latter occupies in the interrelationships between state, regional, and national governments. While the implications of traditional political macrostructures from the perspective of the campesino are more or less the same in the various countries of the continent, the variations that have historically existed make it feasible to describe the systemic interrelationships for the Brazilian case in greater detail and proceed from there to reflect on the situation in other countries.[5]

Coronelismo is the Brazilian version of *gamonalismo* and originated in the imperially appointed *coroneis* (colonels) of the now-extinct *Guarda Nacional* who wielded great prestige and power in the region to which they were assigned. The post was usually given to an influential landowner in an area who used his position to fortify his domination over the *municípios*. Later *coronel* came to designate any landowner or political chief who had a sufficient amount of land, *jagunços* (armed strongmen), and/or voters to play a dominant role in local and state politics.

In the formation of coronelist politics, the year 1841 was of great importance, when the law of 3 December declared that many local officials who had previously been elected were to be appointed by the central government in Rio. Together with the dependence of the provincial presidents upon their appointment by the federal government, the law effected a further political and administrative centralization and an increased power of the emerging national parties over the local electoral clans. On the other hand, the influence of the provincial governments over the municipal administration also increased, since the provincial presidents customarily suggested to the federal government whom they should appoint to the municipal offices. Local powerholders thus came to depend to a significant extent upon presidential favors. Therefore, local political parties tended to center around the provincial president expecting to share in his partiality and power. The most important post to be filled was that of the commander of the *Guarda Nacional;* the *coronel* of the troop usually was or became the leader of the party that was on the side of the government. Besides suggesting the appointments for municipal posts by the central government, the president of the province also influenced the issuing of honorary titles and thus disposed of yet another means for granting favors to the municipal politicians. Thus the *municípios* in the nineteenth century were typically dominated by the *partido do coronel* (party of the *coronel*) ,which was also the *partido do governador* or the *partido do presidente* and had the sole purpose of providing spoils for its members and excluding the opposing clans from sharing responsibility and power. Since they were in charge of police and military operations and had the judicial posts occupied by men of their confidence, the political chiefs got away with various abuses—protectionism, nepotism, intimidations, and infringements upon their opponents' liberty and property. Violent threats and acts on the part of the *jagunços* of the chiefs were the rule in those days. For this reason, the most feasible political strategy for the local population was to jump on the bandwagon of the president's party.

It should be noted, however, that this political concentration took place on the level of the *município*. The rural populations—the *sitiantes* and *moradores* of the *fazendas*—in general remained firmly incorporated in the large estates; they gained and suffered together with their *patrón*.

Although the appointment of many local officials by nonmunicipal authorities contributed significantly to a modification of the *senhorial* power, one of the most important changes in the municipal power structure after the 1820s was brought about by the introduction of universal suffrage and a variety of elective offices. With that institution the number of his dependents became of additional importance for the landlord. Old political feuds received a new expression in various electoral tumults, like the destruction of ballot boxes, intimidation, and terror through the *capangas* of the chiefs. In view of the traditional loyalty, protection, and obedience that characterized the relationship between patrons and dependents, it was not surprising that the former commanded also the vote of the rural masses. The characteristic of the "electoral clan" (Vianna) was, then, its particularistic nature, which also affected the national parties.

The Republican constitution of 1891 had important repercussions upon the *coronelista* power structure. One of the most significant changes was the state governments, which replaced the provincial presidents from the colonial period. Unlike the presidents, the governors did not depend upon the always revocable nomination by the central government; but they became more dependent upon the local *coroneis* who effectively controlled the votes in the *municípios*. Still in the possession of many municipal spoils and in control of large parts of the municipal finances, the governors remained in a position to establish a mutually beneficial *do-ut-des* relationship with the *coroneis*. This gave them a solid political base from which to confront the federal government, which, in turn, forced the federal government to give certain recognition to regional and local interests.

A mutual recognition between federal and state governments corresponded to that between the state governments and the *coroneis* and became known as the *política dos governadores* (politics of the governors). This politics of the governors was institutionalized—though not created—in the late 1890s under President Campo Sales, who, in order to restore the finances of the nation, gave the state governments the disposal over federal spoils and patronage in return for cooperation in the national Congress. In this deal, the powers of the president of the Republic rested in his right to allocate federal funds to the states, nominate federal officials in states and *municípios*, and, in extreme cases, order military intervention in the states on behalf of the dominant regional powers. The powers of the state governors were derived from the local and regional control of the votes by the *coroneis* in accord with the *situação estadual*, which influenced presidential elections and assured that virtually only representatives of the regional oligarchy—the *dégola*—were sent to the federal Congress to check the programs of the government. The politics of the governors consisted, then, of a mutual exchange in which the federal government gave away money, favors, and posts in return for votes and cooperation in Congress.

The strength of the state governments rested precisely in the fact that they formed, on the lower administrative levels, the same kind of compromise that the federal government had with them. They controlled the municipal budgets and allocated funds for public works and services in the *municípios*. Because of their influence in Rio, the governors virtually controlled the nominations not only for state but also for federal offices in the *municípios*. This gave them a strong hold over the *coroneis*, who were all too eager to see that their rivals did not win the governor's favor; in disputes, therefore, the *coroneis* were easily "convinced" by the governors.

On the other hand, the *coroneis* firmly controlled the votes of their dependents and thus managed to impose upon the governors a *política dos coroneis* analogous to the *política dos governadores* on the higher levels. This compromise involved local electoral support for the candidates of the state situation (*situação estadual*) and a free hand for the *coroneis* in local affairs. The *coroneis* thereby elected state and federal deputies. Their influence was not restricted to the nomination of state officials in the *municípios;* the combined mechanisms of the *política dos governadores* and the *política dos coroneis* permitted them also to influence federal appointments to the *municípios*. As a consequence of this *compromiso coronelista,* virtually all municipal officeholders depended on the benevolence of the *coroneis,* and the *coroneis* incurred little challenge when they used their offices to enrich themselves and suppress their opponents; they had the law on their side. This is precisely what made many local elections so violent: it was a matter of being "in" with the party of the governor and having the exclusive power to abuse offices and protect oneself from the potential encroachments of rivaling chiefs. The law and the public offices were means in the individual pursuit of wealth and power, not institutions in their own right, and the guiding motto of the coroneis was: *para os amigos pão, para os inimigos pau.*[6] Significantly, when a local opposition managed to win an election and become recognized in spite of the bad odds, it usually switched to supporting the government, since it needed the spoils and financial support that came from the capital. If the chiefs who had not managed to incorporate themselves into the party of the governor wanted to protect themselves from the harassments of the favorites, they had to rely upon their own private forces of *jagunços.* Thus, organized violence was not only a monopoly of the state; it was maintained by those who had succeeded in subjecting public powers to their private interests as well as by those who did not have access to public resources. Often the only difference between private and regular police was that the latter were on the state payroll and the former not. But even this distinction did not always hold.[7]

POLITICAL STAKES

Under political conditions such as the ones just described, lines of cleavage develop horizontally between different groups who are either in or out of power. All groups are identically structured in a hierarchical manner with state and national politicians in the highest positions and the common people who constitute the clientele of a local powerholder at the bottom. They do not form very cohesive associations and are not centered around common ideologies. Rather, they consist of loose alliances of people and groups with a common stake—the stake of political power, which begins at the local level and has ramifications to the top national positions. Those who are in can control patronage, spoils, public funds, and local administration and justice. Those who are out have no access to such benefits and are at the mercy of their more fortunate competitors who may grab their lands or can utilize the local police to settle legal disputes on their own terms. The frequent prosecution of political adversaries by local powerholders who are in and the extent of their control is indicated by the Brazilian maxim "for the friends bread, for the enemies the stick," cited above. Nuñes Leal comments on the political cleavages in Brazil and the situation of the local opposition in the early twentieth century:

> They do not fight to defeat the government on the municipal terrain in order to strengthen the position of a state or national opposition party; they fight to contest among each other the privilege to back up the government and get protection from it. . . . the situation of the member of the opposition in the municipal sphere is so uncomfortable that as a rule only those remain in the opposition who cannot stay with the government. (1948: 29. My translation)

A political structure of this kind makes it imperative for those in the lowest social strata to seek the protection of a local *coronel* or *caudillo* who will defend them against other landholders trying to take their land, in exchange for loyalty in the polls and, if necessary, readiness to follow their protector in arms. Those campesinos who live on the property of a *hacendado* or *fazendeiro* do not have a choice in this matter anyway because their residence commits them unquestionably to their *patrão*. There exist, therefore, interdependencies and hence solidarities between campesinos and *patrones* that are founded on unilateral exchanges. These solidarities override intraclass solidarities among the campesinos since (1) under conditions of powerlessness they cannot gain protection from one another but only from a strongman, and (2) rivalries between *hacendados* involve all their retainers, so campesinos may fight other campesinos who belong to the clientele of a rival *hacendado*. While these patterns have been observed in many countries, such as Puerto Rico (Landy, 1959: 54–56) and duri..g the Mexican Revolution (Millon, 1969: 113–16), they appear most clearly in Brazil and in Colombia. While the *violencia* in Colombia will be discussed in greater detail below, it may be noted at this point that it arose out of the rivalries of the two competing national parties and their local bosses who used their campesino clientele for their political ambitions. In Colombia, too, the cleavages were originally not along ideological lines (Payne, 1968: 74–95) or along class lines. Rather, each party included the whole spectrum of social classes in the country. A campesino was liberal when his *patrón* was liberal, and he was conservative when his *patrón* was. The bloodiest battles were fought between liberal and conservative campesinos for whom it was a matter of self-preservation that the party of their boss controlled local spoils, patronage, and justice (Daniel, 1965: 15; Dix, 1967: chaps. 8–9). What came to be called *la violencia* in Colombia in the 1930s was basically an intensification of the violence that was endemic in the Colombian political structure since the independence from Spain. This political structure entailed the classic pattern of an exchange in which the national parties delivered spoils and patronage and the local *gamonales* provided the votes (Daniel, 1965: chaps. 2–3; Guillén Martínez, 1963: 139–78; Fluharty, 1957: 230–36). The stakes were all or nothing. Whenever power changed hands, the new party in power would harass the members and the clientele of the defeated incumbents (Daniel, 1965: chap. 3). To oppose the party or government in power meant to risk deprivation of most economic opportunities and the loss of land or life. As Guillén Martínez points out, for the party that was defeated in an election it was better to start a civil war than to comply with the results (1963: 150). Characteristically, in the twentieth century outbreaks of violence frequently followed periods of relative peace after elections turned the incumbent party out of office (for example, in 1930, 1938, and 1946). The peasantry, under these circumstances, had little choice but to become an appendage of whatever political machine their *patrón* belonged to (Guillén Martínez, 1963: 151; see also Dix, 1967: 222).

Suffice it here to refer to other authors who found it feasible to classify political groups as in or out in countries such as Peru in the mid-1960s (Payne, 1965: 269), Colombia (Bailey, 1967: 564; Dix, 1967: 231), and prerevolutionary Cuba (Wolf, 1969: 264–68). The effect is in any case that class conflicts are unlikely to occur as long as members of the lower classes stand to derive better benefits from interclass alliances with their *patrones* than from intraclass coalitions with their fellow workers or campesinos.

POLITICAL PARTIES

Party life in Latin America has traditionally centered around particularistic relationships between *patróns* and clients at the local and regional level. In the nineteenth century, and to some extent still in the twentieth century, political parties especially in rural areas are organized around local and regional *gamonales* and their extended family who are capable of mobilizing the rural vote and dispensing spoils and patronage at the local level. In such a system based on patterns of social power, the need for a more formal party organization is minimal as long as the electorate is relatively small and controllable by the *gamonales* (Dix, 1967: 204). Frequently, larger political parties originated in the nineteenth century out of coalitions between local political bosses with their respective families and followings, which became integrated with other such local coalitions on the provincial and national level. In Brazil, for example, Oliveira Vianna (1949, vol. 1) found it useful to conceive of the emerging political parties in the nineteenth century as local coalitions of "electoral clans" who had to side with the party of the governor in order to share in the spoils and patronage dispensed at the national and state (during the Empire, provincial) level (1949, vol. 1: 277–91, 338, 350).

It is characteristic that conflicts between the traditional political parties in Latin America have centered less around ideological issues than around the incorporation of new or deprived sectors and groups into the national system of spoils. In many countries, relatively enduring parties have grouped around the *conservative* and *liberal* labels. It would be wrong to state that ideologies played no role at all in the party membership. The Conservatives were generally representative of the traditional landowners with aristocratic inclinations and strong beliefs in the sacredness of social hierarchies, authority, and obedience by subordinates; the Liberals were a heterogeneous group of newer sectors: landowners and merchants with commercial interests related to imports and exports, people affected by the French enlightenment and rationalism, and (such as in Colombia) officers of the independence movement who had been rewarded for their services with land grants and found their economic interests hampered by slavery, the Indian reservations (which restricted the availability of cheap labor), and the Church (which held much of the best lands). In Colombia this led to often violent conflicts between the Conservatives and the Liberals in which the dividing issues were the state-Church relationship, slavery, and free trade (Dix, 1967: 231–48). But notwithstanding the ideological dimensions that did exist in traditional party struggles,

the struggle was, after all, primarily within the elite itself, with others serving as Liberal or Conservative camp followers. The Liberals did not seek to destroy the *patterns* of social and economic power, such as the system of large estates, but rather to partake of their benefits. (Dix, 1967: 246)

It is this overriding concern with spoils that reduces the significance of ideological dimensions in party conflicts. Existing differences in the social bases and ideologies are usually tendencies and founded on the political background, not the social status, of the family and on very concrete economic or political interests. The lines of such ideological cleavages tend to be blurred and not defined along status differences. In Colombia, Payne (1968: chap. 4) found in a recent survey of party functionaries that the Conservative and Liberal parties, as well as the factions within them, were not divided on ideological or policy questions, except on strategic matters. In Peru of the 1960s, the lack of ideologies and programs on the part of the parliamentarians was reflected in the parliamentary initiatives, which consisted of "the power endowed upon each representative to personally mobilize a given budget assignation for any purposes that he should determine" and "surname laws" that benefited or hurt a particular individual or sector of the population (Cotler, 1970b: 431). In nineteenth-century Brazil, the very designation *party of the governor* indicated the lack of ideology. Or witness Tannenbaum's discussion with an exiled Honduran army officer in the early twentieth century. Tannenbaum asked him how many parties there were in Honduras.

"Only two: the Red and the Green. I belong to the Green Party," he replied.
"And what is the difference between them?"
After a moment's reflection he said: "Well, there is really no difference between them, only naturally I think that the Green party is better." (Tannenbaum, 1960: 136)

The late development of relatively permanent political parties in many Latin American countries after the achievement of independence is another reflection of the insignificance of programs. In Peru and Ecuador, no permanent parties developed during most of the nineteenth century, and the few attempts to found political societies in the metropoles were limited in membership and short-lived. Governmental succession was mostly regulated through military intervention. In Ecuador the labels *liberal* and *conservative* existed in the nineteenth and have survived in the twentieth century, but these labels carry little weight in the outcomes of elections (Payne, 1968: 127–31). In Colombia, in contrast, permanent organizations formed around the conservative and liberal labels early after independence. But it should be noted that the origin of these labels is confused. The term *liberal* appears to have been in use since 1830 but did not clearly distinguish between political groups, since most politicians adopted it. Payne (1968: 129) suggests that the final clarification came just prior to the presidential election of 1848 when the incumbents adopted the conservative label; "whether arbitrarily, or because it was the next most popular term after 'Liberal,' is not clear."

The functioning of political parties in Latin America to the present day is best explained in terms of the clientelism that pervades the political life of the continent. Clientelism is a political pattern that basically rests on a variety of interconnected exchanges in which (1) in a general manner political parties and governments provide material benefits to their clients in exchange for votes, and (2) more specifically, local organizers deliver the votes of the clientele to a national party in return for local spoils and patronage.[8] Ideological aspects are of minimal importance precisely because parties are held together by the rather material payoffs for their membership and following (Powell, 1970: 422). These payoffs entail:

1. Votes, delivered by the clientele, followers, and hangers-on, either because they expect tangible rewards in return or because they have to follow the wishes of the *patrón* who controls their lives. Those who cannot provide votes (for example, because of literacy requirements) receive little attention. Peru's APRA, an urban-based reformist party, has only hesitantly incorporated the Indian campesinos of the highlands because, as one party official put it, "there was no interest in it, in view of the fact that Indians do not count politically, as they do not vote" (cited by Cotler, 1970b: 431).

2. Patronage. Local "grass roots mobilizers" (Powell, 1970: 416, fn. 27) who deliver the vote to the regional or national parties are rewarded with patronage for themselves and their followers, which has in Latin America usually enabled them to exercise political control over their territory and to harass their opponents.

3. Employment and prospects of social mobility. The party faithfuls and the dues-paying members can expect employment from the government in return for their services to the party (Payne, 1968: 51–73; Landy, 1959: 56; B. Hutchinson, 1966: 21). In Mexico, it has been estimated that by 1910 almost three-quarters of the middle class had found employment within the state apparatus (Wolf, 1969: 15). In general, party politics also provides an avenue for social mobility, prestige, and power (Payne, 1968: 25–50).

4. Public benefits such as the allocation of public works, extension of credit, or, where the powers of the landholders have been effectively challenged, agrarian reform legislation to benefit the campesino (Galjart, 1964: 7; Powell, 1969; 1970: 418–22; Heath, Erasmus, and Buechler, 1969).

5. Security and survival. Those who are powerless and in an economically precarious position can obtain a degree of security under the protection of a powerful *patrón* to whom they give their votes.

What are the alternatives of the campesinos in such a system?

As long as they did not have the right to vote and as long as they were under the total domination of their *patrón* they had either nothing to bargain with or no power to sell their vote to the highest bidder. With the gradual extension of the rural vote in Latin America in the twentieth century, the campesinos gained the potential resources for political bargaining with those *patrones* who offered them the most benefits.[9] But in many areas the expansion of rural suffrage through legislation had the effect of strengthening the local *gamonales* and *coroneis* who, retaining their economic and social leverage, now were able to use the enfranchised campesinos as a political resource they could mobilize vis-à-vis the regional and national governments (Galjart, 1964). The *gamonales* thus retained in a modified form their monopoly as brokers who, according to Eric Wolf,

stand guard over the crucial junctures or synapses of relationships which connect the local system to the larger whole. Their basic function is to relate community-oriented individuals who want to stabilize or improve their life chances, but who lack economic security and political connections, with nation-oriented individuals who operate primarily in terms of the complex cultural forms standardized as national institutions, but whose success in these operations depends on the strength and size of their personal following. (1965: 97)

It was the brokerage function of the *gamonales* that rendered them important in the larger political structures of Latin American societies and made it so difficult for the campesinos to fight them effectively. The campesinos had little to offer in the informal networks of favors by which members of the upper and middle classes were obligated to one another. These networks of mutual obligation still provide access to employment, contracts, and social mobility for their participants and are described in detail in A. Leeds's (1965) discussion of the Brazilian *panelinha*. Other authors have noted the same phenomenon in Peru (Cotler, 1970b: 427) and Latin America in general (R. N. Adams, 1967a: 57–61). Campesinos generally lack the connections necessary to achieve their ends in such a system and, therefore, have to rely on the favors from their *patrones* in such simple matters as filing legal claims with a court, petitioning the government, or finding employment outside the community. Under these conditions, realistic alternatives to following the *patrón* in his political endeavors did not develop until new brokers (teachers, sympathetic lawyers, and so forth) entered their community and political parties developed at the national level that competed with the established *patrones* for the lower-class clientele. These problems will be discussed at greater length in later chapters.

ELECTIONS

Electoral processes have constituted a crucial mechanism in the political structure prevailing in traditional Latin American politics. Campesinos have been, and still are, handicapped in obtaining the vote because many of them are illiterate (which bars them from voting in countries such as Brazil and Peru and used to exclude them in countries such as Bolivia) or do not speak Spanish. Thus, the proportion of campesinos who could vote has traditionally been small. In Brazil of 1930 it is estimated that some 80 percent of the population was rural and that 80 percent was also the rate of illiteracy of the country. The total electorate at that time is estimated to have comprised no more than 1 percent of the total population. Since illiteracy was and is higher in the countryside than in the city (and most of the rural residents were *camponêses*), it is apparent that the proportion of peasant voters must have been even less than 1 percent (Furtado, 1965: 151). In a contemporary regional survey in rural Peru, Cotler (1970a: 554) found that 39 percent of the Indians living in their own communities and 5 percent of those residing on haciendas were registered to vote. Those campesinos who did vote tended to vote with their *patrón* in countries such as Guatemala (Pearson, 1969: 330), Chile (Petras and Zeitlin, 1970: 510), Colombia (Dix, 1967: 204), or Brazil (Blondel, 1957: 57–59, 73). Workers on traditional *engenho* plantations in Brazil, when asked in the 1950s how they might vote in the next election, were apt to give answers such as: "I don't know, I haven't found out how the *patrão* will vote," or "With the *patrão*, Senhor" (Wagley and Harris, 1965: 61).[10] Such answers reflect sentiments of loyalty in many cases; but the campesinos usually also had little choice other than to comply with the orders of the *patrão*, since they needed his favors and protection (Vianna, 1949, vol. 1: 307–12; Blondel, 1957: 57–59, 73). Usually, election day meant for those who voted that they would be trucked into town, have a day off work, and receive a free meal—which could be considered quite a bargain by campesinos with little understanding of politics. Dix writes about contemporary Colombia:

As a rule, those dependent on a patrón look to him for political guidance. They know that to vote against his wishes would be to "lose credit" with him. Some patrones make it a point to hire only those of their own party so that their employees will be more amenable to their political direction. But it is doubtful that most campesinos even conceive of voting in a manner distinct from that of their patrón, or of those local political leaders who in turn owe their positions to him. On election day the function of party officials is to shepherd electors to the polls, to hand them the party ballot, and to ensure that the voters actually cast their ballot for the proper list. (1967: 204)

Observing similar processes in northeast Brazil, Furtado has analyzed the consequences of the rural worker's dependence on the *patrão*:

Neither does he perceive any connection between his "political" conduct—voting in elections—and the conditions of his life. Whatever the outcomes of the elections may be, the local authorities, the only ones whose conduct is reflected in his life, must necessarily please the wills of those who have something to defend, who are the owners of the lands, the machines, the houses, the roads, and everything which (can be found) on the property on which the voter lives. (1964: 148. My translation)

Election laws were frequently geared to facilitate the *patrón*'s supervision over the choice of his workers. In many countries, such as Brazil during the nineteenth century, there was no secret ballot. Chile had an election code until 1958 that allowed each party to print and distribute its own ballots. The implications for the campesinos' voting behavior are obvious:

The *patrones* often simply gave the ballots of the party of their choice to their *inquilinos*, and provided them and nearby peasants with transportation to and from the polling places. With their ballots already provided, the peasants were not likely to ask the local registrar for a different party's ballot—if it occurred to them to do so. Whether provided with the "proper" ballot beforehand or not, their choice of party was, of course, known from the choice of their ballot, and was information easily available to the *patrón*. (Petras and Zeitlin, 1970: 510, fn. 10)

A Puerto Rican caneworker who worked as an election official sympathetically described the plight of his colleagues who lived on the property of the plantation on which they were employed:

The last one we worked with that day—that is, with whom I worked that day—was Don Rafael Garcia. . . . He was the mayordomo overseer at Colonia Destino, and there he was, working alongside me in the polling station. In the other station, on the other side, was Don Benigno Patino, the mayordomo of Colonia Texidor, who threw me out of work and blacklisted me. They used this system so that when the voters came from their colonias to vote, they were confronted with the mayordomos sitting there. And then you could see the fear. They would vote for *their* party for fear that when they went back home they would be thrown out, or some such thing— whatever oppression the mayordomo would think of—and so the voters would vote with them.
    They had a system that almost always told them how one voted. They'd know. Because I've also worked at the table, and when I was interested in knowing how a person voted, I've investigated. (Mintz, 1960: 150)

Political allegiance thus is not determined by class interests, but by personal, family, or communal attachments, and election campaigns "are therefore attempts to 'animate the masses' and to reinforce assured loyalties, rather than to convince" (Dix, 1967: 204–5). Even in the middle of the twentieth century, Brazilian political bosses in rural areas organize the transport of their voters to the polls and personally supervise the vote of their dependents (Blondel, 1957: 90). The interest of a *fazendeiro* in mobilizing his dependents has been shown to depend on the number of candidates running in local elections. With only one candidate, the election is assured without much mobilization, and the turnout is low. When a landholder's candidate is opposed by another party, he is likely to mobilize all his dependents who can vote or learn how to spell their names in crash courses provided by "*escolas temporarias*" (temporary schools), which are established for purely electoral purposes (Blondel, 1957: 73–93). In Chile, landholders encourage their *inquilinos* to vote for the party of their choice by giving them one shoe and promising the other when the desired candidate has in fact been elected. In this manner, *inquilinos* are likely to bring social pressure to bear on recalcitrant peers who oppose the wishes of the *hacendado*. Such tactics were not vitiated by the single ballot introduced in 1958 (Petras and Zeitlin, 1970: 510, fn. 10). Incentives such as these are another instance of the peasant's dilemma in having to choose between his immediate personal interests and his class interests.

It has generally been the case that an incumbent party manipulated elections through the use of loyal local administrators, judges, and police officers. In Colombia, elections have been characterized by "creeping fraud" (benefiting the incumbent) ever since the inception of the Republic. It has been suggested that the only reason the opposition party sometimes won an election was the endemic division in the incumbent party and the possibility for all the "outs" to form a coalition for purposes of the election.

Thus, the division of the ruling party was actually the more common termination of creeping fraud. If the opposition won, it could take office primarily because the "incumbents" were so divided that they could not take concerted action. (Payne, 1968: 126)

Under the Diaz regime in Mexico preceding the revolution of 1910, the government had complete control over the outcome of all elections. This was precisely why elements of the urban intelligentsia proclaimed the revolution; his unsuccessful campaign for an opposition candidate for the governorship in the state of Morelos was a major factor in convincing Emiliano Zapata that the peasantry had nothing to gain from the current regime. In Brazil, after the establishment of the republic in 1891 the state governments used their budget and appointive power over the *municípios* to control local elections and, if necessary, invalidate the outcomes (Nuñes Leal, 1948: 87–88).

Fraud and violence have tended to be endemic in rural (and also urban) political campaigns. In Colombia, violence and fraud were considered normal at election time (Daniel, 1965: chap. 4), but in the 1949 campaign for the presidential election, the abuses of the incumbent Conservatives became scandalous. Liberal voter registrars were expelled from their posts by force; the police terrorized liberal functionaries and voters; voter certificates were taken away from political opponents; lives were lost, houses and property were destroyed, and civil liberties were suspended. On at least one occasion, Liberal campesinos were intercepted by Conservative forces, lost their voter registration certificates, and were issued safe conduct passes in return for a Conservative vote (Guzmán Campos, Fals-Borda, and Umaña Luna, 1962: 250; Daniel, 1965: 58). In Mexico, opponents of the Diaz regime were frequently apprehended by the special rural police forces (the *rurales*) and killed under the protection of the *ley fuga* that permitted the shooting of prisoners trying to escape (Wolf, 1969: 15).

Violence, fraud, and terrorization of opponents and their voters have traditionally been rampant in Brazil and have been described in detail by Vianna (1949, vol. 1: 300–306) and Nuñes Leal (1948: 87–88, 146, 163–67, 174–89). Blondel, describing techniques of election fraud in rural Brazil (1957: 93–100), has reported veritable "mobile voter squadrons" (*esquadrões volantes de eleitores*) who went from precinct to precinct in order to cast their ballots for their political boss (1957: 75). In the 1960s elections were still rather meaningless in many places, at least from the standpoint of the peasants' interests. A member of one of the *ligas camponésas* in Brazil told the CIDA researchers:

When the elections come, the M.'s announce that there is a climate of insecurity in Sapé and ask for state police to guarantee the outcome of the elections. The police arrive and stay there with pointed guns. It's laughable. The M's bring the workers from the factory in trucks. They (the workers) must be nudged by the capangas when the time comes to applaud. (CIDA, 1966a: 315)

From the point of view of the campesinos, politics was a vicious circle. They were totally dependent on their *patrón* and had to vote according to his wishes. The *patrón*'s control over the workers' vote, in turn, made him indispensable for politicians who could ill afford to pass legislation, execute administrative programs, or appoint local and regional officers who could undermine the land-lord's control over his subordinates.

POLITICAL VIOLENCE

As the previous considerations have indicated, violence has traditionally played a crucial role in Latin American politics. The rule of the *caudillo*, "who governs because he can, not because he was elected" (Tannenbaum, 1960: 138), is still pervasive in the twentieth century where the actual or threatened use of force is in many countries a prime mover of governmental action. Payne has found it useful to conceive of contemporary Peruvian interest-group politics as "democracy by violence" (1965: 268–83) in which threats of violence against the executive constitute a permanent aspect of political bargaining. During the most tumultuous years of the Colombian *violencia*, opposing deputies fought gun battles in Parliament (Guzmán Campos, Fals-Borda, and Umaña Luna, 1962: 239–69).

One aspect of the pervasive violence in Latin American politics is the normality of military intervention in regulating governmental succession. This pattern has been predominant in practically all Latin American countries during the nineteenth and twentieth centuries (Kling, 1968; 1969) and is reflected in the cynical comments of Bolivian newspapers, in which the fighting of 1952 was dismissed as "merely the 179th revolution in Bolivia's 126 years of independence" (cited in Heath, 1965).[11] A simple survey of con-temporary Latin American countries reveals that most regimes owe their existence to direct intervention or tacit tolerance by the armed forces.

Similarly, the police have traditionally been an instrument of partisan politics—to maintain not "law and order," but usually "the government and order." The use of the police by politicians to terrorize their opponents and their followers has already been indicated (Guzmán Campos, Fals-Borda, and Umaña Luna, 1962: 252–63). What is particularly interesting with regard to the private function of the police is the blurring of the boundary between those who are on the side of the law and those who are not. Ultimately, those were within the law who were on the side of the winning politicians. The infamous *rurales* in Mexico who ruthlessly purged the countryside from opponents of the regime were recruited from regular police and various kinds of outlaws who had thus found a legal way for continuing what they had been doing before (Tannen-baum, 1929: 140; Wolf, 1969: 14–15). In Brazil during the nine-teenth and early twentieth century, it was frequently only a matter of luck whether those who earned their livelihood through violence ended up as *cangaceiros* (bandits), as *capangas* (hired gunmen) of private *coroneis*, or as members of the mobile police forces, the *forças volantes*, which roamed the northeast chasing bandits or the private troups of political bosses who were rivals of their *coroneis*. Characteristically, all these groups had the same kind of membership, and changes from *cangaço* (outlawry) to *capangagem* and police were possible and frequent. Many outlaws operated from safe territories well into the 1930s where they enjoyed the protection of *coroneis* who provided them with money, supplies, and shelter in return for safety from raids and cooperation in the terrorization of political opponents. A highlight of this situation was the commission of the famous *cangaceiro* Virgulino Ferreira, better known as Lampião, as a captain of the federally enlisted troups that fought the communist *Coluna Prestes* in 1926.[12]

A similar pattern of interaction between official and unofficial violence is found in the Colombian *violencia*, where the distinction between guerrillas, bandits, and police became increasingly difficult to make in the 1950s. Some criminals, freed during the *bogotazo* (the Bogotá riots in 1948), took to the hills and mingled with the politically motivated *cuadrillas* and with campesinos who were driven into a mixture of political guerrilla action and banditry by the prevailing violence and anarchy (Daniel, 1965, esp. chap. 5). Cases are also known where local political bosses entered coalitions with bandits in which protection and arms were exchanged for political assassination (Daniel, 1965: 104), and participants in the *violencia* have stated in interviews that there was little difference between the activities of bandits and the police (Guzmán Campos, Fals-Borda, and Umaña Luna, 1962: 267–68). Also in Colombia, the so-called *pájaros* (literally, birds) intimidated the Liberal population as a private secret police who would kill anybody for whom the Conservatives (and later dictator Rojas Pinilla) had written a contract. The *pájaros* had virtual immunity from police prosecution and were even said to be frequent visitors at local police headquarters (Guzmán Campos, Fals-Borda, and Umaña Luna, 1962: 165–69). Such organizations as the *pájaros* were not unknown in other parts of the continent. For example, the Argentinian dictator Juan Manuel Rosas (1829–1831, 1835–1852) had a similar secret organization in his *majorca*.

The prevalence of violence is paralleled by the relative inability of the courts to punish its perpetrators. The domination of municipal courts by political bosses has been amply demonstrated in countries such as Brazil (Nuñes Leal, 1948: 146–48), Peru (Béjar,

1969: 94–95), and Colombia (CIDA, 1966b: 226–27). The general pattern is that the juridical personnel at the local municipal level, while appointed by the state or national governments, owe their position to the intervention of local *gamonales* and have little freedom to pronounce verdicts against the wishes of their benefactors. A generally regulated judicial career does not exist (Guzmán Campos, Fals-Borda, and Umaña Luna, 1962: 301–98; CIDA, 1966b: 226 for Colombia). In the Colombian *violencia* the impunity of criminals was one of the most severe problems that served to institutionalize political banditry. Bandits and assassins who killed at the order of eminent politicians were acquitted or received minor sentences at the intervention of highly placed officials, depending on their political affiliation and that of the judges. At the same time, the jails were filled with followers and allies of the opposition party (Guzmán Campos, Fals-Borda, and Umaña Luna, 1962: 249–52). An interesting variant of the impunity existed in Brazil well into the twentieth century with the asylum landholders could grant to fugitives from justice. The *direito de couto e homisio*, granted to the large *fazendeiros* by the king of Portugal in the sixteenth century, was the right to give inviolable asylum to anybody (Vianna, 1949, vol. 2: 223, 231–32). It prompted many fugitive slaves and criminals to seek refuge on the large estates of the interior. This brought them into complete dependence on the *fazendeiro* and made them his most devoted followers and least scrupulous *capangas*. The tradition of granting asylum (*coito*) still persisted in some parts of Brazil in the first half of the twentieth century, where many *coiteiros* (landholders harboring fugitives) secretly entertained and supplied *cangaceiros* on their estates and openly refused to let the police chase the bandits on their lands. While some landholders in the more remote areas had often little choice but to protect the *cangaceiros*, lest they risked the loss of lives and property, many of them actually benefited greatly from an alliance with outlaws who would direct their attacks to the *fazendas* of their protector's enemies (Gueiros, 1956: 15, 68).

As has been pointed out frequently (Stokes, 1952; Kling, 1968; 1969), violence is endemic to Latin American politics on the local as well as the national level; it is a "recurring, chronic, and rule-conforming" (Kling, 1969: 196) mechanism of political succession. With the independence of the continent there arose a vacuum of legitimate authority left by the departing king of Spain. There was no legitimate successor to the throne, and political power became the spoils of those who were strong enough to conquer it. Legitimacy existed only in the right of the *caudillo* to make use of the powers he had gathered and to enjoy the fruits of his success as long as he could hold on to it (Tannenbaum, 1960: 145–53). In politics, there was no conflict between might and right: violence was accepted as a legitimate means for the pursuit of power (Kling, 1969: 193); might was right.

For the ordinary campesino who controlled few means of force, all this meant (and often still means) that there were no avenues available for countering the usurpation of the landholders. The CIDA researchers found in Colombia that the most frequent complaints of campesinos centered around their lack of access to legal institutions because they had no recourse against the slowly moving bureaucracy that owed them nothing (CIDA, 1966b: 227). Such bureaucracies can be speedily mobilized, on the other hand, when the local powerholders are filing claims. In 1963, a Peruvian *hacendado* killed one of his tenant farmers. When the rest of his workers took this occasion to file a long list of complaints against the abuses they had suffered in the past, the complainants were sent to prison for violating the freedom of their boss and stealing money and foodstuffs from him (Béjar, 1969: 94–95). Incidents such as this one have been numerous and the experiences of the campesinos have been bitter. Unless they see practical proof that the law can and will help them, they are likely to distrust the judicial administration, which frequently conducts its business in a language they neither understand nor identify as the language of their oppressors. Thus, of 499 Indian campesinos interviewed in the 1960s in the Cuzco region (Peru), 56 percent believed that judges base their decisions on personal influence and on the amount of money paid by the plaintiffs (Cotler, 1970b: 419), and Bolivian campesinos have been found to prefer justice to be dispensed in a Solomic fashion by their local syndicate leaders because they feel, even after the revolution of 1952, that the official "justice belongs to the rich" (Heath, Erasmus, and Buechler, 1969: 190). As a result, they need to seek a protector who mobilizes his political influence if they need to resolve legal matters. They are thus dependent upon lawyers from outside their community to handle their claims, but these lawyers frequently abuse them (Cotler, 1970b: 418–19; Tullis, 1970: chap. 6, esp. 87, fn. 1, 104, 106–8, 120–21).[13] If even such lawyers are unavailable, the only recourse the campesinos have is to join the bandwagon of their *patrón*, try to make a place for themselves through loyalty, and hope that he will be a good *patrón* or an effective *caudillo* (Galjart, 1972: 7–8). They might find the Arab saying congenial that advises, "Kiss the hand that you cannot cut off."

INFLUENCE ON GOVERNMENTAL INSTITUTIONS

While the general influence of large landholders in the national and local politics of Latin American countries has already been indicated with regard to party organization and elections, a few comments may be made with specific reference to the influence of the *gamonales* over administrative offices. In the more remote areas of many countries, municipalities have remained under the control, if not on the property, of the large haciendas of the vicinity. In some Peruvian regions, reports from the 1960s indicate that many landowners accept no authority on their estates other than their own. They are the first to intervene in quarrels between their tenants, in cases of theft, and even in matters of more severe crimes. Traditional local authorities were appointed by, and took their oath before, the hacienda administrators; the provincial government was inactive in the regions (Cotler, 1970b: 424). A district, a province, and even a department may be dominated by a single family or group of families. Corresponding observations have been made in other countries such as Ecuador (CIDA, 1965b: 98), Brazil (Mitchell, 1966–1967: 5; Vinicius Vilaca and Albuquerque, 1965: 34–35), and Colombia (CIDA, 1966b: 224–26). The influence of Brazilian *fazendeiros* on the municipal administrations has been described in many places (Diégues, 1954: 226–31; Nuñes Leal, 1948: 26–27; Harris, 1956: 186–207). One of the main levers of the landholders, apart from their control over local appointments, is their influence in the state and national capitals to mobilize the financial resources on which the municipal governments depend for their regular operations and for the provision of public services. This leverage is especially strong where the *municípios* are notoriously poor (Nuñes Leal, 1948: 27; CIDA, 1966b: 225; Lewis, 1960: 49).

At the national level, the powers of the landholders are reflected in several ways. First, as has been indicated, they can deliver the local votes and, moreover, have access to the informal networks of favors and obligations known as *panelinha* in Brazil (Leeds, 1965) but operating elsewhere as well. This constitutes one of the most important bases of the landholder's power. A second source for their power lies in the electoral systems that frequently provide the landholders with disproportionately large representation in the national parliaments (Furtado, 1965: 151–52; Cotler, 1970b: 422).

A particularly effective way of expanding their influence at the national (and local) level is the landholders' access to multiple positions held at the same time. They often invest their profits from agricultural enterprises in urban and industrial business (CIDA, 1966a: 169–78), or they may hold a variety of institutional offices, as has been shown in most Latin American countries (CIDA, 1965b: 108; White, 1969: 131–32). In Ecuador, for example, members of the influential *Cámara de Agricultura* (a landowners' association) have occupied within a span of twenty-five years such positions as president of the republic (4), legislators, often for several terms (51), cabinet ministers (21), members of the supreme court (3), diplomats (8), high administrative posts, especially directorships of the official bank (14), and provincial and municipal councilmen (4) (CIDA, 1965b: 108). Such institutional membership is quite characteristic in other countries, too (CIDA, 1966c: 259–61 for Peru). Brazil's Senate in the 1960s was controlled by rural landholders (Furtado, 1965: 151), and the majority of Colombia's current Parliamentary deputies are said to be *latifundistas* (*Der Spiegel*, 1971). Even when they do not directly hold offices, landholders still wield significant influence over the occupation of positions touching upon their interests. When the director of INCORA (Colombia's institute for administrating agrarian reform) recently declared that the land invasions of 1970–1971 by Colombian campesinos were an expression of "the *campesinos'* justified distrust of the legal obstacles to agrarian reform" (*Der Spiegel*, 1971), he was fired.

With the landholder's influence on administrative and legislative offices, it was nearly impossible to plan and carry out agrarian reform programs or other social legislation protecting the campesinos. Those programs passed by the legislatures were usually designed to assuage the demands of interest groups or international pressures from the Alliance for Progress; but they have generally been stated either so vaguely that there was considerable room for the discretion of an administration favorable to the landowners,[14] or in a manner that demanded minimal concessions from the *latifundistas* who found easy ways to circumvent the law or actually profit from it (Feder, 1970). This type of avoidance was congenial to the colonial tradition of a dualism between the king's law (protecting the Indians) and the actual customs of exploitation prevailing in the colonies in violation of the law. The royal bureaucracy tended to compromise and thereby "save the King's conscience"; they would report to him that the law had been "obeyed but not enforced" (Tannenbaum, 1960: 156). This tradition is still very much alive in Latin America where social reforms have frequently been moral facades and token concessions to a political clientele or ally. Such reforms tend to lead not to a change in social conditions but to a perpetuation of them by providing an outlet for some of the pressures that might otherwise lead to violent revolts. Social reforms in Latin America have frequently been counterreforms—measures that tend to weaken the position of the very groups that are supposedly helped.[15]

For the peasant, national and local government have traditionally meant very little. National politics appears only as a label of the local powerholders (Hobsbawm, 1967: 49). Harris's (1956) description of the difference between town and village in rural Brazil is quite representative for the traditional politics of other parts of the continent: in the village, there is little interest in politics since the outcome of elections is expected to have little effect on the villagers' living conditions; *o governo*, the government, is an abstract menace represented by the tax collector who takes the villagers' money and never returns anything (Harris, 1956: 201–7; see also similar comments about Mexico by Lewis, 1960: 45). Venezuelan campesinos have expressed very low confidence in their ability to influence political decisions in comparison with all other groups surveyed (Mathiason, 1966: 138–40). Tullis (1970: chap. 6) has provided detailed descriptions of many futile attempts by campesinos to settle their claims through the official legal channels. The responsiveness of local governments to the campesinos' needs has traditionally been limited because of the latter's "contractual inferiority in the face-to-face relations" (Pearse, 1970: 38) with town-dwelling merchants and officials. Thus,

the "Indian" may be required to bring gifts to the alcalde or perform some menial task before a problem of boundaries or inheritance is attended to, and at any point he may be shouted down and the matter ended by the caprice of the official. The unlettered peasant who does not suffer from these cultural disadvantages, i.e., being an Indian is likely to be led into unnecessary complicated and expensive paths when he tries to legalize an inheritance; and no one is surprised if he arrives at the agricultural loan bank after a twenty-mile walk to be told by the clerk to "come back tomorrow." (Pearse, 1970: 38–39)

Fitzgibbon observed about countries with a large Indian population (Guatemala, Bolivia, Peru, Ecuador):

In practically all of those countries or parts of countries, the Indian, after four and a half centuries, is still not "a part of the national life." Politics in the occidental sense remains a monopoly of the white or very-near-white segments of the population. The Indian's contact with the white man's government are usually with the police official, the recruiting officer, or the tax collector. (1950: 124)

CHAPTER 7

Psychocultural Dimensions
of Domination

There are a number of cultural and psychological configurations representing cognitive adaptations to the subordination of peasants in general and of Latin American campesinos in particular. Analogous to Oscar Lewis's conception of the culture of poverty, Everett Rogers (1969: chap. 2) has outlined what he believes to be a universal subculture of peasantry with eight characteristics that are presumed to be universally found among subsistence cultivators: distrust in interpersonal relations, a lack of innovativeness, fatalism, low levels of aspiration, absence of deferred gratification, limited time perspective, familism, dependence on government authority, lack of cosmopolitanism, and low levels of empathy. An obvious weakness of this kind of approach, however, is that it places the cause of the peasants' deprivation on cultural and personality traits while ignoring entirely the repressive objective context within which peasants have to adapt their cultural patterns and personality traits. Williams (1969), for example, found among Peruvian campesinos tendencies to avoid decisions, to perceive the world in crude dichotomies, anxiety, low tolerance for ambiguity, and the search for patronage to be psychosocial correlates of domination. Huizer (1970b; 1972) has persuasively argued that these and related psychocultural configurations represent a "culture of repression" that is primarily not the cause but the consequence of tremendous external constraints and the general exploitation faced by peasants. The culture of repression is a "culture" insofar as it entails realistic adaptations to low control over the social, political, and economic environment. But these adaptations may not be as much founded on socialization and internalized values as on pragmatic and individualized (in other words, not socially shared, transmitted, and sanctioned) habitual responses to deprivation and domination. These responses may over time become sufficiently fortified to constitute initial barriers to new responses once realistic opportunities for improvement or revolt emerge. The thrust of the culture of repression is in the direction of maintaining the peasants' status quo of subordination by restricting their interactions with peers and members of other social groups in the larger society, placing them at the mercy of outside authorities, and adapting their aspirations and expectations to low-action outcomes. It is precisely for this reason that we have to examine in this chapter a number of psychocultural configurations that have been identified in the literature as possible mechanisms whereby domination is perpetuated.

But available evidence also suggests that in the long run peasants respond enthusiastically once they are convinced that innovative or rebellious courses of action not only have realistic chances of success but also bring about drastic changes in existing structures of domination. Psychocultural adaptations to domination are, therefore, consequences of repression, as they can reinforce it. Causation must thus be seen not in unidirectional terms but as a process of mutual determination of culture, personality factors, and objective constraints and opportunities with each one being capable of changing autonomously and thus constituting a source of imbalance in relation to the others.[1] Some psychocultural factors that reinforce and validate dominance-related behaviors among campesinos will be discussed in the following sections.

COGNITIVE CAPACITY

Cognitive capacity is conceived as the degree to which individuals are capable of handling complex cognitions and expanding their repertory of concepts and categories. This variable is significant for the maintenance of dominance patterns because the propensity of subordinates to perceive and value alternative relationships to the current one(s) should increase with an increase in their cognitive capacity. In this regard, campesinos have traditionally been at a disadvantage in comparison with their *patrones*.[2] The landholders had easy access to the large cities and the best educational facilities. They were usually widely traveled men, capable of providing their children with the best education in the country or even abroad. The campesinos, on the other hand, usually did not even have elementary instructions in their communities. Illiteracy still is pervasive among them, opportunities for travel limited. In addition, Indian campesinos frequently did not know Spanish and thus had no way of communicating in their national culture without the help of interpreters—*patrones* and other mestizos who took advantage of their cultural monopoly. Outsiders who might have influenced the campesinos could easily be barred from the community by the *patrón*. Even in contemporary Venezuela, sample surveys

TABLE 2. *Exposure to Media and Level of Information*
(Percent "yes")

	Paucartambo	Sicuani
Has a radio	6	64
Listens to the radio daily	11	49
Has never heard a radio	40	13
Knows how to read and write	6	39
Knows the name of the president of Peru	26	51
Knows who the Incas were	8	42
Knows his own age	34	88
Is bilingual (Spanish/Quechua)	16	62

All differences significant at the .05 level. SOURCE: Cotler, 1970a: 553.

reveal that among all groups campesinos are least exposed to mass media, except radio, and have the least contact with officers of the armed forces, businessmen, student leaders, and foreigners (Mathiason, 1966: 134–35). The extent of cultural isolation among contemporary Indians in the Peruvian highlands is reflected in data from Cotler (1970a), who compared a hacienda village (Paucartambo) with the independent Indian community of Sicuani (Table 2).

Traditional campesino communities, then, have existed in cultural isolation not only in the sense that they lacked access to the symbols of the national culture (Cotler, 1970a: 537–38), but also because their low cognitive capacity (education, outside reference sources) functioned to limit their conceptions of alternatives to the status quo to the benefit of the landowners.[3]

The above considerations are consistent with some insightful interpretations of peasant society and personality in general provided by Bequiraj (1966). Bequiraj suggests that powerlessness and scarcity in peasant societies necessitate cognitive adjustments that entail substitute gratifications in the form of kin attachments and the magnification of momentary euphorias provided by fiestas. Furthermore, the discrepancies between material needs and attainments makes it mandatory to lower expectations to the level of past attainments. The seeming satisfaction of peasants, often alleged, however, is not a function of satisfaction with current outcomes but reflects an accommodation to the high costs of attaining better ones; latent aggressiveness always looms under the surface of this accommodation and breaks open when opportunities arise (Bequiraj, 1966: 9, 14). This sort of response to deprivation is seen by Bequiraj as part of a vicious circle in which accommodation, low cognitive capacity, and low behavior outcomes reinforce each other:

The adjustment of problems rather than an intellectual confrontation of them, keeps differentiation of activities down to the minimum necessary for survival. The individual can scarcely step outside the narrow circle of interactions allowed by the closed familistic group of which he is a member by birth. This narrowness, in turn, restricts the development of the cultural system's level of comprehension, which contains only the knowledge generated by these microsystems. (1966: 36)

PATERNALISM: WORLD VIEWS, VALUES, AND SENTIMENTS

Campesinos who are economically dependent and culturally deprived tend to view the world as basically hostile and power oriented and perceive their *patrón* as the single authority whose confidence and trust must be gained (Cotler, 1970b; CIDA, 1966a: 292). Paternalism is thus not only a sociostructural phenomenon. As Foster (1967a; 1967b) and B. Hutchinson (1966) have indicated, it is deeply rooted in the perceptions, world views, and belief systems of the dependents and as such may even persist in motivating behaviors that have become anachronistic with urbanization and industrialization (Foster, 1967e: chap. 1). The basic tenet of this world view is the "search for the boss" (Harris, 1956; also B. Hutchinson, 1966) or the establishment of "dyadic contracts" (Foster, 1967a; 1967e), expressed in the "feeling of isolation and abandonment" found by H. W. Hutchinson (1957: 65) among those Brazilian workers who worked on an *usina* plantation without a *patrão* and who could only turn to a disinterested overseer.

The search for a protector as a general cultural orientation is reflected not only in the mundane exchanges between *patrones* and clients, but also in the religious sphere. The preferential selection of high-status persons as godfathers for the children has already been discussed. The campesino's relationships with God, Christ, the Virgin Mary, and patron saints have been shown to express in a similar manner this inclination to seek favors and protection from a "supernatural patron." Patron saints are generally treated as intermediaries who, in return for sacrifices (such as candles, flowers, or vows), solicit favors from God for the supplicants desiring a good harvest or recovery from an illness.[4] In this sense the patron saints serve a function analogous to the functions of the cultural, economic, and political brokers on whom the peasant depends to underwrite his livelihood.

Information concerning the nature of the sentiments underlying the *patrón*-dependent relationship is equivocal. On the one hand, there is the almost idyllic picture of the personalistic bond of loyalty and affection linking the *patrón* and the campesino described by Wagley (1960: 183–87), Patch (1960: 140–41), H. W. Hutchinson (1957), and Gillin (1960: 36–37). In this situation the campesinos regarded the landlord as the strict but understanding benefactor, while the *patrón* regarded his workers as "children in his charge, to be disciplined, guided, and occasionally indulged" (Petras and Zeitlin, 1970: 509–11, paraphrasing Reinhard Bendix). On the other hand, there is the equally familiar picture of merciless exploitation and brutal repression of the peasantry, the campesinos' grudging submission, their concealed hostility, and outbursts of violence in which ferocious revenge is taken. There are two possible explanations for this contradiction, each of which may account for the conditions in different areas. On the one hand, reports have shown that subordinated campesinos tend to hide their true character and feelings when they are in the presence of the *patrón* (Holmberg, 1966: 8; Fried, 1962). They either act out their expected roles (childlike, naive, deferent, loyal, and so forth) or suppress their emotions (Fried, 1962). Witness Nuñez del Prado's characterization of the Cuzco (Peru) Indian:

With mestizos, he is suspicious, silent, withdrawn and nearly inaccessible; he offers a passive, and systematic resistance. He is humble, fearful, and inattentive; reticent and evasive in his answers, indecisive in his attitudes. He suppresses and hides his emotions and rarely reveals his disagreements even when he finds himself in fundamental opposition. He is obsequious at times, but this attitude implies that he wants something very specific, that he expects an almost immediate reward. With other natives he is open, communicative, fond of practical jokes, he makes a display of his industry and is ready and willing to cooperate; he shows his feelings and states his opinions without reserve. (1965: 106)

In view of such contradictory behavior in different settings, it may be suspected that in many instances the campesinos' "loyalty" and "affection" displayed in their interactions with landlords are a reflection of necessity and experience, rather than of authentic sentiment. This is not to say that the campesino fakes his behavior when in the presence of superiors; but it may be suggested that his manifest behavior toward superiors is pragmatic, learned, and reinforced by the experience of submission as much as it may be an expression of personality and culture.

On the other hand, in some cases there may be a real difference between areas or estates under harsh or benevolent domination. Hostility and violence may be most prevalent in areas where the landlords subdue their campesinos through force and deprivation, while sentiments of affection and loyalty may exist among campesinos who live under a benevolent rule and whose landlords employ minimal coercion, provide adequately for the workers, and display occasional signs of generosity. Thus, Petras and Zemelman (1972) have provided a wealth of field notes testifying to the perceptions of the *inquilinos* on the Chilean *fundo* Culiprán with regard to the allegiance that must be owed to a "good *patrón*." Particularly, one of the former *empleados* who enjoyed a relatively favored position on the *fundo* observed:

It's better to have security—even if you have to obey orders—than to be more free, as you say, in the city. . . . As for me, the *patrón* was always very good to me because we were brought up together. He's always given me all my food, and everything I have I owe to him. Why should I say anything bad about him? (1972: 121)

So we've had this house for more than one hundred years, and do you know why? Because we've gotten along well with the people who have owned the *fundo*. The *patrones* before gave us land. They thought well of my grandfather, and of my father after him. So we've always led an honorable, good life. (1972: 122)

I used to have a cuadra of the best land wherever I asked for it. And then I sold the produce in the capital. A year ago this month I sold two truckloads of potatoes in Santiago. I paid one thousand pesos a sack for freight and sold two hundred sacks in February. That's why I agreed with the *patrón* about the *regalías*. Even if there are others who don't have as much—who haven't risen as high—because you know that everyone has his place on the ladder. Not everyone can be the same on the fundo. (1972: 124)

Concerning the unionization of the *inquilinos*, this *empleado* observed:

I didn't even want a union when we had a *patrón* because he and I got along. How would I go against my *patrón* when I was on good terms with him and he gave me all the privileges: pasture for the animals, and milk cows. How could I go against him? I'm not saying that the others don't have a right to form a union. I'm not unreasonable. If they didn't get along with the *patrón*, then I can almost say that they have a right. (1972: 127)

While not all *inquilinos* on this *fundo* shared the *empleado*'s solidarity with the *patrón*, Petras and Zemelman's detailed documentation (1972: 107–45) shows manifestations of paternalism among all the respondents, reflected in their perceptions of the fact that for them the *patrón* was a bad one who deserved being thrown off the *fundo*; by the same token, the *inquilinos* (including their leader) were hesitant to support a takeover on a neighboring *fundo* because its owner was known to be a good *patrón* (1972: 116). As the leader of the union expressed in general terms:

If there's a good humanitarian *patrón*, then it's better to stay at home with your *regalías* and with that *patrón* than to work in community. One lives more peacefully and there are more guarantees, and the people are well treated. (1972: 135)

In general, the observations of these *inquilinos* well reflect the general structure of paternalistic social relations. They are founded on certain benefits that the subordinates receive from the *patrón*, but it is very significant that these benefits are not equally distributed among the subordinates. Those receiving exceptional benefits expressed high solidarity with the *patrón* and clearly perceived that solidarity with their peers was not in their best interest. Social relations on the traditional *fundo* were thus particularistic relations between individuals, rather than universalistic relations between classes, an observation that is underscored by the *inquilinos'* repeated distinctions between good and bad *patrones* and the observation by the *empleado* that those on the *fundo* who did not share in the generosity of the *patrón* "almost" had a right to revolt.

The above observations suggest that the expression of paternalistic sentiments toward the *patrón* is by no means universal among Latin American campesinos. Where it occurs, there will be cases in which it represents merely the economically sanctioned and tangibly reinforced acting out of the subordinate role; there will be other cases in which the campesinos have genuine sentimental ties with their *patrones* that are underwritten by favorable treatment. Whenever campesinos solidarize themselves in this fashion with their *patrones*, they do so at the expense of horizontal solidarity within their own class and thus help perpetuate exploitative social structures in which a few of the subordinates can gain a relatively favorable position while the rest of them remain oppressed.

CHARACTER STRUCTURE AND EVERYDAY WORLD

Knowledge of the personalities and character structures of campesinos is generally derived from ethnographic descriptions that are extremely insightful and in general agreement. Quantitative measurements and psychological tests, however, are relatively sparse. The general picture that emerges from the available reports indicates that the character traits related to traditional dependence and domination are not conducive to independent and self-reliant action on the part of the campesinos.

An example of such character traits is the *encogido* syndrome identified by Erasmus (1968), which entails timidity and a tendency to be withdrawn and avoid persons of higher status except when they are needed as intermediaries. Erasmus did not necessarily consider the *encogido* syndrome an immutable character trait and observed himself that peasants in northwestern Mexico at certain times have changed to the aggressive and self-assertive *entrón*—an observation that Huizer (1970b: 309) has related to the peasants' increased contacts with one another and their joint participation in union activities.

A character orientation consistent with dependence and scarcity is the *speculativeness* that has been observed among rural dwellers in several countries. A. Leeds (1957: 468–72) provides a detailed account of such an orientation among cacao workers in northeastern Brazil; it involves a view that wealth was due to luck and chance rather than hard work and that gambling and lotteries were the most appropriate ways to strike it rich. Foster (1964) makes similar observations in rural Mexico and shows the reflection of this orientation in the popularity of "treasure tales." Speculativeness has been conceived as a realistic adaptation to depravation, "marginal gratification" (A. Leeds, 1957: 451–63), scarcity, and a static economy in which the desired goods are in limited supply (Foster, 1964; 1967b).

Another character trait A. Leeds (1957: 472–78) describes is *immediacy*, in other words, a disposition to seek direct gratification without deferment. Such a disposition has been frequently observed among peasants (Rogers, 1969). As Leeds points out correctly, immediacy is a realistic response to scarcity and depravation, where the demands of day-to-day survival make long-range planning and future-orientedness meaningless.

One of the few studies of village communities in Latin America with a specifically psychological focus is Fromm and Maccoby's (1970) formal investigation of social character in a Mexican village. Some of their findings are worth presenting in detail.

The village they studied had been part of a hacienda before the revolution, and the authors suggest that the mentality of dependence of the villagers has persisted to the present day. One general character orientation that was notably weak among the villagers was "*productiveness*" (1970: 88). Having a productive character orientation means that a person

experiences himself as the embodiment of his powers and is the "actor"; that he feels himself as the subject of his power, that he is not alienated from his powers, i.e., that they are not masked from him and transferred to an idolized object, person, or institution. (1970: 71)

While very few persons with such a character orientation were found in the village, the majority of the respondents were scored as either dominantly "*receptive*" (44 percent) or "*hoarding*" (31 percent) (1970: 86–88). Fromm and Maccoby describe these two character orientations:

In the receptive orientation a person feels "the source of all good" to be outside, and believes that the only way to get what he wants—be it something material, be it affection, love, knowledge, pleasure—is to receive it from that outside source. As far as the acquisition of material things is concerned, the receptive character, in extreme cases, finds it difficult to work at all, and expects things to be given to him as rewards for being so "good"—or perhaps because he is "ill" or "in need." In less extreme cases he prefers to work under or for somebody, and tends to feel that what he gets is given to him because of the boss's "goodness," rather than as a result of his own work, and as something to which he has a right. . . . being loved by anybody is such an overwhelming experience for them that they "fall for" anybody who gives them love or what looks like love. (1970: 69–70)

The hoarding orientation . . . makes people have little faith in anything new they might get from the outside world; their security is based upon hoarding and saving, while spending is felt to be a threat. They surround themselves, as it were, by a protective wall, and their main aim is to bring as much as possible into this fortified position and let as little as possible out of it. (1970: 71)

The hoarding orientation may be expected to lead to security-oriented behaviors and a tendency to minimize risks and not "rock the boat" of the status quo. But from the point of view of this study, the dominance of the receptive orientation among the villagers is most interesting, since it characterizes precisely the person who seeks the paternalistic protection of a *patrón*.[5]

Another revealing aspect of Fromm and Maccoby's study is their exploration of those dimensions of character in the village that pertain to "sociopolitical relatedness." They find that the most frequent orientations along this dimension are submissiveness (49 percent) and acceptance of traditional authority (20 percent) (1970: 89–90). While submissiveness is defined in clinical psychodynamic terms (1970: 80–81), acceptance of traditional authority is discussed as a sociocultural phenomenon. The person characterized by this orientation

accepts a traditional authoritarian pattern. He does not challenge his fixed social structure, including the idea that those in power deserve respect, that children should subordinate their wills to the dictates of parents. Yet, the traditional peasant does not believe that force makes right, nor does his identity rest on identifying himself with power. The traditional pattern of relationships gives him a sense of continuity, security, meaning. (1970: 81)

A personality trait that has been found to be characteristic of many peasants in Latin America and elsewhere is their fatalistic belief in the immutability of their destiny. Niehoff and Anderson (1966), who surveyed a large number of communities in different societies, found fatalism expressed in three types: (1) beliefs in the superior power of supernatural beings who control man's destiny, (2) "situational" fatalism, an "apathy based on a real understanding of limited possibilities for improvements, usually of an economic nature" (1966: 275), and (3) "project negativism," a skepticism about the benefits of concrete programs for improvements.

Students of Latin American village communities have found fatalism to be characteristic of many campesino personalities and cultures. Fromm and Maccoby found fatalism one of the main obstacles to the success of a cooperative program they instigated (1970: chap. 10). Foster (1967e: 118–20) pointed to some cultural expressions of fatalism in the villagers of Tzintzuntzán, Mexico. They attribute (and thereby excuse) undesirable behaviors not to the actors' volitions but to the vices and weaknesses that *make* people act the way they do; a person's occupation is *su destino* (his destiny). Cotler provides indicators of fatalism among Peruvian Indians in his data comparing the hacienda village of Paucartambo with the independent community of Sicuani:

TABLE 3. *Presence of Fatalistic Conceptions*
(Percent in agreement with statement)

	Paucartambo	Sicuani
The Indian is born to obey	86	40
Destiny cannot be changed	84	62
Some people are born to rule and others to obey	90	66
It is not worth making plans for the future	70	46

All differences significant at the .05 level.   SOURCE: Cotler, 1970a: 555.

It should be pointed out that these data[6] can be interpreted only with caution, mainly because the questions given to the respondents are likely to have evoked stereotyped response sets. As has been pointed out by Villanueva (1967: 32), the non-Indian interviewers may have appeared to the Indian respondents as other bosses, in front of whom the stereotyped role of the Indian had to be acted out. This is especially likely to have been the case with the first and the third items, which directly referred to the Indians' attitudes about their authority relationships.

Fatalism is generally observed among groups with little mastery over nature or their social relations. Thus, the pessimistic views rural workers in Itabuna, Brazil, expressed about their chances for improving their conditions were founded on their realistic assessment of stagnant wages, rising food prices, perpetual indebtedness, and a continuous deficit in their balance of earnings and expenses. Characteristically, among the group of workers interviewed by Geraldo Semenzato, only one was optimistic about his future prospect in view of the confidence he would create with his employer (CIDA, 1966a: 255).[7]

Foster suggests that fatalism is "the best adjustment the individual can make to an apparently hopeless situation" (1962: 66–67). Once such an adaptation is made, however, it reduces the individual's capacity to actively improve his life chances even if the objective possibilities for such improvements have increased. However, it would be wrong to conclude that fatalistic peasants have an immutable personality structure that renders them inherently incapable of taking their destiny into their own hands. If persistent and, if necessary, dramatic events convince them that activity, innovativeness, or rebellion provides realistic prospects for improvement, they will adopt these means. This argument is borne out by corresponding community intervention strategies (Huizer, 1972) and by the findings from Fromm and Maccoby's experimental program in a Mexican village (1970: chap. 10), which indicate that passivity, submissiveness, and fatalism among deprived people can be overcome under two joint conditions: on the one hand, the actors undergo experiences that open their minds, broaden their consciousness, and induce them to critically examine their current situation; on the other hand, it is crucial that previous objective constraints are weakened or disappear, and self-reliant behaviors yield visible and concrete results. The repressive constraints, which make fatalism often a realistic response to overwhelming controls, are reflected in the subjective perceptions of Ecuadorian *colonos,* interviewed by the CIDA investigator (CIDA, 1965b: 163–64). One of them described his world:

I practically do not know where I was born. My mother died. I never learned how to read or write. I believe I am something like 53 years old. Half of that time I have lived on the same farm. We are 30 colonos. The obligation is to work two weeks per month, according to the orders of the *patrón.* I have a small plot. I plant a little bit of corn only to see it spoil, because it is on *tierra de temporal* [unirrigated lands]; there is no water. I also have pasture rights, but some animals died because there is no water. One plants corn, and the *patrón* plants also wheat. The *hacienda* is on the upper parts of the mountain. This year has been a good one.

Asked whether he would like to own his plot, the *colono* replied: "The poor man has to remain a *colono* all his life and until he dies." Another *colono* in the group described his plot on the *tierra de temporal*, his work obligations, and the planting and selling of his crops. When asked whether he was, then, very content, he replied:

I have been living on this hacienda for thirty-five years. All my sons have been born here. If the *patrón* kicked me out, what would happen? I have a little cow and a little goat. I don't have more. What I produce is barely enough to survive. When could you save money? You don't progress. The land is good. We have conducted ourselves well. You have to conduct yourself well, otherwise the *patrón* will fire you. You have worked for so many years, and everything goes to the hacienda, always. You have to do what the *patrón* tells you to. He forbade us to form cooperatives, syndicates. Everybody is for himself. Everybody suffers silently (*Cada uno aguanta*). (My translation)

These few statements describe in a nutshell the everyday world experienced by the dependent *colono* under the "culture of repression"; in spite of their shortness, they are quite comprehensive and characteristic of the experience of many campesinos. There is illiteracy and lack of education, and the world is small. The campesinos know little beyond the horizons of the hacienda on which they spend most of their lives. They are dependent on, and dominated by, the *patrón*. They are poor and barely manage to survive. Life is full of crises (for example, death of the animals) and insecurity: they cannot control their destiny but have to hope for a good year and must guard themselves from being fired by the *patrón*, whose good graces they must maintain. They have little chance for advancement because they cannot accumulate by saving and producing, and they recognize their powerlessness and hopelessness in the face of overwhelming odds against them. The generalized state of fear that Holmberg (1966) found among Peruvian serfs is all-pervasive among these Ecuadorian Indians as well. Too oppressed to organize themselves, they suffer silently.

SELF-CONCEPTS

The self-concepts of traditional campesinos have frequently been found to be negative and to reflect an internalization of lower-class status (Tumin, 1952: 234–50). If campesinos are continually treated by their supervisors as incapable of self-reliant behavior and have few alternative reference sources besides their peers, who receive the same treatment, it is likely that they come to look at themselves through the eyes of their *patrón* and to conceive of themselves as unable to take responsibilities or as born to obey the *patrón* (Cotler, 1970a: 555; 1970b: 417). This internalization of dependence is reflected in observations made by Ernest Gruening in 1923 when he asked peons of a hacienda in Mexico why they did not wish to receive *ejidos*.[8] They replied, "If we got them, we wouldn't be able to take care of them." When asked who had told them so, they referred to the *patrón* and the padre (cited in White, 1969: 131). In a Guatemalan community, Tumin (1952: 170) reported that the Indians identified themselves as poor, sick, and hardworking people whose destiny was given by God. Therefore, they had little resentment for their exploitation by the *Ladino* local upper class.

Apart from low self-confidence, outright self-depreciation has been observed among villagers in several communities. Harris (1956: 95, 98–100), for example, described how rural workers in Brazil expressed internalized disdain for their humble manual work when they laughed as the *fazendeiro* lent a hand at cleaning brushes as a joke. Fromm and Maccoby (1970: chap. 10) note that boys in a Mexican village expect little praise from their elders for work they have done; the elders, in turn, expect little good to come out of the boys' cooperative activities and feel that the boys are not worth the investigators' effort. The authors note:

This attitude of always expecting failure is common to peasants in Latin America; Hirschman makes the significant suggestion that for many Latin Americans *success is disconcerting because it demands a radical change in one's view of the world.* (1970: 220. My italics)

In other words, this statement suggests that failure is consonant with past experience and future expectations; success would lead to the experience of cognitive dissonance. This problem may underlie many instances of skepticism encountered in rural areas. Lewis (1959: 57) provides another example of this in his account of Conchita, eldest daughter to the peasant Pedro Martínez, who was sent to school to become a teacher. Her father underwent great sacrifices to pay for her education, while the neighbors were critical; they warned Pedro that he was striving too high for a poor man and that his daughter could not be trusted away from home. This skepticism was validated and reinforced when Conchita had to abandon her first position because the school principal had made her pregnant. Other manifestations of self-depreciation are expressed in the expectations of failure in interpersonal relations that have been observed in a Peruvian community (Simmons, 1965).

An interesting aspect of the campesinos' self-concepts is related to the connotation of the term *Indian* in the Central American and Andean countries. Even though indigenous movements have sought to revive the Indian heritage, the term *Indian* has generally negative connotations. For example, witness Heath's list of epithets applied to the Bolivian Aymara:

anxious, apprehensive, brutal, careless, closed, cruel, depressed, dirty, dishonest, distrustful, doubtful, drunken, dull, fearful, filthy, gloomy, hostile, ignorant, insecure, irresponsible, jealous, malevolent, malicious, melancholic, morose, negative, pessimistic, pugnatious, quarrelsome, rancorous, reticent, silent, sinister, slovenly, stolid, sullen, suspicious, tense, thieving, treacherous, truculent, uncommunicative, unimaginative, unsmiling, untrustworthy, violent, and vindictive. (1969: 179)

Those who identified themselves as Indian were quite aware of the negative connotations the term had. As long as they were subject to a castelike ascribed position, individuals who identified themselves as Indian placed themselves in a fixed social status with very low prestige. Patch suggests, "This traditional force of immobility justified the continuing payment by 'Indians' of many obligations—in money, in kind, in service, and in humble deference—to the benefit of that class which claimed the mantle of aristocratic status" (1960: 138).

It should be noted, however, that again these negative self-images are unlikely to be the primary cause of the campesinos' deprivation. Time and again such perceptions have disappeared with the disappearance of the fundamental structural constraints. After the Bolivian revolution, for example, which freed the Indians from the landowners and gave them a degree of autonomy unheard of before, the term *Indian* has been rejected and come into disuse. In its place, the term *campesino* is used as a residential and occupational category, without the connotations of submission, humility, and low-caste ascription (Heath, 1969: 207–8; R. J. Alexander, 1958: 75–76). Similar changes are taking place in Peru (Bourricaud, 1961: 33). In this sense it is "more realistic to think of subcultural systems and the personalities they nourish as responses to real situations. Peasants have a 'limited view of the world', not because this is a universal of peasant psychology, but because of the real absence of alternatives."

CHAPTER 8

Horizontal Relations and Solidarity in the Peasant Community

Until 1953, interpretations of peasant societies more or less followed Redfield's (1930) description of a homogeneous, isolated, and integrated community, a gemeinschaft in which there was much contentment and little conflict. Lewis's (1953) article and subsequent works challenge this interpretation, charging that Redfield glossed over manifestations of violence, disruption, cruelty, disease, suffering, and political schisms. Lewis's restudy of Tepoztlán reveals an overriding individualism in institutions and personalities, a lack of cooperation, tensions within and between the villages of the *municipio*, as well as an overriding quality of fear, envy, and distrust in interpersonal relations. Lewis's view has since received support from Foster, who reviewed pertinent evidence from a variety of other studies (1960–1961; 1967c) and provided data from his own investigations in Tzintzuntzán, Mexico (1967e). Banfield's (1958) analysis of "amoral familism" provides further evidence, albeit controversial, on the issue; Bequiraj's (1966) interpretation reveals the peasant community as a coercive and repressive system.

I have followed essentially the interpretations of Lewis and Foster. It should be recognized that integration and solidarity are by no means completely absent in Latin American peasant communities. But they are clearly limited in many communities, principally due to scarcity and repression. It is precisely scarcity and repression that have resulted in circular patterns of causation by creating a number of influential factors mitigating against the development of intense and lasting horizontal ties. Some of these factors will be analyzed in this chapter.

PSYCHO-CULTURAL DIMENSIONS OF CONFLICT

A pervasive quality of fear and mistrust among campesinos has been described by a number of authors in countries such as Mexico (Foster, 1967e; Fromm and Maccoby, 1970: 37–39), Guatemala

(Nash, 1967: 100–103; Gillin, 1951: 114–19), and Colombia (Reichel-Dolmatoff and Reichel-Dolmatoff, 1961: 396–405). In a Venezuelan sample, about half of the responding campesinos preferred the proverb Never trust anyone but yourself over Trust in people, and you will go a long way (Mathiason, 1966: 134). In a characteristic passage, Foster summarizes this common phenomenon in Tzintzuntzán, Mexico:

Timidity and fear, of the known and the unknown, of the real or only the suspected threat, mark everyone's behavior. People fear poverty, old age, the death of their spouses, of their children, and above all their own deaths while they are still young, because this will leave their small children alone in a hostile world where no one will tend them the way their parents should. Gossip is feared, eavesdropping is feared, envy is feared, fierce dogs are feared, and sleeping alone is feared. House doors are usually kept closed all day long, and at night they are wedged shut with heavy poles. (1967e: 103)

Fear of aggression is most prominent. This aggression is manifested in visible acts, but the less visible forms of magic aggression, witchcraft, envy, and gossip give rise to even greater anxiety and suspicion (Reichel-Dolmatoff and Reichel-Dolmatoff, 1961: 247–54, 396–405; Gillin, 1951: 114–17; Lewis, 1959: 43; Foster, 1967e: 91–96, 103–8, 153–60; Wolf, 1955: 460).

Exploitativeness is another aspect characterizing the character structure of individual campesinos and the quality of the relations among them. This trait involves a disposition to take advantage of fortunate circumstances to obtain personal benefits or to exploit others without regard to what in other cultures would be called "fairness." For example, Foster (1967e: 109–12) points out that in Tzintzuntzán it is not considered morally wrong if officials use their position to gain personal advantages; making the most of fortuitous circumstances or abusing authority is expected as normal behavior (see also Reina, 1959: 45). A. Leeds (1957: 463–72) observes that cacao workers in Brazil expected to be taken advantage of by the government, employers, and peers and took for granted the legitimacy of exploiting, in turn, official agencies, employers, peers, customers, and women. In other parts of the continent, observers have reported that campesinos see nothing wrong in turning against their peers as informers (*soplones*), supervisors, or enforcers of penalties (Tullis, 1970: chap. 6; Vazquez, 1963; Heath, Erasmus, and Buechler, 1969: 100–101). While such persons are not very popular, campesinos generally do not blame those who obey orders for taking advantage of the opportunity to receive extra privileges and admit that they would act the same way if they had the chance. It should be noted that exploitativeness is not a trait unique to campesinos but is anchored in the sociopolitical structure of most Latin American countries and practiced by all classes.

SOCIAL RELATIONS IN THE PEASANT COMMUNITY

In a general atmosphere of fear and mistrust, peasants throughout the world have retreated into the family as the basic unit of solidarity whose interests override all others and as the only source of security. Family individualism, Banfield's (1958) "amoral familism," has been a commonplace in the anthropological literature on rural Latin America (for example, Foster, Reichel-Dolmatoff and Reichel-Dolmatoff, Lewis).[1] Again, the existence of competition and conflict among the upper classes in Latin American countries points to the fact that family individualism is not a peculiarly lower-class phenomenon.

Kin solidarity among campesinos is a form of social security and an economic necessity under conditions of scarcity and uncertainty about the future—conditions that prevail in most peasant societies. The economic functions of kin solidarity are best illuminated when the pattern breaks down. Fried (1962), for example, provides some insightful case studies of anxieties among individuals in a Peruvian community who fell ill and could not fulfil their labor obligations to the *patrón*, thus risking the loss of their land. Under conditions of illness the villagers would normally turn first to members of their household, then to members of the extended family, and in the last resort to the *minka*, a type of festive labor remunerated by food, coca, and alcohol. The individuals involved in Fried's study were unfortunate because they had no relatives or had quarrels with them, had no *compadres*, and did not have the means to sponsor a *minka*. In general, "neighbors" (a concept that did not exist in the village) would not give help unless they were under kin obligations; the importance of having a wife and children to fulfill one's obligations was stressed. The economic aspect of familism is also apparent among Venezuelan campesinos who, in response to a battery of items dealing with "family deviance," differed from all other groups surveyed by placing greatest sanctions against "economic crimes" such as a lazy son refusing to work or a wife working outside the home (Mathiason, 1966: 131–32). Familistic in-group attachment among Venezuelan campesinos was also reflected in their disproportionately high identification with the proverb Those who are not your friends are probably your enemies instead of with an opposite statement, and most campesinos also reported that they did not have a person outside the family to whom they could confide their most intimate problems (Mathiason, 1966: 132). Lewis (1959: 43) has also reported conflict in a Mexican peasant family over the need for the sons' labor. The wife of a Brazilian rural laborer expressed a related concern: "It's an unhappiness when a mother dies, but it's a terrible tragedy when a father dies because a family is left destitute. When a child dies, there is one less mouth to feed and the baby goes to heaven sinless" (A. Leeds, 1957: 459).

There is a quality of delicacy and tenuousness in the social relations of Latin American peasant communities. Emphasis is often placed on respect, sobriety, and formal courtesy; emotions are not to be shown, and a stoic face (*cara de palo*) must be maintained (Reichel-Dolmatoff and Reichel-Dolmatoff, 1961: 441–42; Nash, 1967: 98–99). Alcohol is often needed to loosen up interpersonal relations on special occasions such as fiestas (Simmons, 1965), and villagers have shown great sensibility to intended or unintended insults, which makes them prone to engage in brawls and even vendettas for trifle reasons (Fals-Borda, 1955: 208–11). Intimate friendship among nonkin is frequently absent (Nash, 1967: 72–73) or contains a paradoxical element of fragility, treacherousness, and uncertainty (Foster, 1967e: 100–103).[2]

Ritual kinship (*compadrazgo*) is generally seen as a mechanism that strengthens horizontal solidarity in the rural community beyond the family and provides for assistance and social security in times of need (Foster, 1967e: 81–85; Martínez, 1963a; Fried, 1962; a summary is in Sayres, 1956). The exchanges involved between godparents, however, are not always without tensions altogether. Helping a *compadre* is often onerous, although assistance is seldom declined. In a Brazilian village, a man who took the child of a deceased *compadre* into his care remarked about his new burden: "His care is something I can barely manage, but what if God had willed such a fate on one of my children!" (Siegel, 1957: 251). Foster (1967e: 80) found in Tzintzuntzán that nearly all villages, if pressed, admitted to hostility in some of their *compadrazgos*. Spielberg (1968) found in a small Guatemalan village that was rife with conflict and hostilities that the villagers preferred to maintain proper social distance with one another and select *compadres* from the outside, on the basis that they could not trust one another:

Intravillage *compadrazgo* would have the undesirable effect of committing a person to a variety of long-term, explicit, reciprocal obligations and would expose the initiator to danger should the compadre choose to exploit the relationship for selfish purposes. (Spielberg, 1968: 209)

In two Colombian villages, Sayres (1956) found that hostilities underlying some relationships among *compadres* were prevented from becoming manifest only by social sanctions. Such suppressed hostilities rendered the relationships ambivalent and affirmed that the system as a whole can be viewed not only as a design for providing personal support and social cohesion but as a program of psychologically constructing and socially enervating restraints and controls. . . . engendering negative effect and concurrently inhibiting its release. (Sayres, 1956: 352)

The degree to which various forms of cooperativeness prevail varies among Latin American rural communities. Fromm and Maccoby found many manifestations of anticooperative attitudes in a Mexican village (1970: 39, 206–10), related to distrust and fatalism. On the other hand, certain forms of cooperation have been traditional in the Indian communities of Central and South America. One of these is the *faena*, the voluntary and shared contribution of labor to public-works projects. Thus, the same villagers who were found to have a high degree of anticooperativeness by Fromm and Maccoby did rather well in the performance of public works (1970: 206). A high participation rate on *faenas* in a Peruvian village has also been reported by Fuenzalida (1968: 181–87). Other forms of cooperation involve exchanges more directly. There are spontaneous and ritual exchanges of gifts that have been found to facilitate credit, good will (Foster, 1967a: 215–16; Beals, 1970), and solidarity (Reichel-Dolmatoff and Reichel-Dolmatoff, 1961: 247–54), and various types of exchange labor have been widely employed throughout the continent. Exchange labor in the strict sense involves the reciprocal lending of equivalent services among two individuals at different times; it has been most prominent where smallholders had little cash for wages or did not have enough members in their family to take care of the work at peak periods (Erasmus, 1965; Carter, 1964: 49–56). Festive labor (*minka*) involves the sponsoring of a "work party" by an individual who is obligated to provide food and drinks for his workers. *Minkas* tend to involve individuals with unequal status and have bestowed a certain amount of prestige upon the sponsor where conspicuous giving was a means to obtain esteem (Erasmus, 1965). While labor exchanges tend to foster solidarity, a degree of ambivalence has been observed in this form of cooperation, too. Especially festive labor appears to be becoming less prominent because the quality of the work is often poor, its costs are high, and the worker-guests are difficult to control (Erasmus, 1965: 184–89). In this connection, the observations of the Reichel-Dolmatoffs in Aritama, Colombia, are particularly interesting. Festive labor was quite common in this village, particularly for the construction of private houses. While participation in such work parties was a sign of friendship and thus highly valued, it at the same time gave rise to anxieties about who would show up (a measure of esteem for the sponsor) and suspicions of the workers' motives. A bypasser would occasionally pick up some small piece of work at a party to show his respect and friendship to the sponsor; but such assistance might cast doubt upon the helper's motives—he could want to create obligations that would have to be paid back in the future. Such help, as well as the smallest gifts (for example, a cigarette) were generally interpreted as bait, and villagers preferred to pay for these rather than be subject to unspecified obligations in the future (1961: 257–58). Such responses were in part related to the particular attitudes toward work in Aritama. Work was manual work, dirty work, part of the burden of poverty, and God's punishment (in contrast to employment, a sinecure that carried prestige). Thus, work was not gladly accepted, since it proved that the worker was in need—a humiliating admission. The negotiation of work contracts was thus an art that required delicacy and diplomacy and was usually performed by an intermediary. Great emphasis was placed on avoiding the implication that the workers were in need or in inferior bargaining positions. Workers took their time before accepting a contract even if they were badly in need. They showed their independence by accepting a contract grudgingly, insisting that they were doing the employer a favor, and by doing slow and poor-quality work (1961: 260–64; see also Erasmus, 1965: 188, for references to other places). Interestingly, people in Aritama preferred to work outside the village where they were not known and where there was no need to keep up a front. Outside the village they would even work harder and for lower wages and deliver better quality (Reichel-Dolmatoff and Reichel-Dolmatoff, 1961: 265–66).

Thus cooperation in many Latin American rural communities is intimately related to economic scarcity and the personal need of individuals to guard themselves against incurring future obligations and inferior bargaining positions. *Compadrazgo*, labor and gift exchanges, can give rise to solidarity among the participants as well as undermine this same solidarity. Cooperation, where it exists, is rewarding as well as threatening to individuals; it is "too costly to be enjoyed and too rewarding to be given up" (Bequiraj, 1966: 36).

THE DYADIC CONTRACT MODEL

The preceding observations can be integrated under the "dyadic contract" model developed by Foster (1961; 1963; 1967a). Living in a hostile world full of crises, the individual campesino's first need is to protect (defend) himself and his family from danger and misfortune. Protection and defense accrue from living *sin com-*

promisos, without compromises, in other words, by guarding one's personal dignity and avoiding the incurring of obligations that cannot be repaid in kind. Yet, paradoxically, the campesino constantly needs to seek to establish social relations with other individuals in order to secure the things he cannot provide for himself. The dyadic contract provides an opportunity to provide for these things. It implies a relationship that is informal (not recognized by law), unenforceable, and noncorporate (between individuals qua individuals, not as members of groups or institutions). Dyadic contracts provide an opportunity for exchanging tangible benefits and services (which may be complementary in nature) as well as symbolic and ritual services. While the exchange of tangible benefits has obvious economic and political implications, symbolic exchanges of small gifts or food are essential expressions of solidarity by which the partners indicate to each other their interest in maintaining the relationship. Symbolic offerings such as food must be accepted, unless the receiver wishes to terminate the relationship. It is essential for a dyadic contract that a balance in the exchange is never struck. In a continual process, each benefit provided creates new obligations for the receiver and thus symbolizes the existence of the relationship. A contract ceases when a balance is struck and neither partner feels obliged or interested in granting further benefits to the other. The implicit contractual character of such relationships is reflected in the manner in which benefits are received. Gifts are received with a minimum show of gratefulness, since they are perceived not as signs of generosity but rather as an attempt to create obligations that will have to be repaid at some later time. Nevertheless once a dyadic contract is established, participants derive a great deal of emotional gratification from the exchange. Symbolic gifts are highly valued precisely because they indicate to the receiver the interest of the giver in the relationship.

Dyadic contracts occur at different levels. Horizontal exchanges between equals have been called "colleague contracts" by Foster, whereas contracts between individuals with different social statuses are "patron-client" contracts (see also Wolf, 1966b). The latter can involve landlords, professionals, and a number of other desirable towndwelling individuals as well as supernatural patrons such as God, the Virgin Mary, or the various patron saints. Patrons, human or supernatural, are selected according to pragmatic criteria on the basis of need.

The significance of the dyadic contract model for this study rests in the following: (1) Solidarity among equals as well as among individuals with different statuses is derived from the benefits exchanged in their interrelationships; (2) the selection of partners follows pragmatic criteria; (3) the exchanges involved not only create solidarity among the interactants but at the same time generate tensions related to (a) anxiety over the other's willingness to continue the relationship, and (b) the need for each individual to avoid receiving benefits that he cannot repay in kind and that thus entail unspecified future obligations; (4) it can be postulated that patron-client contracts can undermine the solidarity in colleague contracts when they provide superior (or more needed) benefits than the latter to the campesinos, while increases in the relative attractiveness of colleague contracts tend to undermine vertical solidarities between patrons and clients.

SOCIAL EQUILIBRIUM AND SCARCITY: AN INTERPRETATION

Culture can be analyzed as a response to the security needs of a community (Gillin, 1951). Security, according to Gillin (1951: 1), is "a state of affairs in which an individual or group may anticipate with confidence that wants will be satisfied . . . according to expectations." The degree to which security becomes an overriding cultural concern should vary from one society to the next, in accordance with the degree to which scarcity and dependence prevail. Peasant societies typically are characterized by high degrees of scarcity and dependence. The villagers of Tzintzuntzán, for example,

see themselves facing a hostile and dangerous world, from birth until death, in which the good things in life are in short supply, and in which existence itself is constantly threatened by hunger, illness, death, abuse by neighbors, and spoilation by powerful people outside the community. Society and culture provide the Tzintzuntzeños with formal institutions and behavior patterns within the framework of which they struggle to "defend" themselves and their families in this essentially unequal battle. (Foster, 1967a: 213)

The precariousness of the economic balance for Latin American rural dwellers is generally acknowledged. Their life is characterized by a perpetual struggle to get by; money is always short, borrowing helps them survive until the next harvest or payday, and any illness is a catastrophe (Fried, 1962; Lewis, 1959: 43). Mintz's (1960) recording of a Puerto Rican caneworker's life story reveals the everyday concerns of the rural poor: illness, unemployment, loss of the house, pregnancy of the wife while he was unemployed, death of the children, and political repression. In the face of such odds, any risk can result in starvation; the course of life is like a walk on a tightrope both psychologically and socially (Foster,

1967e: 142–43). Individual ambition and innovativeness are perceived as threats to the whole community, and the maintenance of given social patterns becomes mandatory (Foster, 1967e: 136–52). In this situation, "defensive ignorance" about cultural alternatives to existing behaviors prevents threats to the social and psychological equilibrium in the village and helps to maintain the "uninterrupted routine" of "traditional patterns" (Wolf, 1955: 459–60).

Data from four Peruvian villages in different regions suggest that personal strain is common in rural communities and accounts for much of the variation in manifestations of conflict. Measuring personal strain by self-perceived psychosomatic symptoms, Kellert, Williams, White, and Alberti (1967) found among other things that (1) the degree of strain was most highly related to levels of literacy, education (both negatively), and age (positively); (2) women experienced higher levels of strain than men; (3) single, never married individuals experienced least strain; widowed, divorced, and separated individuals experienced most strain. Apart from these general findings, strain was found to be significantly associated with manifestations of conflict and cooperation: (1) the less the strain, the greater the likelihood of membership in voluntary organizations; (2) the greater the strain, the greater the perception of envy in the community (Table 4); (3) the less the strain, the less likely individuals are to report much or some conflict in the village, and the more likely individuals are to identify with the "group with modern ideas" (as opposed to the "group with old customs"); (4) the less the strain, the more future-oriented individuals are, the more optimistic they are about the future, and the less fatalistic they are (although fatalism was generally found to be high).

TABLE 4. *Perception of envy in four Peruvian villages by level of strain*
(Percent replying "hardly anyone" to the question: "Do you believe other people envy you?")

	Village			
Level of Strain	Chancay Valley*#	Arequipa	Montaro Valley**#	Cuzco
High	22	8	12	13
Medium high	29	9	15	23
Medium low	25	11	13	32
Low	41	19	26	45
N	457	267	1,112	498

*p .05   **p .01   #bivariate regression, p ≤ .05 for slope.
SOURCE: Kellert, Williams, White, and Alberti, 1967: 407.

Foster (1967b; 1967e: chap. 6) has developed a comprehensive rationale that can explain many of the conflict symptoms in peasant communities. He argues that there is an implicit, unverbalized cognitive orientation underlying peasant behavior, which he called the "image of limited good." This image implies

that broad areas of peasant behavior are patterned in such fashion as to suggest that peasants view their social, economic, and natural universes— their total environment—as one in which all the desired things such as land, wealth, health, friendship and love, manliness and honor, respect and status, power and influence, security and safety, *exist in finite quantity* and are *always in short short supply*, as far as the peasant is concerned. Not only do these and all other "good things" exist in finite and limited quantities, but in addition *there is no way directly within peasant power to increase the available quantities*. (Foster, 1967b: 304)

As a corollary of this principle, improvements in the situation of some individuals imply a disadvantage for at least some others, and a significant improvement for one constitutes a threat to all. As a result, peasant societies tend to be characterized by extreme individualism where each individual (and his family) jealously guards his position and sanctions actions that threaten the traditional order of things or accrue undue advantages to some. Envy and hidden aggression are manifested in numerous forms, and even compliments can constitute an act of aggression by suggesting that some individuals are unduly outstanding. Foster shows that various manifestations of conservatism and conflict in the peasant community (for example, economic behavior, friendship, machismo) can be subsumed under the image of limited good. On the other hand, the open aspects of the peasant community (in other words, its subordinated position within the larger, city-dominated society) make it possible for individuals to accrue gains from outside sources. Such gains are acceptable in the community since they do not take away valued things from other members. Such outside sources of "goods" are luck and fate (which explains a preoccupation with lotteries and treasure tales [Foster, 1964; A. Leeds, 1957]) on the one hand and the search for (human and supernatural) patrons on the other. Acts designed to improve the individual's "luck position" (Foster, 1967e: 318) and to elicit favors from a patron are thus considered acceptable. But such actions tend to be individualistic in nature, as everybody seeks to obtain benefits for himself.[3]

Where the image of limited good prevails, then, the individual feels powerless to improve his destiny by himself. He constantly has to be on guard to defend his tenuous position against encroachments from others who stand to gain from his loss. Benefits are, therefore, not accrued from intraclass solidarity but from powerful patrons whose favors must be elicited through loyalty, deference, and the sacrifice of personal autonomy.[4] In this manner the search for dyadic contracts, in both vertical and horizontal social relations, has been a particularistic adaptation with the end of pursuing individual and immediately pressing interests. This pattern has been a countervailing force to the articulation of collective interests and thus has mitigated against the formation of class solidarity among campesinos. It could, therefore, be expected that the collapse of the traditional dyadic relations between *patrones* and campesinos would be a major contributing condition opening up the possibility for campesino movements.

Alternatives for Campesinos
A Theoretical Model
and Implications for Change

TRIADIC EXCHANGE AND UNILATERAL DEPENDENCE

The analysis in Chapters 4 to 7 reveals on the one hand the typical patterns of "internal colonialism" (González-Casanova, 1969), in which vertical exchanges and dependencies between campesinos and landlords have traditionally been reinforced by coercion, economic pressures, social organization, political structures, and psychocultural configurations. On the other hand, horizontal solidarity among campesinos has been mitigated by these same factors as well as by relevant dimensions of the socioeconomic organization within their community. Vertical exchanges and a relative lack of horizontal solidarity thus reinforce the traditional pattern of domination in rural Latin America. While solidarity with the *patrón* has been a matter of survival for the individual campesino, it has been obtained at the high cost of humiliation, lack of autonomy, and deprivation; on the other hand, horizontal solidarity has rarely been totally absent in the campesino community, as is testified by exchanges of material and symbolic benefits and by expressive solidarizations on ceremonial occasions. Thus, the individual campesino has been faced with the task of maintaining a tenuous balance at the point where vertical and horizontal exchanges intersect. Both horizontal and vertical exchanges have provided positive as well as negative reinforcements to the individual campesino. Powerlessness and dependence have traditionally tipped that balance in favor of vertical ties; changes in power and dependence relations are, therefore, expected to strengthen horizontal solidarities to a point where collective action against the *patrón* becomes increasingly feasible.

Scarcity and dependence have thus mitigated the development of campesino solidarity in two ways. First, they encouraged the development of behavior patterns that were consistent with the image of limited good, described by Foster. In light of this image, collective gains for the campesino community are inconceivable; exchanges within the community can have only limited utility, and individuals have constantly to be on guard against each other, for any gain by one individual constitutes a threat to all the others. Second, scarcity and dependence have encouraged the establishment of patron-client relationships between individual campesinos and the landholders or other power figures. These relationships were individualized, particularistic, and involved exchanges of economic assistance and protection in return for deference, loyalty, informant services, and political support, including force (Wolf, 1966b). Such relationships became imperative for the campesino to the extent that the landlord exercised total control over his means of subsistence and his access to alternative sources of supply; the relationships became feasible when the formal institutional structure of the larger society was weak and unable to supply necessary goods and services at the terminal levels for him (Wolf, 1966b: 17). Once a *patrón* ceased to mediate the delivery of goods and services from the larger society to the campesinos, or once he became unable to maintain his traditional controls, alternative adaptations became increasingly attractive for the campesinos, including the formation of solidarity movements at the horizontal level.

When differential control over vital resources gives rise to an initial differentiation of power and the establishment of unilateral exchanges, subordinates are likely to experience cognitive inconsistency between perceived actual outcomes and desired outcomes. If power differentials are significant, they will tend to restore consistency not by actions but by redefinitions of their environment. If the unilateral exchanges are legitimized by the benefits the superior supplies to the subordinates, subordinates are likely to respond by adjusting their evaluations, in other words, by lowering their aspirations to the level of their actual (perceived) outcomes. In that case, subordination is justified by the differential value of the mutually supplied benefits. This situation is characteristic for the benevolent paternalism and the traditionalistic attachment of campesinos to a *patrón*. If, however, unilateral exchanges are maintained mainly by coercion and not by superior benefits, then subordinates are more likely to attempt a restoration of consistency by adjusting some of their perceptions. This response is characteristic for campesinos who explain their undesirably low outcomes as being a result of their lack of control over their natural and human environment, by the will of fate, luck, or God, against which they are powerless; or they may lower their expectations of future outcomes; they may also define alternative adaptations as nonexistent, unrealistic, or too costly—which may or may not involve cognitive distortions. Such perceptual adjustments, whether realistic or not in the face of changing circumstances, are generally founded on long, futile attempts to improve outcomes.

From these considerations a number of corollaries follow. As campesinos have a tradition of extremely low control over their social environment, they can, as a rule, not be expected to form organized movements, unless their power resources relative to those of the landholders improve. This does not preclude the outbreak of spontaneous resistance and violence under deteriorating conditions that threaten the subsistence of the campesinos; such attempts have been numerous, but they were generally uncoordinated and shortlived as long as the traditional balance of power prevailed. If shifts in the balance of power do occur, the development of campesino movements is contingent on the degree to which existing relations with the landlords were legitimated. With a high degree of legitimacy (benevolent paternalism), changing evaluations (values, goals, exchange rates) will motivate campesinos to renegotiate their position and, if necessary, to actively oppose the landholders. With a low degree of legitimacy, a change in perceptions (of alternatives, expectations of success) will be a more decisive instigator of campesino movements. Also, under conditions of benevolent paternalism, a decline in the *patrón*'s ability to provide the traditional benefits to his campesinos will motivate the latter more than a decline in his control over the means of institutionalized violence. In forced exchanges, on the other hand, a change in the landholder's relative control over means of coercion will spark more resistance than a decline of the benefits that had not been just to begin with.

Chapters 3 to 8 provide an analysis that permits us to assert that traditional *patrón*-campesino and campesino-campesino relationships in Latin America fit the model of unilateral dependence in triadic exchanges developed in Chapter 3. Having outlined the institutional parameters that contribute to the maintenance of this pattern, we can now state a number of propositions that predict that changes in one or more of these parameters will encourage the development of campesino movements:

Proposition 1: In *patrón*-campesino relationships, campesinos will actively seek improved outcomes in these or alternative relationships when they attain access to new resources or when the previous controls barring them from alternative resources break down.

Proposition 2: In *patrón*-campesino relationships, campesinos will actively seek improved outcomes in these or alternative relationships when alternative suppliers can provide better benefits than the old *patrón* or supply the same benefits as the old *patrón* at lower cost to the campesinos.

Proposition 3: In *patrón*-campesino relationships, campesinos will actively seek improved outcomes in these or alternative relationships if there is a deterioration in the outcomes from these relationships.

Proposition 4: In *patrón*-campesino relationships, a change in some evaluations on the part of the campesinos (values, goals, exchange rates) will induce them to (a) do without what the *patrón* has to offer, (b) pay less than before for the traditional benefits supplied by the *patrón*, or (c) demand greater benefits than before from the *patrón*.

Proposition 5: In *patrón*-campesino relationships, campesinos will actively seek improved outcomes in these or alternative relationships if there is a change in their perceptions of the balance of force and power, of the accessibility of alternative resources and suppliers of needed benefits, or of alternative outcomes.

Proposition 6: In *patrón*-campesino relationships, the greater an increase in the power of the campesinos relative to that of the *patrón*, (a) the greater the likelihood that they will actively seek improved outcomes in these or alternative relationships, and (b) the less the likelihood that they will cognitively adjust to these relationships or cognitively respond to changes in them.

A NOTE ON EVIDENCE

The preceding propositions will guide the formulation of more specific hypotheses in the following chapters. These hypotheses, in turn, will be examined in the light of existing evidence on campesino movements in Latin America. This examination will necessarily have the character of a historical analysis, and an attempt will be made to interpret and order the available evidence in a manner that permits us to assess the plausibility of the exchange and power theory formulated in Chapter 3. Quantitative comparisons have been available occasionally, but most of the evidence has a more qualitative character, indicating the structural and psychological contexts within which campesino movements have occurred. These are some of the shortcomings to be recognized:

1. Hypotheses have been formulated so that they state associations between constructs, not between empirical indicators. The review of the evidence following the hypotheses will, however, indicate the nature of empirical observations necessary to evaluate the hypotheses. Since the data used to evaluate the hypotheses were not gathered for the purpose of this study, a further specification of measures would have been fruitless.

2. Most of the propositions involve changes in an independent variable followed by specified changes in a dependent variable. No

attempt was made to specify in each case how soon the change in the dependent variable should follow the change in the independent variable. While the nature of the evidence did not permit the specification of such temporal qualifiers, the materials explored may assist future investigators in attempting such refinements.

3. No attempts at systematic quantification were made, as the data had to be taken from where they were available. Thus there is no specification of the universe of peasant movements in Latin America, and no evidence was available as to the representativeness of the observations recorded. The analysis has been quite selective with a focus (a) on movements on which data were available, and (b) on those movements, and on those countries, that were of greater significance in the twentieth century. The observations are thus for the most part restricted to the major movements in Brazil, Peru, Bolivia, Mexico, Venezuela, Chile, and Guatemala. Furthermore, no tally has been taken as to how many instances there were of a particular phenomenon associated with campesino movements, and there was no possibility to compare campesino movements with control groups where no such movements occurred.

4. The focus of this study was analytical, not geographical. Thus, the chapters have been ordered in terms of significant variables, which then were examined in the context of different campesino movements. It was felt that this sort of analysis has been lacking in the literature. As a result, there is no in-depth analysis of individual movements. But many excellent analyses of this kind already exist and provide data for comparative purposes. The concentration on variables has also led to a procedure that examines every factor individually. It is recognized that peasant movements occur in a context where these factors interact systematically. While the systemic aspects of campesino movements will be highlighted, the effort will be concentrated on the examination of the contributing factors separately.

What has been done in this study is a search of the major campesino movements in Latin America for the occurrence of the processes postulated in the theory. The question was asked retrospectively: what factors have been associated with the different campesino movements on which we have data? And where can we explain the presence of certain observed phenomena by reference to the theory proposed above?

The aim of this survey, then, is to review available evidence in such a manner that future hypotheses can be derived from a general body of theory and formulated in terms precise enough to direct more refined empirical investigations. Future students may find that the evidence presented here justifies the use of an exchange and power model to analyze Latin American campesino movements. Or they may conclude that the evidence does not enhance the plausibility of such a theory for that purpose. In either case, the present effort will have served its purpose.

PART III

Imbalances in Traditional Parameters of Domination and Campesino Movements in Latin America

CHAPTER 10

Imbalances in Economic Relations

As has been pointed out in previous chapters, a principal obstacle to campesino movements has traditionally been their lack of economic resources and the monopoly the landowners have over the campesinos' means of subsistence.[1] If we add the assumption that deteriorating returns in a social relationship undermine the legitimacy of that relationship, Propositions 1, 2, and 3 can be transformed into four hypotheses:

Hypothesis 1: In *patrón*-campesino relationships, campesinos tend to act toward obtaining improved benefits if the benefits obtained from the *patrón* deteriorate or are threatening to deteriorate.

Hypothesis 2: In *patrón*-campesino relationships, peasants will act toward obtaining improved benefits when they gain access to new economic resources that enable them to either provide needed benefits themselves, bargain with the *patrón* for better benefits, or enter into bargaining with alternative suppliers.

Hypothesis 3: In *patrón*-campesino relationships, campesinos tend to act toward obtaining improved benefits if alternative suppliers can offer them better or cheaper economic benefits than their *patrón*.

Hypothesis 4: In *patrón*-campesino relationships, campesinos tend to act toward obtaining improved benefits when they or their "allies" can bear the economic costs of such actions.

Hypothesis 1. Economic decline in general, and a deterioration of the benefits from the traditional relationship with the *patrón* in particular, appears to be the most significant economic factor for campesino movements in Latin America. Such deterioration has been reflected in long-range trends in the levels of living and in the socioeconomic status of campesinos (Smith, 1969: 49–51), in the inability or refusal of the *patrones* to continue supplying the traditional benefits, or in increased exactions on the part of the landlords. A deterioration of outcomes decreases the attractiveness and the legitimacy of a relationship for the campesino. Indeed, most campesino movements in Latin America have had a conservative origin in the sense that at least initially they aimed at restoring or affirming what were considered traditional rights. They were generally precipitated by a gradual erosion or a rapid deterioration in the traditional status quo (Huizer, 1970b: 397–98; Griffin, 1969; 1976; Barraclough, 1973; Pearse, 1975: 88–102, chap. 6; Migdal, 1974: chap. 5). Some of the processes that can erode the campesinos' status quo are: deterioration in the campesinos' socioeconomic status following prior improvements, long-term encroachments of Indian lands by mestizo and criollo outsiders, unwillingness or inability of *patrones* to provide traditional benefits to the campesinos, and increased demands by the landholders.

Taking the lead from Tocqueville's (1955) analysis of the fall of the *ancien régime* in France, Davies (1962) has suggested that revolutions arise when certain social groups experience a decline or stagnation in their socioeconomic status after a period of relative improvement. While this approach is probably too simple to account for the variation and complexity of revolutionary movements, it points out one salient precedent of many upheavals (Huizer, 1972: 142–43, 181). The origin and growth of the Brazilian *ligas camponêsas* and of the campesino movements in La Convención, Peru, and Ucureña, Bolivia, can be traced to the processes described by Davies. The Brazilian peasant leagues arose in the mid-1950s out of a mutual benefit society formed by the tenants of the *engenho* Galiléia (Pernambuco), in response to the owners' attempt to evict them after a decade of relative prosperity, security, and freedom from interference by the landlord (Correia de Andrade, 1963: 108, 115, 241–55). In La Convención, Peru, it was the campesinos' previous economic success with the planting of coffee that strengthened and motivated their resistance to the landlord's attempts to wrest their lands from them and increase their labor obligations (Craig, 1969; Hobsbawm, 1969). In Ucureña, Bolivia, it was the initial success of the campesino syndicate in securing land that unified the peons in their resistance to new encroachments by the landowners (Dandler, 1969; 1971). The violent dispossession of gained campesino lands in Venezuela, executed after the 1948 coup d'etat, together with the visible torture and harassment of syndicate leaders, strengthened the solidarity of the campesinos and their respect for the syndicates (Huizer, 1967: 217–18).

The continual encroachments on Indian lands by the ruling groups have resulted in a long history of campesino uprisings in Bolivia, Peru, Colombia, and Mexico. While under colonial rule, the Indians enjoyed a measure of protection from the crown against the colonists, but they lost this support after the wars of independence. In Bolivia, a decree of 1866, signed into law in 1868, declared all lands to be state property and obliged the Indian communities to pay heavy taxes or lose the right to their lands. The *leyes de exvinculación*, which aimed to abolish communal property and establish private property, had similar effects and were enforced vigorously, often accompanied by fraudulent manipulations of mestizo land grabbers (Shazo, n.d.). The Indian communities resisted but were usually subdued violently (Huizer, 1967: 143–45; Antezana, 1969). Antezana (cited in Huizer, 1967: 144) estimated that between 1861 and 1944 more than two thousand rebellions and movements arose in response to loss of land and forced servitude. Against this historical background, the Indian movement had always been subdued only temporarily in Bolivia until it won its victory in the 1950s. The historical background of campesino movements in the Peruvian highlands is similar. For centuries, land grabbers had encroached upon the indigenous *comunidades* and were frequently met with resistance that had to be suppressed violently (Tullis, 1970: 76–81). Tenants and sharecroppers on the haciendas did not fare much better, and violent confrontations had been common long before the campesino movement became more widespread and coordinated in the 1960s.

One of the principal causes of these conflicts appears to be attributable to the desire of many *latifundistas* to evict campesinos from their plots or to demand from them more onerous obligations, after in the course of several years they had accomplished valuable improvements such as clearing the lands, cultivation, and the planting of permanent plants, such as coffee, cacao, or coca. (CIDA, 1966c: 215. My translation)

Large-scale alienations of Indian lands also took place in Mexico and Chile (Thiesenhusen, 1968: 413–16) during the second half of the nineteenth century. In Mexico, the liberal reform laws of 1856, which prohibited corporate ownership of land by civil and ecclesiastical authorities, undermined the traditional Indian system of collective ownership by allotting properties to individual Indians administering a plot. As the concept of private property had little meaning to the Indians, they were helpless in the face of the commoditization of lands and fell easy prey to *hacendados* and corporations acquiring their lands by force, purchase, and/or legal ruse (Buve, 1972; White, 1969: 114–15; Wolf, 1969: 12–18; Huizer, 1967: 3–8; Whetten, 1948: 85–89). In defense of their disintegrating traditional community, Indians arose in numerous rebellions and wars throughout the nineteenth century but were unable to halt the loss of their lands (Buve, 1972: 1–3; Meyer, 1973; Silva-Herzog, 1959: 105–7). At the end of the Diaz administration in 1910, lands were concentrated in the hands of a few large *hacendados* or corporations, and the great majority of the Indians were reduced to indebted peons and workers on the haciendas or were trying to ward off violent encroachments on what little land was left to them (Huizer, 1967: 3–8). It was in defending village lands against neighboring *hacendados* that the Zapatista movement had its origin.

Against the historical background of long-standing deprivation and repression, it is usually an individual repressive act, an increased exaction by the landholder, or increased taxes that set off the development of campesino reactions (Galjart, 1972: 2). A former *inquilino* on the Chilean *fundo* Culiprán recalled the motivations for the revolt that eventually led to the expropriation of the estate:

[the *patrón*] said that there was a raise in the minimum wages since the first of May. He always paid us at the end of the month—the last Saturday of the month. But he didn't warn us at all about the cuts he was thinking of making. Then he called us to be paid at night on the sixth of June, and he didn't say anything about it then either, but he had made tremendous cuts: nine thousand for pasturing our animals, three thousand a year for the use of his carts and he took six hundred pesos per month for bread and charged for water. He was about to take off for our tools, too.

Those who work as day laborers (*voluntarios*) and only work six or seven days a month came out owing him money. They didn't make enough to pay and had to try to pay him the next month. That was when we said to ourselves, "We can't allow this." (Petras and Zemelman, 1972: 132)

Furthermore, once moderate organizations for airing grievances have been established, they frequently become radicalized by the intransigent reactions of the landholders. In both situations, the legitimacy of given dominance relations is dramatically undermined, or the illegitimacy of the relation is underscored. In his analysis of five campesino communities in the Peruvian highlands, Tullis (1970: chaps. 6, 7) clearly demonstrates the link between declining outcomes (new demands by *patrones*, negation of old privileges) for the campesinos and intransigence by the *patrones* on the one hand, and the development and intensification of campesino organizations on the other (also see Alberti, 1970a: 126–27). In the valley of La Convención, Peru, campesino organizations arose when the landlords tried to reclaim the improved lands and coffee trees from their *arrendires* and demand new *condiciones* (work obligations) precisely for the times that the *arrendires* needed to tend to their own production (Craig, 1969: 284; also Landsberger, 1969a: 24–25). In Bolivian instances of prerevolutionary violence, *patrones* who demanded too much of their peons were simply shot (Heath, Erasmus, and Buechler, 1969: 125). A student of Colombian rural unrest in the 1930s and 1940s concludes his observations, "In the nonviolent zones, the agrarian struggles were the result of an offensive on the part of the *latifundistas*, whose intention was to throw the peasants off their land, or else to take revenge for the events in the previous years" (Gilhodès, 1970: 427). In Ucureña, Bolivia, fraudulent manipulations by land-owners, which obstructed the campesinos' prospects of buying their own lands, had a unifying effect for the emerging rural syndicate (Dandler, 1969; 1971; Patch, 1960: 120–21). The peasant leagues in Brazil gained their first momentum in the mid-1950s when the owner of the *engenho* Galiléia persecuted the members of a mutual benefit society and tried to evict them from the land that they had worked for decades under relative autonomy (Correia de Andrade, 1963: 241–55). At later times, violent clashes between landowners and members of the leagues were provoked by the owners' *capangas*, who attacked workers and destroyed their houses (CIDA, 1966c: 230–34). The growth of the Zapatista movement in Mexico began with the development of defense councils set up by villagers against the terror of land-hungry *hacendados* (White, 1969; Wolf, 1969: chap. 1; Fromm and Maccoby, 1970: 34; Huizer, 1970a: 376–77).

The refusals of landowners to supply the traditional benefits to their tenant-laborers or to meet their raised demands are frequently a result of their own difficulties in maintaining the viability of their estates in the face of a changing politico-economic environment at the periphery of the capitalist world economy. At the periphery, it is much more problematic to resolve the inherent contradictions of capitalist development, which the first industrializing nations could respond to via the colonial exploitation of cheap labor, raw materials, mining enterprises, and food imports. Contemporary areas at the periphery not only lack the access to such cheap resources but, moreover, have to compete in the world economy with the more advanced nations and corporations. Given, furthermore, the historical formation of their limited economies, contemporary Third World nations tend to be exposed to a vicious circle of low productivity and precarious profit rates compensated by minimal wages, which, in turn, limit the internal market and thus stand in the way of incentives for higher capital investments.[2] Within this situation, the transformation of peasants into capitalist farmers, into an agricultural labor force remunerated by wages or salaries, or their shift into nonagricultural occupations is limited. A large number of them tend to remain in agriculture for lack of promising alternatives, although different family members may seek various kinds of temporary or regular work to supplement the decreasing income derived from agriculture.[3]

It is such a deterioration of peasant incomes and the limitations of other sources of subsistence that have provoked much resistance in Latin America against landlords whose patronage has become decreasingly feasible for the Latin American peasant communities. Long-range economic trends at the national and international level have adversely affected the campesinos' level of living in several countries and thus may have decreased the feasibility of many traditional social relationships for them. Mexico, for example, during the second half of the nineteenth century up to the revolution of 1910 experienced declining food production, rising food prices, and stationary agricultural wages, while during the same time a very large number of campesinos lost their lands (White, 1969: 120–21; Silva-Herzog, 1959: 104–5, 127–28; Wolf, 1969: 19–21). The buildup of the peasant movement in Bolivia after the Chaco war (1932–1935) coincided with a spiraling inflation (Heath, Erasmus, and Buechler, 1969: 197) that was unchecked until 1956. The growth of the peasant movement in Venezuela was preceded by the great depression of the 1930s and by a stagnation of the export-based agricultural sector in which a small group of landowners was able to transfer the impact of the recession onto the masses of peasants, most of whom experienced a worsening of their economic position (Powell, 1969: 63–64). As Powell notes,

The erosion of the rural economy from the 1920's onward was accompanied by a certain amount of rural unrest and occasionally violent outbursts. Surface indications of the tensions which resulted as the peasants were pushed closer to the margin of survival included violent as well as legal landlord-tenant conflicts, changes and resistance to changes in landlord-*colono* or landlord-sharecropper arrangements, scattered land invasions, and even isolated attempts at guerrilla warfare. (1969: 64)

Similarly, in Colombia it has been noted that land invasions and strikes by agricultural workers in the 1920s and 1930s followed times of demographic pressure, rises in the cost of living brought about by the monopoly of the company stores, inflation, and export difficulties (Gilhodès, 1970: 413, 421–22).

Such economic difficulties at the national level affected the status of the campesinos directly through unemployment or rising prices, but the indirect effects resulting from economic difficulties on the part of the *patrones* were often more important, since they hampered the latter's ability to make do with the traditional services of their tenant-workers or to provide the traditional compensations for them. Economic pressures on the landowners thus diminished their ability to legitimize their domination over the campesinos. The convent that owned the lands over which the labor conflicts in Ucureña arose, for example, was faced with heavy debts and decreasing returns (Dandler, 1971: 100), and after the revolution of 1952 the most frequent complaints the campesino syndicates filed with the government arbitrators (*Inspectores de Trabajo Agrario*) were against landholders whose financial straits prevented them from fulfilling their contracts with the laborers (Heath, Erasmus, and Buechler, 1969: 117). In a number of communities surveyed in Peru, economic pressures also reduced the bargaining powers of landlords vis-à-vis their mobilized campesinos (Tullis, 1970: chap. 6; Alberti, 1970a: 123, 126–27, 130). The peasant and rural workers' organizations in northeast Brazil flourished during the decade (1955–1964) in which the economic pressures on the sugar planters and industry were particularly severe. The crisis in the sugar sector was to a large extent due to the owners' traditional practice of responding to improving market conditions by extending their area under cultivation rather than by intensifying their methods of production. Under relatively unfavorable market conditions, they would reduce the area under cultivation and rent more land to their workers for their subsistence. The workers then were left relatively independent and only had to render their obligatory work days at below-market compensation (*cambão*). During World War II, the world market for sugar was relatively restricted, and production was curbed. Thus, the tenant-workers received relatively large plots of land for their subsistence and enjoyed a prolonged period during which they had sufficient land, food, and freedom from obligations to enjoy a measure of security. In the years following the end of World War II, conditions in the international market improved drastically, and the internal demand for sugar also rose sharply. As a result, the northeastern plantation and factory owners sought to utilize every piece of land available, and the additional lands tended to be those of inferior quality. This raised the cost of production. Furthermore, as all lands were used for commercial production, the workers had to be remunerated in wages rather than in kind. As a result, the cost of labor increased without a corresponding increase in productivity. In the face of competition from the more modernized sugar industry of the south, the plantation and factory owners in the northeast were forced to increase production (by incorporating their workers' lands) and at the same time keep their labor costs low by reducing wages to whatever level they could get away with. These practices contributed to the rising tensions between owners and workers and to the breakup of the traditional paternalistic labor relations (Lopes, 1966: 198–99). The workers felt the additional pressure from the lack of jobs and rising food prices, since the lands previously used for food production were now used for commercial exploitation. (For a more detailed analysis, see Furtado, 1964: 149–53; also Lopes, 1964: 14; 1966: 198).

The situation was gloomy in the mid-1960s. One-fourth of the sugar factories in the state of Pernambuco were forced to close in 1965, creating unemployment for some 150,000 workers (Foland, 1968, no. 22: 2; F. Mitchell, 1966–1967, no. 11: 5). In 1966, the money became tight. The *Instituto de Açucar e Alcool* (which buys all sugar and regulates the prices) was indebted to the factories, the factories could not pay their workers, who often for months received only promises or worthless token money for exchange at the empty company stores (F. Mitchell, 1966–1967, no. 11). The crisis even spread to the town, where merchants went bankrupt for lack of paying customers (Foland, 1968: no. 23). The situation for the workers became truly catastrophic. In spite of newly enforced minimum wages, they actually often received less money than before, food prices had risen sharply, and there was mass unemployment and starvation (F. Mitchell, 1966–1967, no. 11; Foland, 1968, nos. 22, 23; CIDA, 1966c). In at least one town, an infant mortality rate of 100 percent was reported (Foland, 1968, no. 23: 5). The owners, pressed by their workers, by newly enforced minimum wages, and by declining returns, were simply unable to provide adequate means of subsistence for their workers and either were forced to close their operations or in some instances squandered what little resources they had—attempting to cling to their accustomed life-styles or hoping that the government would buy up their estates out of pity for the workers (F. Mitchell, 1966–1967, no. 11: 5–6, 8). The initial development of the peasant movements arose in the mid-1950s as a response to the landlords' attempts to incorporate the workers' and tenants' lands into their commercial production. The economic pressures described above gave rise to new flare-ups and violence in the mid-1960s (Foland, 1968, nos. 23, 24; F. Mitchell, 1966–1967, no. 11: 4), even after the peasant and worker organizations had been suppressed in the 1964 coup d'etat.

The historical evidence cited in this section suggests that a deterioration in the economic status of the elite is frequently an important precedent of peasant movements. This general point has been previously made by other authors (Landsberger, 1969a: 23–25; Moore, 1966: 472–73). When the economic pressures on the landholders are passed on to their tenant-laborers through a variety of labor-repressive measures (Whyte, 1970: 21; Moore, 1966: 473), the legitimacy of their domination is undermined. The price the subordinates have to pay for the landlords' favors may then become too high to make submission worthwhile for them.

Hypothesis 2. The notion that revolutionary movements are usually not carried out by the poorest and most destitute strata of the population has had a long standing in the social science literature (Brinton, 1965: 250–51; Tocqueville, 1955: 174–77; Davies, 1962). A variant of this theme has been voiced by Francisco Julião, organizer and leader of the Brazilian *ligas camponêsas*, in his contention that peasants with some control over land have better economic and financial resources than the salaried rural workers and that the former are more readily organizable (Julião, 1962). While the success of rural labor syndicates in northeast Brazil has not substantiated Julião's specific predictions, evidence from Latin America suggests indeed that campesino movements arise under conditions of at least minimal economic security (Galjart, 1972: 8). Huizer, for example, has made the tentative empirical generalization that in Mexico, Peru, Venezuela, Bolivia, and Brazil campesino movements were most numerous in the less marginal regions of the countries, and that campesinos with relatively independent work who lived above the subsistence level were more likely to organize than were those with less economic resources (Huizer, 1969; 1970a: 396–97; also Landsberger, 1969a: 39–40). In Ucureña, Bolivia, Dandler (1971: 122, 190) has observed that campesinos who were able to acquire landed property could free themselves from the landowner's domination. Indeed, control over land has always been recognized by campesinos as their main objective in their conflicts with their *patrones*. Another crucial resource is the ability to pay the often staggering cost for lawyers and court fees in the settlement of land disputes (for some good examples in Peru, see Tullis, 1970: chap. 6). In general, the development of independent economic resources without assistance from outside the campesino community is a relatively rare phenomenon, although great sacrifices have been made in holding out on strikes and in taking up collections of money. The most significant exception to this pattern is probably the campesino movement of La Convención in Peru, where the scarcity of labor (Craig, 1967: 10–13) and the relative wealth of the campesinos enabled the latter to hold out for years on a long boycott against the landowners beginning in 1962 (Craig, 1967: 39–40). Craig also notes that the autonomous development in the valley in the 1950s gave rise to "an unusual

Latin American phenomenon of a rural labor union organizing itself from the bottom up—rather than being organized and directed from the outside" (1967: 40).

Hypothesis 3. One aspect of this hypothesis refers to alternative sources of supply open to the campesinos, which means simply that they leave their relationship with the *patrón*. Such alternatives involve temporary or permanent migration, change of employer, change of occupation, or a combination of these. These types of alternatives do not represent proper campesino movements, since they usually do not imply any reaction against the *patrones*. There have been, however, individual cases where campesinos have been able to play rival landowners against each other and thus to receive better terms from landowners who disputed the land claims of their *patrón* (Tullis, 1970: 103–6; Alberti, 1970a: 112).

New brokers have frequently become alternative providers of needed economic benefits to campesinos. The campesino movements in La Convención, Peru, most clearly benefited from the emergence of new middlemen (*rescatistas*). These were local store owners and town merchants who bypassed the *hacendados* and dealt directly with the campesinos by selling them goods, granting them credit and loans, and marketing their produce (Craig, 1967: 33, 50).

An alternative supplier of particular interest for this study is the peasant community itself. That issue will be taken up in a later chapter.

Hypothesis 4. Economic support from political allies and sympathizers has played an important role in many peasant movements. Political parties and especially urban labor movements have on numerous occasions provided funds and lawyers to campesino organizations (Huizer, 1969: 404). The poverty-stricken sugar workers in Cabo, Pernambuco, Brazil, were able to sustain their strike against the plantation owners with the help of free food from some local merchants and from the Church (Foland, 1968, no. 24: 11). In some countries, such as Venezuela and some areas of Bolivia, many local campesino organizations arose in response to organizing efforts from the outside (political parties, urban labor movements, rural labor movements expanding from other areas). It is significant that rural syndicates in these two countries received quick and broad-based support from the campesinos when they had the power to grant immediate and tangible benefits such as land, food coupons, arms, and political influence (Mathiason, 1966; Powell, 1969; Heath, 1969: 185; Huizer, 1967: 153).[4]

CHAPTER II

Imbalances in Changing
Social Relations

In this chapter some general social implications of propositions 1, 2, and 3 will be considered. While the treatment of the specific economic and political aspects of these propositions will be reserved for subsequent chapters, this chapter will argue that there have been two major interrelated factors contributing to the emergence of campesino movements: the breakup of traditional patronage relations (Galjart, 1972: 11–12) and the emergence of new patrons for the campesinos (Landberger, 1969a: 23–25; Eisenstadt and Roniger, 1980: 76–77).

THE BREAKUP OF TRADITIONAL PATRONAGE RELATIONS

Proposition 1 implies two possibilities: Either campesinos may utilize newly emerging resources, or the institutional controls preventing campesinos from utilizing existing resources may break down (Eisenstadt and Roniger, 1980: 70–71). The most important controls over the campesinos' resources have traditionally been the isolation of their communities within the domain of the hacienda, which gave the landholders a virtual monopoly over power and authority (Petras and Zemelman, 1972: 44). We may thus hypothesize:

Hypothesis 5: When the isolation of the traditional hacienda domain breaks down and campesinos gain access to institutions and resources of the larger society, the likelihood of campesino movements increases.

The breakdown of infrastructural constraints isolating the campesinos from the larger society (Migdal, 1974: chap. 7, 229–36) is manifested in the extension of transportation and communication facilities as well as in increasing contacts with towns. While systematic evidence for this hypothesis is sparse, the significance of infrastructural improvements for the development of campesino movements has been best described for the valley of La Convención, Peru. Here the power monopoly of the *hacendados* has been steadily eroded since 1881 when one of the landowners donated one-third of his land for the creation of a town and commercial center; here the merchants could not be expelled at the whims of the *hacendados* on whose land they had been operating previously (Craig, 1969: 281; 1967: 24–25). More market centers emerged after the valley had been linked to the rest of the country by road and railroad in 1928 and 1933, mostly resulting from the railroad right-of-way development. In these communities, independent merchants and middlemen represented brokers who were alternatives to the *hacendados* (Craig, 1967: 26–27, 50–52). The accessibility to campesinos of urban centers as the location of alternative resources has also been pointed out for the campesino movement in the Cochabamba valley of Bolivia (Dandler, 1971: 122). Similarly, Alberti (1970a: 119), in his analysis of the disintegration of a traditional hacienda, points out that the increasing contacts of the resident tenant-workers with inhabitants of nearby indigenous communities led them to a reevaluation of their own situation.

The breakdown of political constraints on the campesinos, as well as the actual utilization of new alternatives, will be discussed further below.

As has been shown, the domination of the traditional landholder over his tenant-workers has rested not only on his power and capacity for constraining the peasants, but also (in variable degrees) on the legitimation derived from his paternalistic services rendered to the subordinates. We may thus hypothesize from Proposition 3:

Hypothesis 6: In *patrón*-campesino relationships, the likelihood of campesino movements increases as the paternalistic benefits from the relationship decline for the campesinos.

As a general observation, Huizer (1969: 389) has remarked that campesino organizations in Latin America have been least frequent on haciendas where the paternalistic exchanges between landlords and tenant-workers have remained intact. In Bolivia, the campesinos took the harshest revenge on their landlords after the revolution of 1952 in areas where the domination had been mostly based on coercion and least on mutual benefits (Malloy, 1970: 202). The breakup of the traditional paternalistic relationship between landlords and tenant-workers has in many cases left a vacuum of insecurity for the workers. H. W. Hutchinson has described a strong sense of loss in northeastern Brazil where the paternalism of the traditional plantation had ceded to widespread bureaucratization in the sugar factories (1957: 65, 70–71; see also Wagley, 1960:

215–16). Furthermore, the recent attempts to enforce minimum wages and social security legislation in the northeast diminished the occasional paternalistic fringe benefits without eliminating the workers' need for them (Foland, 1968, no. 22: 6–7). The wife of an *usineiro* (owner of a sugar factory) has commented with considerable justification:

Our system has always operated on the basis of paternalism, I admit it. But at least there was a basis. Now the owners no longer have that margin of profit which they can devote to services to the workers. Furthermore, the state is moving in with its bureaucratic apparatus of social welfare—there are the institutions of social provision, and the syndicates—the owners are losing their sense of responsibility. It is a new kind of paternalism, but it is impersonal and it does not function well. It breaks up the old system, and the worker is left with nothing. (Foland, 1968, no. 22: 11)

Absentee ownership is an important factor in the frequent breakup of paternalistic domination (Galjar, 1972: 12). While it is not unusual for campesinos to seek out the administrator of the estate as a substitute *patrón* (H. W. Hutchinson, 1957: 50–51; see also Lopes, 1964: 15), absentee ownership in conjunction with an economic decline of the estate appears to have undermined the status of the owner vis-à-vis his tenant-workers on many estates. Tullis (1970: chap. 6) has documented the salience of this factor in the emergence of campesino movements on several haciendas in Peru. Tullis's observations have been confirmed by Alberti in his more detailed analysis of one of these same haciendas:

The first period which goes up to 1944 exemplified the *hacienda* system with prevailing conditions of balanced exchange with the use of power. . . .
. . . from oral reports of those subjected to the demands of the old *patrón*, their compliance was not extracted from them. There was an element of legitimation in the exercise of that power which transformed it into authority. . . .
. . . it seems that the old Landa lived in the *hacienda* most of the time, thus directly participating in the organization of the activities for the exploitation of the *hacienda*. This perhaps made him more aware of the needs of the peons and so he was able to reward or take away, as the circumstances dictated according to his conscience. His presence there added a note of personal contact which is so important in a subordinate-superordinate relationship. In essence, he played convincingly the role of the benevolent master. This was generally recognized by all the people of Tingo at that time. "He was a good man; he cared for us," they unanimously reported.
. . . The second period, which goes from 1944 until 1956, is typical of the *hacienda* system characterized by unbalanced exchange; here the exercise of power and the generation of an opposition movement prevailed. . . .
What made the balance of exchange relationships tilt to the perceived disadvantage of the peons was a change in the social relationship between the peons and the new *patrón* and particularly a change in those intangibles

which the old *patrón* managed so well to furnish the peons and thus to reciprocate for the personal services received. . . . Those intangibles which the new (absentee)*patrón* failed to reciprocate were particularly "in protection and general care" for his peons. (1970a: 110, 115)

Observations in Colombia during the 1950s have also suggested that rural conflict and land invasions by campesinos were most frequent in cases "when an absentee owner had subdivided his property and rented out individual lots without making any managerial or financial contribution of his own" (Hirschmann, 1965: 195–96). In Guatemala, it has been noted that the success of the Arévalo and Árbenz governments in unionizing the rural labor force has been decidedly less marked among the stable laborers residing on the plantations than among the more mobile workers who did not enjoy the paternalistic benefits of their landlords (R. N. Adams, 1960: 251–52). In a case study of peasant mobilization on a Chilean *fundo*, Petras and Zemelman (1969; 1972) report that the tenants initially reacted to the owners' attempts to rationalize some aspects of the social relations on the *fundo* (withdrawing the traditional *regalía* or payments in kind in favor of monetary remuneration) by perceiving them as a threat to their daily existence and as indication of the owner's untrustworthiness. The peasants preferred the traditional particularistic ties with the *patrón* to contractual and universalistic ones. "For most rank-and-file peasants, the breakdown of paternalism was an important event in the chain that led to the revolt" (1969: 27; 1972: 30–31).

ALTERNATIVE PATRONS

The last hypothesis to be considered in this chapter is derived from Proposition 2 (Eisenstadt and Roniger, 1980: 77):

Hypothesis 7: In *patrón*-campesino relationships, the emergence or accessibility of alternative suppliers of the benefits campesinos receive from the *patrones* increases the likelihood of campesino movements.

The type of supplier to be considered at this point is the "cultural broker," introduced above.

As Wagley (1964: 45–46) has noted, traditional brokers such as the *patrón* or the padre (who used to monopolize the campesinos' links with the larger society) have become increasingly challenged by new brokers (teachers, lawyers, merchants, urban politicians, labor leaders) in recent years. It is important to consider the emergence of such new brokers in the context of new power domains that encroach upon the traditional domain of the haciendas, most notably the government (R. N. Adams, 1967a: 226–31, 238–47; 1967b; Sharpe, 1977, chap. 9). Thus, the individual campesino occupies a series of roles within a complex of "multiple-power domains" and thereby "has a number of alternative channels of access to power. By holding positions in a series of domains, he has access to derivative power that lets him play one organization against another, each of which in turn operates with access to the power of the government" (R. N. Adams, 1967a: 241). In the context of these structural transformations of the larger society, the exchanges between landlords and campesinos undergo drastic changes. The brokerage monopoly of the landlord breaks down, alternative brokers emerge whose interests, in various degrees, conflict with those of the landholders, and the expansion of the governmental domain begins to include the campesino directly and no longer the landlord as an intermediary.

These processes have taken place in all Latin American countries. A number of scholars have taken these observations as a point of departure for developing a model for campesino movements in terms of a triangle that is open at the base. Figure 1 represents an ideal-typical model of traditional campesino relationships. P designates the *patrón*, C the campesinos, R the institutional and other resources available in the larger society (government, courts, banks, markets, and so forth), and the connecting lines represent channels of communication, brokerage, power, and exchange. In this model, lines of exchange and communication between campesinos are practically nonexistent; they are related to one another indirectly through the *patrón*, who, in turn, also controls the links of the campesinos to the institutions and resources of the larger society. The development of campesino movements is hampered by their lack of horizontal solidarity and exchanges and by their dependence on the *patrón*, whose brokerage and protection is more vital for the individual campesino than the benefits he can receive in exchanges with his peers. The domination of the *patrón* weakens when his brokerage monopoly breaks down and the campesinos can gain access to outside resources directly or through alternative brokers, designated B in Figures 2

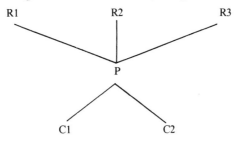

FIGURE 1. Traditional *patrón*-campesino relationships.

and 3. To the extent that the "usefulness" of campesinos to alternative brokers is contingent on their joint activities (for example, as a bloc of voters, organizational members, money collectors, or militia), these alternative brokers may foster the development of horizontal solidarity and organization among the campesinos. This is represented in Figures 2 and 3, where the triangle becomes closed at its base and integrated within a complex of other triangles. The conceptualization of campesino movements in terms of the closing triangle has been developed by Cotler (1969) and subsequently employed by Whyte (1970), Tullis (1970: 43–45), Dandler (1969: 4–16; 1971: 64–75), and Alberti (1970a: 90–96; 1970b). In these studies, the authors have found the model to be most appropriate to account for their empirical findings concerning the campesino movements of Peru and Bolivia. Observations from other countries in Latin America suggest a similar pattern. As the emergence of alternative brokers is primarily due to power shifts, the issue will have to be taken up again in Chapter 12.

NEW BROKERS

The changing roles of government and political parties in campesino movements, to be discussed at greater length below, have set the power parameters for the successful emergence of other brokers. Among these other new brokers, lawyers have been universally instrumental at manipulating legal resources for the

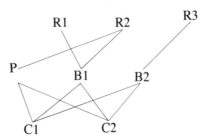

FIGURE 2. *Patrón*-campesino relationships and the emergence of alternative brokers.

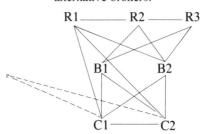

FIGURE 3. Campesino solidarity and new brokers.

benefit of the campesinos in the recognition of organizations, in the settlement of land or labor disputes, in deliberations about strategies, and in the provision of political connections. It is equally tue, however, that lawyers have often been the worst exploiters of their peasant clients. In Peru, for example, many lawyers have involved campesinos in endless litigations over land-ownership and boundaries, so draining the financial resources of their clients that the latter became impoverished. It is notable that such legal disputes (which a 1965 study found to exist in 653 out of 754 rural communities surveyed), which are artificially prolonged by the lawyers, undermine class solidarity among the campesinos, as they generally pit individual campesinos and whole communities against one another (Whyte and Williams, 1968: 8–12).

Teachers, students, and other intellectuals have also played crucial roles in a number of campesino movements. Individual politicians have provided valuable help through protection, legislation, and political connections. One of the best known cases involves Francisco Julião, a lawyer and state deputy in the Brazilian state of Pernambuco at the time that the *moradores* of the *engenho* Galiléia needed legal and political support in their struggle with their landlord. Julião found his cause and an expanding political base in the *ligas camponêsas* whose mentor, organizer, and leader he became. The *ligas* benefited from his political connections and the material gains he could provide; Julião, in turn, greatly enhanced his political career through his leadership of the *ligas* (A. Leeds, 1964).

Industrial and mining unions have frequently aided campesino movements by providing funds, counsel, lawyers, indoctrination, organizers, and political pressure in the capital. Various forms of such peasant-worker alliances have existed in Brazil, Peru, Bolivia, Chile, and Guatemala. It should be observed, however, that labor support for the campesinos has not always been reliable, as campesinos and workers do not necessarily share common interests (Galjart, 1972: 9; Stavenhagen, 1969) and coalitions with other groups may demand different courses of action from the workers. One of the most notable instances of this sort was the deal Carranza made with the Mexican workers in 1916, whereby the workers were granted freedom to organize and call strikes in return for their formation of six "red battalions" to help fight the Zapatista armies.

The Catholic Church has emerged in the 1950s and 1960s as another sponsor of campesino organizations. The Christian Union Movement of Peru (MOSICP), founded in 1954 as an organization for urban workers, extended its interests to rural workers in 1956 and eventually formed the Federation of Latin American Peasants in conjunction with the Christian Democratic party in the Arequipa region. After a split in the organization in 1963, MOSICP was confined to the province of Ayaviri (northern Puno), supported by the foreign priests of the area, with the purpose of organizing the indigenous population to limit the expansion of the more radical organizations of the area (Cotler and Portocarrero, 1969: 320). In Chile, Church-sponsored unions have achieved significant break-throughs in collective bargaining (see below). It is notable that these unions have tended not to challenge the legitimacy of the existing agrarian structure but to obtain improvements for rural workers within that structure by using their leverage on the government as a means to gain concessions from the landowners. Such a strategy can only be successful with wage laborers (who need higher remunerations and better working conditions), not with sharecroppers and tenants whose goal is control and owner-ship of land—a more radical objective (Petras, 1966).[1] In north-eastern Brazil, the Catholic Church began to organize rural syndi-cates in 1961 as a counterweight to the more radical organizations of Julião and the Communist party; by the end of 1963 it claimed a membership of 200,000 (Kadt, 1967: 214). Although this movement was subdivided into groups with different strategies, different leaders on the whole shared a reformist orientation that stressed legalism, negotiations rather than strikes, and the need to obtain benefits for the rural workers through intervention within the existing political structure (Wilkie, 1964; Kadt, 1967; Moraes, 1970; Hewitt, 1969). In Guatemala the Social Christian Peasant Movement was founded by Christian Democrats in 1962. The movement was rather small, not very radical in its orientation, and unenthusiastically tolerated by the government (Pearson, 1969: 372; Murphy, 1970: 476). The Church was not active in the organi-zation, although individual priests participated. Traditionally, the Church in Guatemala has not only legitimized the rule of the landed elite, but has also actively intervened (through individual priests) in the labor conflicts during the Arévalo-Arbenz regime by de-nouncing the *Confederación Nacional Campesina de Guatemala* (CNCG) as communist and demanding that the campesinos choose between communism and Christianity (Pearson, 1969: 367–69).[2]

In summary, brokers have played an important role in stimulat-ing campesino mobilization. The discussion, however, also suggests that the activities of brokers did not necessarily contri-bute to the emancipation of their clientele. Many brokers out-rightly manipulated campesinos solely for their own political or economic interests. Other brokers with reformist political ideologies or who deliberately took action as a counterforce to more militant organizers set inherent limits to the success of the movements they led. These issues will be discussed below in various contexts.

BROKERAGE THROUGH CAMPESINO ORGANIZATIONS

The brokerage functions of campesino organizations have been manifested notably in the leadership provided by the organizers, who generally have had greater knowledge, experience, connections, and other resources to manipulate the institutions of the larger society and guide the campesinos in their dealings with an outside world from which they had been largely excluded under the domination of their old *patrones*.[3] Thus, the history of campesino movements in Latin America is also a history of their leaders. Among the best known are Emiliano Zapata in Mexico, Francisco Julião in Brazil, Hugo Blanco in Peru, and José Rojas in Bolivia. But while these are personalities known for their more spectacular achievements, campesino organizations have always operated with a large number of organizers, mediators, advisers, influence peddlers, "ward heelers," and other officials at all political levels who may or may not have had the personal charisma of the above-mentioned figures. What distinguished most of these was that their education, skills, or experiences enabled them to provide brokerage services to campesinos with little understanding of, and control over, national or regional politics. Many of them were not campesinos, and especially the national leadership of campesino federations tended to be provided by urban intellectuals, lawyers, politicians, labor leaders, and sometimes members of the clergy.[4] This situation has been characteristic for the Chilean ASICH, analyzed by Landsberger (1969b: esp. 265–66), for the Brazilian peasant leagues and rural syndicates (Moraes, 1970; Hewitt, 1969: 386–87), the Guatemalan movement (Pearson, 1969: 346–50), Venezuela (Powell, 1969: 80–84), and Peru's FENCAP (Quijano, 1965; Cotler and Portocarrero, 1969: 306–7). At the local level, leadership was frequently provided by teachers (Otilio Montaño in Mexico), local businessmen (the Caceres brothers in Peru), or priests (padres Melo and Crespo in Brazil). The indigenous leadership for campesino organizations tended to be provided by individuals who had traveled abroad (Rojas in Ucureña), lived in the city (Zapata in Mexico), had experience with industrial labor or mining unions (Tullis, 1970: chap. 6), and an above-average level of schooling. Thus, typical characteristics of the early union leaders in the valley of La Convención included having been a migrant prior to union involvement, prior experience in other occupations, an above-average level of education, bilingualism (Spanish-Quechua), and a higher level of acculturation to the dominant culture (Craig, 1967: 37–38). For Venezuela, Powell (1969; 1971) has provided extensive statistical data that highlight the brokerage functions of leaders in the *Federación Campesina de Venezuela* (FCV). Thus, leadership rank within the FCV is directly associated with education and leaders as a whole have more education than nonleaders (1971: 126). Furthermore, the higher the rank of the FCV leaders, the smaller the proportion of leaders whose fathers were campesinos and the larger the proportion of those whose fathers were professionals (1971: 126). At all levels of leadership in the FCV, there is a consistent career pattern that begins with party membership, continues with participation in the urban labor movement, and last includes membership in the FCV; also within each organization (party, urban labor union, FCV) there is a consistent pattern of declining length of membership as one moves down from the national to the local leadership levels (1971: 128). These data are consistent with the observation that (1) membership in the FCV originated at the national level and was then diffused to the local levels, and (2) the local leadership of the FCV has been recruited from political parties and the labor movement. Commenting on this observation, Powell (1969: 83–84) has pointed out that even the high proportion of campesino FCV leaders at the local levels is largely a reflection of campesinos returning to their communities after having lived in the cities and after having had contact with the urban political and labor movements. The brokerage function of the FCV is further manifested in the type of activities typically reported. Between 65 and 69 percent of the local syndicates sampled reported petitioning various government ministries and agencies for matters such as roads, land, housing projects, schools, and sanitary and health projects; 78 percent helped their members to obtain farm credit from the responsible government agency; and 80.5 percent reported discussing general community problems (1971: 143). Last, FCV leaders reported more frequent contacts with political leaders than their followers and nonaffiliated campesinos (1971: 154). While one has to be cautious in generalizing from the FCV to other Latin American campesino organizations, the relative influence of nonagrarian personalities and of campesinos with experiences outside their communities appears to be common throughout the continent (Quijano, 1967: 324–26).

Examples. Some case descriptions may illustrate relevant aspects of leadership patterns in campesino movements. In

Ucureña, Bolivia, the campesino syndicate was founded by campesino veterans returning from the Chaco war after 1935, with the help of a sympathetic small landowner, a lawyer, and the schoolteacher Juan Guerra. Guerra's brokerage was essential in the achievement of the syndicate's goals. He was born in a town of the Cochabamba valleys, was a member of the PIR party, and had influential friends in the departmental and national administration. His friends provided needed support for the nascent movement, and through him the syndicate transacted its negotiations with its own lawyer, the governmental officials involved in the case, banks, and the lawyer of the monastery whose lands the syndicate claimed. In 1942 an amalgamated school-syndicate organization was formed and Guerra was elected its formal leader. In 1946, José Rojas became the formal leader of the syndicate. He had had experience outside the valley and, more important, had quasi "learned the trade" of brokerage through his association with Guerra, through getting acquainted with the details of the negotiations as an assistant to Guerra, and through his meetings with politicians. A significant transaction he undertook in 1947 was the mustering of campesino votes for a PIR candidate whom he knew personally and who subsequently pressed for legislation favorable to the syndicate (for a more detailed discussion, see Dandler, 1969; 1971). After the revolution of 1952, campesino syndicates became practically identical with local government in many areas of the country due to the dual position of syndicate leaders as political patrons (see also Malloy, 1970: 211–14) and to the amalgamation of rural syndicates, governmental bodies, and political parties (see also Barnes Marshall, 1970). Dual role holding in political party and campesino organization has also been noted in Venezuela, where the close links between these organizations are similar to those in Bolivia. Typically, a secretary general of the campesino syndicate would hold the post of agrarian secretary on the party executive committee at the national or local level. Such dual role holding is most common in Venezuela, and the two roles are so fused that a potential conflict of interest is not even conceived as a realistic possibility (Powell, 1969: 84–86).

While the above discussion has emphasized the role of outside leadership and support for campesino movements, it should not be forgotten that indigenous leaders have achieved spectacular success as well as catalyzed solidarity in small-scale movements. In some cases the leadership of these personalities rested on their ability to manipulate patronage networks for the benefit of the campesinos, as in the case of José Rojas and Hilarion Grájeda in Bolivia (Dandler, 1971). In other cases it rested on the personal charisma and the ability to guide successful armed campaigns. The latter was characteristic of Emiliano Zapata in Mexico, who gained fame first as a defender of village lands and later as a commander of some twenty thousand peasant guerrillas who received the faithful support of the villages (food, information about the enemy) in return for guaranteed security and the distribution of practically all the lands in the state of Morelos to the peasants (Huizer, 1967: 14).

In conclusion, then, campesino movements can be conceived as functional equivalents of the traditional *patrones* insofar as they provide services to their followers. In this sense they constitute new system linkages that integrate the rural masses with the urban-industrial sectors of the macrosociety and, in this sense, they have been characterized in terms of a "triumph of outside-oriented forces" (Migdal, 1974: 15). Such continuities with the traditional social structures notwithstanding, a crucial characteristic of the new protectors of the campesinos is the fact that they do not necessarily represent politico-economic interests that are completely opposed to the objective class interests of the campesinos. While relations of dominance and dependence between the campesinos and their "new *patrones*" occur frequently, it is important to observe that the new sponsors characteristically are not landowners but lawyers, schoolteachers, priests, urban labor functionaries, or campesinos themselves. Their position does not place them into a direct class relationship with the campesinos. Consequently, campesinos who solidarize themselves with one of these new sponsors do not *necessarily* subvert their objective class interests. It should be noted that such solidarizations have typically been the result not of *common* but of *complementary* interests of the new patrons and their clients. As a result, there are a number of inherent dilemmas in such vertical alliances. If the government is a new patron of campesinos, it will require general legitimacy and acceptance among a majority of the political groups in the society (unless it rules by coercion alone) and thus is likely to have to compromise the interests of its campesino clientele. Or the government may have to compromise between the goals of the campesinos and a presumed national interest; the "developmentalist" policies of the Mexican government after 1940 exemplify this dilemma (Huizer, 1970c: 486–87). Finally, there is always the potential conflict between the patron's self-interests and those of their clientele; many campesino leaders have indeed placed a premium on their own political ambitions and conducted themselves much like their former *patrones*. This continuation of traditional social patterns, however, has also been observed in cases where campesinos are not necessarily manipulated by cynical opportunists. Heath (1973), for example, has shown how among the Aymaras of the Bolivian Yungas, after the revolution of 1952, there were many "old patrons in new roles" and "new patrons in old roles." The point is that with a favorable balance of power, especially of coercive power, campesinos could tip the pendulum decisively in their favor. In this sense we can surmise that with the ascendance of new political groupings in the late nineteenth and twentieth centuries the formation or durable campesino organizations for the first time became objectively possible in Latin America, as the immediate self-interest if the individual campesino becomes consistent at least with the interests of his particular group (community, organization), if not with the objective interests of his class.

CHAPTER 12

Imbalances in Power Relations

SHIFTS IN CONTROL OVER POLITICAL RESOURCES

As the monopoly of the landholders over access to political power and force has been their primary resource in keeping the campesinos in their place, campesino movements are expected to be encouraged when they can gain independent access to institutional, political, and coercive resources, when the landlords' controls diminish (as a consequence of macrostructural changes in the larger society), or when alternative power brokers can effectively challenge the monopoly of the traditional landholders (Galjart, 1972:7–9). All of these factors have been associated with Latin American campesino movements, to various degrees and in various combinations.

As has been pointed out in Chapter 11 at a more general level, the emergence of new cultural brokers in rural Latin America has been related to the emergence of multiple power domains under the umbrella of the central governments. Urbanization and industrialization, with the concomitant development of new economic interest groups and of urban mass electorates uncontrolled by the provincial political bosses, have generally shifted the focus of political power to nationally oriented parties and politicians, even though important political brokerage is still exercised by local and provincial politicans.[1]

The use or threatened use of force is the ultimate resource for maintaining power relations. Therefore, we modify Proposition 1:

Hypothesis 8: Where force or the threat of force is a contributing factor in the stabilization of *patrón*-campesino relationships, a decline in the *patrón*'s access to, or control over, means of coercion and/or an improvement in the campesinos' access and/or control increases the likelihood of campesino movements.

In his *Anatomy of Revolution,* Brinton (1965: 253) concludes, "No government is likely to be overthrown from within its territory until it loses the ability to make adequate use of its military and police powers."[2] A similar generalization might be suggested for conflicts within the domain of landed estates. While landowners frequently have their own private police to maintain order on their estates, the owners' powers are ultimately derived from their ability to monopolize the institutionalized means of coercion from the larger society for their purposes.

In the past, Latin American landholders have been able to rely on the assistance of the police, the militia, or the military in confrontations with their campesinos. In view of the aforementioned power shifts at the national level, the control over institutional means of coercion can no longer be taken for granted by the landholders (Galjart, 1972: 9). When the worker and peasant organizations in northeast Brazil were prospering, the landholders had a more limited (but by no means completely lacking) influence over the police forces, which were frequently neutral and occasionally even intervened against landholders (Hewitt, 1969: 379). Where peasant leagues were threatened by the police, high-level parliamentarians would visit the leagues and thus protect the peasants from being attacked (Moraes, 1970: 465). Invasions of haciendas in Peru have been aided by the general knowledge or expectation that this time the police would not open fire upon the invaders (Tullis, 1970: 142). Similar observations have been made in the case of several Chilean invasions (McCoy, 1967; Petras and Zemelman, 1972).

The most significant countries where the campesinos' control over means of coercion has been a pivotal factor in the relative success of their movements have been Mexico and Bolivia.[3]

During the Mexican revolution, the peasant armies of Emiliano Zapata and Pancho Villa were the backbone of the agrarian movement for almost a decade, and it was only the strength of these armies that compelled the middle-class leaders of the "revolution" to enact agrarian reform legislation. While these observations are too well known to warrant more detailed documentation (White, 1969; Huizer, 1967; 1970a; Wolf, 1969: chap. 1), it is worth pointing out that the association of peasant success with military strength continued into the 1950s. Under the Cárdenas government, vigorous land distribution programs could be enacted only on the strength of the peasant militias, which were more reliable in countering the continuing "white terror" of the landholders and clergy than the regular army (Huizer, 1967: 66–88, 121–40).

The Bolivian revolution of 1952 began with the seizure of power by *Movimiento Nacional Revolucionario* (MNR), which mainly represented a group of army officers, miners, and disenchanted members of the intelligentsia and middle class. Initially the MNR was only moderately interested in agrarian reforms, but it was soon spurred into taking a stand as land invasions and rural violence spread in the Cochabamba valley. Here, based on the organizational experience of the Ucureña syndicate, campesinos seized various haciendas, drove off the owners, and equipped themselves with the arms they found on the haciendas. It was after an unsuccessful attempt to replace the leader of the syndicate, José Rojas, that the government decided to spearhead the movement it could not contain. Subsequently, organizers of the MNR, the miners union, and the campesino syndicates in the Cochabamba valley spread the movement to other areas in the country. Simultaneously, the government organized armed workers and peasant militias, dismantled the army, and thereby shifted the balance of force in favor of the campesinos and workers. It was the initial violence by the campesinos that moved the tenuously established government to take a radical agrarian stand; the armed peasant militias in subsequent years made it possible to enforce the agrarian reforms:

It is difficult to overestimate the impact of the revolution, even recognizing the fact that a *campesino* used to spend as much as two-thirds of his time doing unpaid work and often demeaning work for a landlord, and now has no such obligations. It is equally true, and perhaps more dramatically impressive, that *campesinos* who had been legally forbidden to wear arms until 1952, were then given rifles, machine guns, and mortars so that they soon constituted a force stronger than the army. (Heath, Erasmus, and Buechler, 1969: 383–84)[4]

Another institutional resource to be considered is the judicial system. Accordingly, we hypothesize:

Hypothesis 9: In *patrón*-campesino relationships, a decrease in the *patrón*'s control over courts and other legal resources, and/or an increase in the access of campesinos to such resources, will increase the likelihood of campesino organizations.

In Ucureña, Bolivia, a court decision vitiating previous actions taken by the *hacendados* of the region against the campesinos greatly aided the nascent syndicate in the valley as early as 1942 (Dandler, 1971:86–87). Tullis (1970: chap. 6) cites a number of occasions where the success of campesino organizations in the courts had a snowballing effect on nonmembers and other organizations. Indeed, the visible success of campesino movements appears to have an accelerating effect on the undecided, as is shown perhaps most spectacularly in the case of Bolivia after 1952.

Legal recognition is a related factor that greatly encourages the development of formal campesino organizations. Traditionally, rural labor laws have been restrictive in Latin America, so until recently only a few rural syndicates existed, and those could ill afford to take a militant stand lest they wished to be banned (Menges, 1968: 2–3; Walker Linares, 1953; Murphy, 1970; Price, 1964). When the legal recognition of a rural union becomes easier to achieve, when the right to strike and bargain collectively is granted, *and* when the government enforces these rights, then rural organizations arise rapidly. Within a few months of the promulgation of the new labor statute in Brazil in 1963, some two thousand rural unions sprang up with a membership of between fifty and three thousand each (Huizer, 1967: 187). Murphy (1970) has shown how closely the increase and decrease in the number of rural unions in Guatemala is associated with changing legal-political tides, and similar observations can be made in Brazil (Price, 1964: 68–69).

In fact, the observer is struck by the optimism and energy that campesinos have manifested in relentless efforts to form organizations, bargain, and settle land disputes within the legal-institutional framework, and by the great sacrifices they undergo to collect lawyers' fees (for examples, see Tullis, 1970: chap. 6). It is reasonable to assume that such legalism is less a reflection of the campesinos' faith in the system of justice of their country than of their weak position vis-à-vis their landlords in direct bargaining or of their inability to organize strikes without having to fear the organized violence of the upper classes. A lawyer, politician, or otherwise influential person, however, is able to manipulate the legal system in a manner similar to that used by the landlords. When campesinos have no resources for direct bargaining, the only strategy open to them is to tap the resources a power broker has within the larger society.

There is, however, an important qualification to be made to the above comments. The most radical campesino movements appear to arise *not* when legal resources become accessible, but when these fail to respond to organized legal demands made by the campesinos, or when violence by the landlord precludes legal means. What Chalmers Johnson has called "elite intransigence," and the general resistance of institutional structures to moderate demands, appears to have radicalized campesino movements in Latin America (Huizer, 1969: 389, 393; 1970a: 398; Tullis, 1970; Alberti, 1970b; also Malloy, 1970: 317–41). As an empirical generalization, it appears thus that (1) an opening of legal channels to campesinos will encourage the development of formal campesino organizations (for example, rural syndicates) *if* the landlord cannot or will not use coercion, and (2) the resilience of the legal system and other institutional structures to moderate campesino goals will encourage radical, spontaneous, and extralegal reactions by the campesinos.[5]

The last potential power resource to be considered here is the vote. In Chapter 9 it was argued that in the past campesinos were either barred from elections or had little freedom (if the knowledge) to choose candidates other than those selected by the *patrón*. In recent years some changes have taken place in this regard, and we may hypothesize according to Proposition 1:

Hypothesis 10: Campesino movements are likely to develop in areas that have witnessed a decline in the landlords' ability to supervise and control the vote of the campesinos.

Campesinos who are able to vote without supervision are free to give their vote to whomever promises them most; as an aggregate, they then constitute a reservoir of voters that can attract the attention of politicians and ward heelers. Craig (1967: 49) has related the success of the movement in the valley of La Convención to the campesinos' ability to vote. In Bolivia, the campesinos were given the vote by the MNR after 1952 in order to ensure a reliable electoral basis of support for the regime. In Chile, the electoral law of 1958, which provided for elections by single ballots, has greatly aided the access to peasants for the reform-oriented and more radical parties (Petras and Zeitlin, 1970: 510–11; Petras and Zemelman, 1969: 8–9). In Brazil, the government of Goulart was obviously aware of the voting potential existing in the rural syndicates. Shortly before the coup of 1964, the minister of labor stated among the goals of his ministry with regard to rural unionization: establishment of two thousand syndicates; organization of the rural union movement so that it could act politically; establishment of a union tax; distribution of identification cards; civil and electoral registration of 3 million new voters (Price, 1964: 69). In Venezuela, the *Acción Democrática* was dependent on the votes of the peasantry, whose cause it had championed for a long time (Mathiason, 1966: 122–23).

The breakdown of the landlords' control and the opening up of new or alternative institutional resources provide the structural framework within which effective peasant mobilization becomes possible. To account for the mechanisms by which this process is set into motion, we hypothesize:

Hypothesis 11: The probability that campesino movements develop increases with the degree to which new political brokers can integrate these movements into the national power structures.

New power brokers, as has been discussed in Chapter 10, may or may not be indigenous campesinos, they may be individuals or associates of interest groups, and they may be inside or outside the government. While some new brokers may align themselves with the campesinos for purely altruistic reasons without receiving even indirect returns, most of them do indeed benefit from their brokerage services by using their campesino followers as a resource for bargaining with third parties (governments, political parties, labor unions, legislators, landholders). In the following, the political brokerage of governments and parties will be examined.

THE ROLE OF GOVERNMENT AND POLITICAL PARTIES

With the expanding power domain of the state in Latin American countries, the different branches of the government as well as the national political parties have come to play increasingly important roles in the formation and success of campesino movements. They exercise their discretionary influence by granting legal recognition to rural unions (or actually organizing them from above), by passing and enforcing laws that facilitate rural movements, by determining the trend of court decisions, by providing various forms of material support for campesino organizations, and by setting the policies for police or military intervention. The nature of the governmental influence on campesino movements has been erratic and characterized by frequent reversals. While it is true that in many instances governments have had to yield to pressures brought about by the campesinos and that in some countries campesino movements have obtained a degree of autonomy after initial periods of government sponsorship (Quijano, 1967: 320–24), the more significant empirical generalization is that the fate of campesino movements—both formal and spontaneous—has on the whole been closely associated with the policies and fates of allies and antagonists in the government and in the political parties.

Guatemala. In the 1920s and 1930s, some rural labor agitation occurred in Guatemala, but under the stern rule of the dictator Jorge Úbico local rebellions were quickly suppressed and formal organizations were virtually nonexistent. The overthrow of Úbico in 1944 and the presidency of Juan José Arévalo marked the emergence of a regime that favored, encouraged, and organized peasants and rural laborers as a means of obtaining electoral and armed support against the old landed elite. During the regime of Arévalo and his successor Jacobo Árbenz (1944–1954), some 1,500 confederated unions with 180,000 to 190,000 members arose, protected and organized by the governmental coalition and by government-instructed labor courts; following the promulgation of agrarian reform laws, 835,083 *manzanas*[6] of lands were expropriated and redistributed. The rural unions functioned as intermediaries, which, for the first time, incorporated the peasantry into the national political structure by circumventing the traditional controls exercised by the landowners. It has been noted that the rural syndicates effectively broke up the paternalistic concepts underlying the traditional *patrón*-campesino relationships. With the overthrow of the Árbenz regime in 1954, the rural unions and leagues were prohibited, forcefully repressed, or reduced to relatively ineffective associations. Expropriated lands were given back to their former owners. The labor code of 1955 made unionization practically impossible. In 1964, ten rural unions were found to exist; subsequently they increased in numbers (to around one hundred in 1967), but not in efficiency. The policies of the regime in power have determined the fate of rural unions in Guatemala (R. N. Adams, 1960; Murphy, 1970; Snee, 1969; Pearson, 1969; Huizer, 1967: 203–8; 1972: 136–40) and currently entail a precarious balance between repression and accommodation.

Venezuela. The background of the Venezuelan campesino organizations can be seen in the economic depression following World War I. Occasional rural unrest and land invasions reflected a deterioration of the campesinos' economic position, but neither an organized peasant movement nor political parties could develop until the end of the Gomez dictatorship in 1935. After that year, a number of political groupings formed, among them what was to become the *Acción Democratica* (AD). Encouraged by the promulgation of a relatively liberal labor code in 1936, the AD sought to establish its electoral base by organizing the campesinos into federated syndicates. Some two hundred professional organizers scouted the countryside to recruit talented local leadership and build up a grass-roots organization, but under the leadership of the urban-based AD. By 1945 significant progress had been made in the establishment of seventy-seven legalized rural unions and some five hundred unofficial groups altogether. The coup d'etat of 1945, which brought the AD to power, spurred the development of campesino as well as industrial labor unions under the main sponsorship of the AD. Between 1945 and 1948, the AD secured a monolithic control over the labor movement in the country by means of patronage and subtle repression of rival organizations. Universal franchise was granted, and vigorous efforts at voter mobilization among the peasantry were made. In the elections of 1946, the AD received 80 percent of the popular vote. The AD strengthened its campesino organizations by leasing lands and granting credits to its members. After the coup of 1945 established the dictatorship of Pérez Jiménez, the campesinos lost practically all of their recent gains, and the syndicates were forcefully repressed. For ten years, party and campesino organizations subsisted underground or in exile. Another coup in 1958 restored the political parties, and the AD again assumed the leadership of the government on the basis of its support among the labor movement. Massive land reform programs were carried out. In 1966, the *Federación Campesina de Venezuela* (FCV) included 3,476 local unions with a membership of around 550,000, and over 100,000 campesino families in over 700 *asentimientos* had benefited from the redistribution of over 5 million acres. Credit, extension services, and technological assistance constituted an integral part of the program. The functioning and success of the FCV are intrinsically linked to its virtual incorporation into the AD and the AD's corresponding control over the distribution of spoils. The state and local leaders functioned again as power brokers between the AD and the campesinos. They would exchange political loyalty from the campesinos for the concrete benefits they could obtain from the government; they could bargain with the government, in turn, for the provision of material benefits to their campesino clientele by delivering votes (Powell, 1969; 1970; 1971; Mathiason, 1966; Huizer, 1967: 211–20; 1972: 108–14).

Bolivia. Apart from Guatemala and Venezuela, Bolivia is the third country in Latin America in which a nationally organized movement has been fostered by the government in power. After the Chaco war (1932–1935), in which Bolivia was disastrously defeated, the power monopoly of the *rosca,* the ruling elite, began to be challenged by newly forming progressive-radical parties: the *Partido de Izquierda Revolucionario* (PIR, independent Marxist), the *Partido Obrero Revolucionario* (POR, Trotskyite), and the *Movimiento Nacionalista Revolucionario* (MNR, liberal intellectuals, disenchanted army officers, later joined by tin miners and ex-PIR members). In 1943 a coup brought to the presidency Major Gualberto Villaroel, who included a number of MNR members in his cabinet and actively supported the emergent peasant movements against the landholders through the promulgation and enforcement of supreme decrees and through symbolic personal appearances at mass gatherings of Indians. In the meantime, the campesino syndicate of Ucureña had developed in 1936 with some initial success, but it received later setbacks under unresponsive governments. In the 1940s the syndicate reemerged under the leadership of José Rojas when a sympathetic PIR member was elected deputy for the province of Cliza. The campesino movement was set back again with the fall of the Villaroel government in the coup of 1946 and the exile of the MNR leader, Victor Paz Estenssoro. After several unsuccessful rebellions and a nullified election in 1951, the MNR obtained power in 1952 with the help of carabineros and armed workers. As was described above, successful campesino uprisings in the Cochabamba valley forced the tenuously established government coalition to join the bandwagon of the agrarian movement after an initial period of indifference and after its attempt to replace José Rojas by MNR followers had been unsuccessful. Once the decision had been made, the MNR committed itself radically to the agrarian cause. Members and supporters of the governing coalition (including miners and intellectuals) carried the campesino syndicalization into the parts of the country where there was no organized movement, and agrarian reform laws were enacted and vigorously carried out. The peasantry received a general franchise, land, self-government, food coupons, schools, hospitals, arms to form powerful militias, and other benefits. Local campesino syndicates, organized hierarchically in a national confederation, were institutionly linked to the MNR political machine and the government through the brokerage functions of local and regional leaders. In many ways, the secretary-general of the local syndicates replaced the old *patrón* as a provider and protector, with the important difference, of course, that he did not own the land. He was capable of tapping the institutional resources of the government and could thus provide material benefits and services to the members of the syndicate, while he ensured the favor of the party and government through his control over the members' cooperation, votes, and armed support (Heath, Erasmus, and Buechler, 1969: 80–81; Heath, 1969; Patch, 1960: 124–28; 1963; Dandler, 1969; 1971; Huizer, 1967: 147–49; 1972: 88–105). The reinstitutionalization of national armed forces and a series of coup d'etats in the 1970s have broken up the initially strong political position of the Bolivian peasantry as well as weakened the strength of the mine workers' unions.

Peru. In Peru there have been no government-sponsored campesino unions, but the fate of the various movements in the twentieth century again reflects the ups and downs of governmental protection and tolerance. The largest recognized peasant and workers unions (FTAB, FENCAP) have been long under the influence and direction of the APRA party and have followed that party's accommodative orientation toward obtaining better benefits from existing arrangements rather than challenging the legitimation of the given social order. The established parties have shown little interest in sponsoring campesino movements, as Cotler and Portocarrero have pointed out (1969: 313), because the largely illiterate campesinos could not vote and because the lack of the syndicates' legal recognition made them unattractive as receivers of political patronage. Some of the communist-influenced organizations (for example, the CCP) showed a more radical stand than most other syndicates, presumably due to the organizations' total lack of access to institutional resources. In historical perspective, campesino organizations have had varying degrees of success, depending on the nature of governmental policies. The election of a sympathetic president, for example, has characteristically sparked widespread campesino agitation and land invasions in the expectation of later legalization through agrarian reform. This situation existed when Manuel Prado (1956) and Fernando Belaúnde (1963) campaigned and were elected. Both presidents have initiated a number of measures in favor of moderate campesino organization. Prado's "open policies" (1956–1958) stimulated the formation of the Provincial Campesino Federation of Cuzco and Lares in 1958 (Craig, 1969: 286); in a later decree he abolished the dreaded *condiciones* and recognized some land invasions de facto. Under Belaúnde a moderate agrarian reform law was promulgated. Both Prado and Belaúnde dealt harshly with the more radical movements. In a study of campesino movements in the Chancay valley, for example, Matos Mar (1967) has neatly traced the ups and downs of campesino movements in terms of the rise and fall of regimes. In the 1930s the first independent syndicates were founded and harshly repressed. In 1945, APRA organizers sought to expand their base of support in the valley by founding some syndicates that were temporarily quite successful in bargaining for higher wages. The organization was broken up when the military coup of 1948 brought General Odría to the presidency. After Odría was ousted in 1956, the syndical movement began to develop again. It was now possible but difficult to form an organization because the process was lengthy and uncertain and required support from the ministry of labor, industrial labor unions, and lawyers with the right connections. In the meantime, the landowners were free to harass and expel the members of the syndicates. In 1960, a serious conflict broke out on one hacienda due to the landholder's intransigence. The provincial federation solidarized itself with the syndicate, and subsequently the police intervened and broke up the federation. During the same time a relatively moderate organization formed under the protection of FENCAP that maintained its status by not rocking the political equilibrium of the valley.

In the 1960s, peasant organizations on a national scale emerged (Villanueva, 1967; Blanco, 1972). Many of them were sponsored by political parties, mainly the Christian Democrats, Acción Popular, APRA, and the Communist party (Bourque, 1971; also Dew, 1969). As the preceeding overview suggests, varying tides in Peruvian politics accounted for varying degrees of elasticity in the constraints operating against the formation of campesino movements. Some regimes suppressed all movements, others allowed moderate movements that did not constitute a threat to the existing social structure (Alberti, 1970b; Cotler and Portocarrero, 1969; Matos Mar, 1967; Craig, 1967; 1969; Huizer, 1967: 161–75; 1972: 114–24; CIDA, 1966c).

The military coup in 1968 entailed a significant, although not stable, rebalancing in the political and economic conflicts between traditional rural *hacendados* and the growing urban-industrial bourgeoisie of Peru. The new government was committed to large-scale agrarian reforms that effectively eliminated the political and economic domination of the traditional landlords. The old structure was replaced by strict governmental controls over key products in agriculture with an emphasis on collective peasant production. While such programs might lead to an eventual emancipation of the peasantry as a social class maintained not only at, but even below, the level of simple reproduction, rural collectivization as such does not have to entail such a radical change if new governmental controls over agricultural production continue to subsidize industrialization through price controls over foods and raw materials.

Agricultural collectivization in Peru has tended to weaken peasant mobilizations, which have tended to become monopolized by organizations under the control of the military government. In terms of the material outcomes of peasants from their collectivization under centralized politico-economic control by the government, there is little evidence that their net benefits from their formal co-ownership of land, sugar mills, and other rural productive units have augmented their incomes or life-styles (Petras and Havens, 1979; Valderama, 1976; Guillet, 1979: chap. 9; Petras and Laporte, 1971).

Brazil. While a good deal of grass-roots organization has existed in the peasant leagues and rural syndicates of rural Brazil and particularly of the rural northeast, the regional and national leadership has in general been provided by nonrural groups and individuals. Governmental support for the rural movement was significant in the 1955 expropriation of the *engenho* Galiléia by the state legislature of Pernambuco that legitimized the first peasant league under Francisco Julião, in the active support of Pernambuco Governor Miguel Arraes for the rural movement, in the promulgation and attempted enforcement of the rural labor statute of 1964, and in the active interest of President Goulart in mobilizing the rural population under his political banner. In Brazil the rural population found itself participating in multiple-power domains, where the Julião group, the Church, a number of Marxist parties, the Goulart government, and Arraes "competed for the privilege of organizing Pernambucan peasants" (Hewitt, 1969: 374–75). The competing leaders and organizations built their following in competing leagues and syndicates. Even the government founded its own rural syndicates. It has been suggested, however, that by 1964 the rural movement "seemed to be on the way to unification under the control of organizers of the Communist Party, supported monetarily and legally by Goulart" (Hewitt, 1969: 395), since his government "commanded both the monetary and the legal resources to inhibit independent action within the rural labor movement and to force unions into a national confederation fully controlled by the government" (Hewitt, 1969: 395–96). The achievements of the rural organizations have been paid for dearly by the peasants. But ultimately, these accomplishments would not have been possible without the "gifts" (permission to strike, laws, administration) from the government (Galjart, 1964; 1965; A. Leeds, 1964; Hewitt, 1969: 396; for a dissident point of view, see Huizer, 1965). Between 1962 and 1964, the federal government thus became a substitute for the *patrão* by handing out favors to its faithful followers. The military coup of April 1964 abruptly ended the movement. Most of the leagues and syndicates were dissolved, and the leaders were jailed or exiled. Some of the Church-sponsored syndicates have been allowed to continue, but they have little room for independent operation. After the deteriorating living conditions in the northeast led to new tension and even a strike in the village of Cabo (Pernambuco), conducted by the Church-sponsored syndicate under Padre Melo, it is significant to note that the negotiations were not conducted by the elected president of the syndicate, but by Padre Melo, who walked arm in arm with the minister of labor up and down the streets of the village until they reached an agreement. Afterward the president of the syndicate was rather rudely informed by the minister that the strikers' demands were granted by the government. At his departure, the minister "paternally patted Padre Melo and the top of his . . . head" (Foland, 1968, no. 24: 6). The president of the syndicate, a local worker, expressed privately his disenchantment with the autocratic rule of the padre and the uselessness of a syndicate that was run by the government (Foland, 1968, no. 24).[7]

Mexico.[8] During the Mexican revolution the peasant armies of Zapata and Villa forced the government to establish an agrarian reform program that eventually destroyed the large haciendas and redistributed large areas of land among the campesinos. The process has been far from complete, however. After the end of the large-scale fighting, the access of the individual rural communities to the benefits of the agrarian revolution depended primarily on the nature of their relationships with the state and federal governments. Already in 1916 the failure of the Carranza government to expropriate large estates had been caused by American intervention (Huizer, 1967: 29–30). After the 1920s various institutional arrangements were set up to systematically incorporate the organized campesinos into the ruling party; both on the national and on the state level, campesinos were organized directly by the government and incorporated into a system of spoils and patronage from which there was no escape (Huizer, 1967: 50–52, 61–63, 65). Land distribution and the granting of legal status to *ejidos* depended on the political orientation of the government. Thus, during the Calles administration (1928–1934) little emphasis was placed on the execution of agrarian reforms, whereas Cárdenas, both as a president (1934–1940) and previously as governor of the state of Michoacán, took a decisive stand against the still struggling landowners. Under his administration, a vigorous program of land distribution was carried out, frequently with the aid of campesino militias armed by the government. In 1935 the *Confederación Nacional Campesina* (CNC) was founded as an integral part of the ruling PRM party; it became the vehicle through which the government distributed spoils and patronage and received organized support in return. Actions on agrarian problems thus originated at the top of the party hierarchy and filtered down to the local syndicates. Huizer has summarized Silva-Herzog's critique of these practices:

Improvements for the workers were not so much conquered in hard struggle against employers and police, but to a great extent simply thanks to government support. From this resulted that many labour and peasant leaders became politicians, and many politicians became peasant leaders. Thus, political success in the official party was frequently based more on personal favors and "friendships." (1967: 99)

In 1945 a rival and more aggressive confederation of peasants' and workers unions' (UGOCM) was founded by dissident labor leaders. But the government refused legal recognition to the organization and intervened militarily to impose its own leadership on the movement. The *Central Campesino Independiente* (CCI), founded in 1961 by a group of socialists, as well as most subsequently founded peasant organizations, have been at best isolated from larger and potentially threatening popular support. But the more typical response of the government has been to first seek the co-option and disreputation of the leadership by offering them personal benefits (money, positions, cars, and so forth); if these measures failed, threats, abductions and physical attacks, including murders, as well as large-scale military interventions tended to be the end result, as has usually been the case with militant peasant mobilizations in Mexico since 1920. While such repression and "arrangements" through co-option have been characteristic of peasant mobilizations in Latin America in general, this process of maintaining political balances has advanced in Mexico to a high degree of efficiency, as is represented by the adaptations and power maintenance of the revolutionary party since 1910. The key to this maintenance of political power appears to be the artful and cynical maintenance of a balance between competing and opposing interest groups (including, more specifically, also class relations). In this process, the possibility of radical social reforms is precluded, and political programs are adapted to shifting balances of interests, dependence, and power relations (Kaufman Purcell and Purcell, 1980). For a more general discussion of these issues, see Chapter 15.

Chile. The Chilean movement did not reach large proportions until the Christian Democratic party under Eduardo Frei won the presidency in 1964. Prior to that time, several legal and political obstacles kept rural unions small in number, isolated, and legally restrained from collective bargaining (Menges, 1968: 2–3; Walker Linares, 1953).[9] There have been incidents, however, where labor disputes arose in the countryside in the early 1950s. Landsberger (1969b) has described in detail the events of a warning strike and subsequent shutout of workers on some twenty vineyards near the town of Molina. The initial action had been taken by the local groups independently of the *Acción Sindical Chilena* (ASICH), a Catholic workers federation, but the leaders of the federation did intervene on behalf of the strikers after the minister of the interior sent in troops and jailed some of the syndicate leaders at the request of the landowners. Characteristically, the bargaining did not take place between the union and the owners but at the highest political levels. The archbishop of Santiago and the president of the federation were able to convince President Ibañez in a private audience that the owners as well as the workers had broken the law and that the latter were good Catholics but not communists. The president grudgingly accepted that position and ordered the ministers of labor and agriculture (who had joined the meeting later) to go to Molina and put pressure on the owners. The two ministers and two top representatives of ASICH drove to Molina in one car but separated ten miles from Molina to "keep up appearances" (Landsberger, 1969b: 216–17). In Molina, the two government officials met in seclusion with the landowners and came out with an agreement that was signed not only by representatives of the workers and the owners, but also by the two ministers, in the presence of the state governor, the labor inspector, the officer in charge of the carabineros, and others.

The agreement represented a victory for the strikers—a novel phenomenon in Chile. Efforts to mobilize the peasantry politically had been taken sporadically in the past; but these were periodic vote-getting efforts, abandoned once the elections were over. As Petras and Zemelman have observed about one *fundo*,

conflict and mobilization within the farm coincided with national political mobilizations organized by insurgent, urban-based, leftist movements which sought public office. The long periods of quiescence coincided largely with periods in which urban insurgents were holding ministerial offices, when parliamentary activity predominated, or when the laws proscribed radical political groups. (1969: 13)

After the election of Frei in 1964, the political climate for campesino organizations became more favorable (Kay, 1976). A new labor law was prepared by the Congress, and new instructions favorable to campesino organizations were issued to the labor inspectors by the new minister of the interior, William Thayer (Petras, 1966: 24–25). (Thayer, incidentally, had been actively involved in the vineyard workers strike of 1953 as legal adviser and negotiator for ASICH; see Landsberger, 1969b: 216). As a result, peasant organizations were formed on a national scale, in each case sponsored by major political parties (chiefly the Christian Democrats and the Socialist/Communist parties) or Catholic Church groups. These parties and Church groups took the major initiative in creating peasant organizations as a means for competing among each other for the support of the newly enfranchised peasant clientele (Menges, 1968). In this favorable political climate a number of successful localized peasant revolts and takeovers occurred, always with the active support of prominent politicians, which neutralized the influence of the landholders over police and other political institutions (Petras and Zemelman, 1969; 1972; McCoy, 1967; Thiesenhusen, 1968). The Christian Peasant Union (UCC) under Héctor Alarcón achieved a breakthrough in the mid-1960s by settling the first collective contract with rural employers (Petras, 1966: 21). Alarcón, in an interview with James Petras, was cautiously optimistic about the future of his organization. He pointed out that the UCC provided electoral support for the ruling Christian Democratic party, but that this support was from a position of independence and by no means unconditional. He expressed a great deal of skepticism about current reform activities, especially about the tendency of government bodies to neglect their agrarian programs and concentrate on the formation of their own rural unions in competition with the UCC (Petras, 1966).

Under the *Unidad Popular* government of Salvador Allende (1970–1973), campesino movements stepped up their militance, since organizers could expect the government not to mobilize its repressive apparatus against the population while emancipation was the core of the official policy (NACLA, 1973: 66–78; Sonntag, 1972; Barraclough and Fernández, 1974; Johnson, ed., 1973; Winn and Kay, 1974; Garcés, 1974; Barraclough et al., 1974). It was the failure of the Allende government to balance its relations with a coalition of military officers and significant segments of the upper and middle classes that led to the violent overthrow of 1973. This overthrow highlights an extreme situation—in contrast to the Mexican case—where an authentic radical movement (1) obtained power through regular institutionalized channels and (2) was unable or unwilling to balance its position against opponents either through compromises or repression.

The comparative analysis presented here suggests that in spite of the diversity of situations encountered in the seven countries described, some important uniformities emerge. In general, the degree of success for campesino movements has been directly related to the degree of support they have received from governments and political parties. While campesinos have often formed organizations that were able to put pressure on the government, the degree of their political autonomy was variable and a direct function of their control over power resources, in other words, arms and votes. Campesino movements have been relatively successful when high-level political sponsors have (1) directly organized the campesino movements from the outside, (2) had to bargain with the campesinos for military or electoral support in return for legal and administrative measures, (3) intervened militarily on behalf of the campesinos, or (4) at least adopted a neutral stand and thereby deprived the landholders of their traditional control over institutional means of repression. While these measures, over a long period of time, have been erratic and frequently reversed, the trend is clearly toward an incorporation of the campesino into the national political system. This trend is characterized by a steady decline of the landholders' monopoly and control over institutional resources and means of constraint and by an increasing attractiveness of the peasantry as a political ally due to their capacity to vote and/or lend armed support. These developments, in turn, have encouraged the development of clientelistic politics and the emergence of political sponsors who need what the peasants can provide and who can reciprocate in kind (Powell, 1970).

The nature of this new "political factor" (Lord, 1967), however, remains ambivalent. From the foregoing analysis it becomes evident that campesino mobilization cannot be equated with campesino emancipation; and movements that have emancipatory potential and initial success can become co-opted over a number of decades or repressed in the wake of new governments or a military coup. Thus, the opening of political structures and the weakening political position of the landholders do not protect the campesinos from repression by the new political interests. And the incorporation of the peasantry into the clientelistic bargaining process does not ensure that they can participate from an autonomous bargaining position. These issues will be further discussed in Chapter 15.

POWER AND ACTIVE RESPONSES TO IMBALANCES

According to Proposition 6, the tendency of campesinos to respond actively to imbalances should increase as their relative powers increase. There are no studies designed to test this proposition. Therefore, only a few interpretive observations will be offered here.

As Chapter 7 has suggested, cognitive adaptations of various kinds to subordination and low status have been common among Latin American campesinos in the form of acceptance, legitimation, or fatalism. But this is not to say that campesinos are necessarily content with their situation and that they would not wish to have a better life. Thus, when opportunities are perceived to arise, it may not be too difficult to shed the protective shield of low expectations and rationalizations. The evidence from the preceding sections strongly suggests that power is indeed a pivotal mediator of responses to cognitive inconsistency, since a shift in the balance of power in favor of the campesinos has been one of the most reliable concomitants of campesino movements. This observation suggests that campesinos, in general, have in the past accommodated to more or less paternalistic relationships with their landlords due to powerlessness and a lack of alternatives, rather than to a particularly positive value placed on these relationships.

CHAPTER 13

Benefits from Horizontal Solidarity for Campesinos

According to Hypothesis 3, campesinos will actively seek to improve their outcomes when alternative suppliers can provide better or less costly benefits to them than the *patrón*. It can be argued that campesino organizations fulfill precisely that purpose and thus constitute functional equivalents to the traditional landholders. In previous chapters, the brokerage and leadership functions of campesino organizations have been analyzed. But beyond these services, campesino organizations have also typically provided a number of tangible benefits to their clientele that made them attractive as brokers.

TANGIBLE BENEFITS FROM CAMPESINO ORGANIZATIONS

The direct benefits campesinos tend to receive from their unions are usually those formerly provided irregularly and sparsely by the *patrón* or supposed to be delivered by the various branches of government.[1] The most immediate services provided by unions and leagues have been the lending of know-how and assistance in the handling of grievances and claims filed with governmental and judicial bodies. Characteristic for many Latin American countries is Powell's (1969: 72) observation that if Venezuelan campesinos had specific grievances against individual landholders, they would generally have little knowledge of what to do. "The union organizers provided an attractive logic for 'what to do,' and the response of the local campesino leaders and their following provided the necessary mass base of support 'to do it.' " Among the most notable services of campesino organizations has been the provision of legal assistance in countries such as Peru, Chile, Bolivia, Brazil, and Guatemala. One of the most spectacular successes was achieved in the northeast Brazilian state of Pernambuco by lawyer and state deputy Francisco Julião, whose political and legal intervention on behalf of the nascent peasant leagues secured protection and favorable legislation for his clientele (Hewitt, 1969;

Moraes, 1970). In most cases, these direct benefits are closely linked with the brokerage functions of the campesino movements. Thus, the above-mentioned activities of the Venezuelan FCV (Powell, 1971: 143) constitute brokerage activities designed to obtain needed benefits for the members. The value of these services is reflected in the increasing budgetary support for agrarian reform (Powell, 1971: 164) and in the number of credits extended to campesinos by the government (Powell, 1971: 165).

The primary benefits campesinos expect from their organizations are, of course, the redistribution of land and/or favorable settlements in labor disputes. Characteristically, campesino organizations have had the greatest appeal and largest support when and where they could provide these services—although the causal patterns for this relationship are complex and by no means linear. Cases in point are the northeast Brazilian peasant leagues and rural syndicates in the early 1960s (Hewitt, 1969; Moraes, 1970), the swelling of the Bolivian campesino organizations after the revolution of 1952 (Heath, 1969), the support of the campesinos in Morelos, Mexico, for Emiliano Zapata (White, 1969; Huizer, 1970a; Womack, 1969), the campesino movements in the Mantaro and La Convención valleys of Peru (Tullis, 1970; Craig, 1969), the success of the Venezuelan Peasant Federation (Powell, 1969), and possibly the surge of campesino activities in Chile following the election of Salvador Allende as president. But the services provided by campesino organizations to their clientele go further than that. In some countries, campesino organizations at times have assumed virtually all governmental functions at the local and regional levels. The powerful secretaries general in the Bolivian campesino syndicates, for example, have often dispensed justice much like the former landlords used to do on their haciendas; they saw to it that schools were built, teachers were hired, and various public utilities were instituted (Heath, 1969). Indeed, the spectacular growth of the Bolivian campesino movements after the revolution of 1952 must be seen clearly as a function of the far-reaching benefits that revolution brought to the campesinos in the form of arms, voting power, local autonomy, and food bonuses (Heath, 1969; Heath, Erasmus, and Buechler, 1969). In northeast Brazil, the various rural organizations during the early 1960s provided, apart from support in labor conflicts, a number of those paternalistic fringe benefits the workers and tenants used to receive irregularly and insufficiently from their landlords—such as medical and dental assistance (Hewitt, 1969: 394).

In the context of the preceding discussion it is well to remember that the reception of benefits from an organization produces dependence on this organization if grass-roots participation is limited and controlled, and if benefits tend to be received from above rather than given in response to demands. In such a case, campesinos are subject to domination and manipulation similar to the traditional patterns. A case in point is Mexico, where Stavenhagen has aptly summarized the dependence of the *ejido* on a number of sponsor-organizations:

> The ejido is directly linked with various governmental agencies. It depends on the Department of Agriculture for anything related to tenure itself. . . . It depends on the *Banco de Crédito Ejidal*. It receives credit, *via* the formation of credit societies or cooperatives. In zones of migration it depends on the secretariat of hydraulic resources for the distribution of water. Furthermore, it is directly linked to national politics through a chain [of organizations]: *ejido* commissariates—regional *campesino* committees—state leagues of agrarian communities—the national *campesino* federation. (1970: 38. My translation)

HORIZONTAL SOLIDARITY IN THE PEASANT COMMUNITY

In the preceding section alternative suppliers in higher status positions have been considered (campesino organizations and other brokers). But it is conceivable that alternative suppliers can emerge from within the campesino community itself, either as individuals or as a corporate group. One application of Hypothesis 3 is, therefore, that campesino solidarity is likely to develop when the benefits from horizontal solidarities within the community increase relative to those derived from the traditional relationships with the *patrón*.

Under conditions of scarcity, campesinos frequently compete among each other for the limited supply of "good things," to use Foster's phrase. For example, the municipality of Tepotzlán experienced a series of occasionally violent disputes between different villages over the utilization and commercial exploitation of communal lands, in which some villages sought to gain economic advantages for themselves without sharing the benefits with the rest of the community (Lewis, 1960: 47). In Peru and Bolivia numerous village rivalries over land rights have been reported, especially after *hacendados* had to give up part of their domain. A typical case would involve a conflict between the ex-*colonos* of a hacienda and a nearby indigenous community over the original claims to the abandoned lands; some of the most prolonged court cases have involved campesinos as both plaintiffs and defendants (Clark, 1969; Craig, 1967: 72; Tullis, 1970: 81–84, chap. 6; Alberti, 1970a: 70–83).[2] In such situations, campesinos gain little from horizontal exchanges.

The association of cooperation, expressive solidarity, and mutual benefits with the formation of both formal and informal campesino movements can be intuitively grasped from the current literature, but little evidence is available that could specify the processes and sequences in which these associations develop. Thus, it is difficult to determine from the present evidence whether campesino movements arise in response to increased horizontal solidarity (exchanges) among the campesinos, or whether increased horizontal solidarity is a result of successful campesino movements. It is reasonable to suspect that there are variations in the temporal sequences of solidarity formation and that there is a high degree of interaction as well as mutual determination among these variables. The following observations should, therefore, be cautiously interpreted.

If Hypothesis 3 holds true for campesinos being themselves alternative providers, it should be expected that willingness for cooperation increases in the community as the benefits to be derived from such cooperation increase. This means that (1) expectations of tangible benefits and of success will motivate the participation in joint or cooperative efforts by individuals, (2) past success in cooperative or joint efforts will encourage new participants to join and old ones to persevere and increase their efforts, and (3) increased unity and solidarity will be perceived and expressively symbolized after cooperative and joint efforts have been successful.

There is some evidence in support of these hypotheses. Galjart, for example, has observed that successful projects such as school construction have aided in the mobilization of campesinos (1972: 13). Huizer, on the basis of his extensive fieldwork as a community development worker, has cogently concluded that the expectations of the campesinos for radical improvements in their position will induce them to cooperate on community projects even after initial resistance and distrust (1972: chap. 2). Various forms of cooperation have been adapted by the Aymara in Bolivia under the leadership of the established syndicate in the expectation that cooperation is a crucial tool for reaching the campesinos' goals (Heath, 1969: 191), and the inhabitants of the Peruvian village of Tingo enthusiastically devoted more time for new tasks under the *faena* in the expectation that such efforts would help in the achievement of a corporate status independent of the landowner (Alberti, 1970a: 129, 133). More will be said about expectation in the following chapter.

The effect of past benefits from cooperation and joint activity upon the motivation of old and new members has also been observed. The initial success of the Ucureña syndicate in the early 1940s greatly encouraged the membership and attracted new members (Dandler, 1971: 83–88). The villagers of Tingo kept up their high degree of participation in communal projects long after they had achieved their goals; they clearly stood out in comparison with neighboring villages (Alberti, 1970a: 147–50). Successful mutual aid societies have often been the basis on which full-fledged campesino syndicates developed, as is witnessed by the origin of the Brazilian peasant leagues or the development of rural syndicates in the valley of Chancay, Peru (Matos Mar, 1967: 4). These observations support Landsberger's thesis that the establishment of peasant organizations is "made easier" by previous communal and cooperative experience (1969a: 43–44). But it may be suggested that such past experience does not just facilitate the development of peasant organizations; it provides also the benefits to the members of the rural community that make horizontal solidarity attractive to begin with.

Symbolic manifestations of expressive solidarity as a consequence of successful campesino organization have been reported by Craig in the valley of La Convención, Peru. After the campesinos here gained a measure of independence through their organized efforts, communities developed around commercial centers, stores, and projects for school construction (Craig, 1967: 93). Craig also developed a Guttman scale of five items measuring key informants' perceptions of different aspects of solidarity in thirty-five communities (1967: 70). These items, in the order of their importance (frequency), were (1) absence of competing peasant labor unions in the community; (2) positive change in unity among people since 1960; (3) high willingness to cooperate in community projects; (4) absence of widespread disputes over land boundaries; (5) high unity in the community at the present time (coefficient of reproducibility: .94). If the phenomena described in the five items occur in a temporal sequence, then this scale suggests that the perception of high unity in the community (item 5) is preceded by (benefits from) a high degree of cooperation among the members (item 3) and by the absence of intravillage conflict (items 1 and 4). Thus, Craig concluded, "In order to attain at least minimum solidarity there must have been something of a positive nature which transpired within the community during the preceding five years to increase community unity" (1967: 71).

Participation in rural syndicates, where not subject to repression, appears to have had the effect of widening the social ties of individuals beyond the limited family circle. Thus, the traditional labor exchange among the Aymara in Bolivia (*aini*), which was

TABLE 5. *Attitude toward Human Relations by Venezuelan Campesinos, by Sindicato Attendance and Community Status*

	Asentados		Non-Asentados	
N	105	49	59	81
Attend sindicato	Yes	No	Yes	No
Proverb Choice:				
1. "An eye for an eye, a tooth for a tooth"	9%	37%	5%	19%
or				
2. "To forgive is better than to condemn"	91%	63%	95%	81%
	100%	100%	100%	100%

SOURCE: Mathiason, 1966: 152.

restricted to members of the kin group, came to be extended to whole communities after the establishment of syndical rule (Heath, 1969: 191). For Venezuela, survey data are available that indicate that *sindicato* members are more likely than nonmembers to say that they have been members of a group where all were friends and from which they received full satisfaction (Mathiason, 1966: 151). Furthermore, union members who lived on *asentamientos* (agrarian reform settlements) are more likely to say that they have a person outside their family in whom they confide (31 percent) than those who do not live on such settlements (12 percent). Union participants are more likely to have an open attitude toward human relations than nonparticipants (Mathiason, 1966: 152), as is reflected in Table 5.

While the association of perceived campesino solidarity with hostility toward the landlord is consistent with the argument that horizontal exchanges among campesinos develop concomitantly with a deterioration of vertical exchanges, this argument remains tautological unless independent measures of the variables can be found. Little evidence of this nature exists, but it may be useful to refer to the findings of Craig (1967: 78) that campesino unity was related to the perception that the *hacendado* was not a member of the community, and to Mintz and Wolf's observation in a historical and comparative perspective that the tendency of peasants to seek ritual kinship ties with patrons of a higher status decreases as the powers and contributions of the patrons decline (1967).

CHAPTER 14

Cognitive Dimensions of Imbalance

While cultural values and ideologies are important dimensions in the formation of revolutionary movements (Skocpol, 1979: 168–71; Landsberger, 1969a: 41–42, 46, 51–54), this chapter will focus on cognitive inconsistency, which develops when within a cognitive context there is an incompatibility between perceptions and evaluations of an object, between different perceptions, or between different evaluations. Inconsistencies thus originate from either changing perceptions or changing definitions.

CHANGES IN COGNITIVE CAPACITY

An increase in an individual's cognitive capacity (his capacity to handle complex and differentiated cognitions) will tend to (1) increase the number of alternative behaviors of which he is aware and (2) thereby raise his comparison level for alternatives, which, in turn, increases the likelihood that his evaluation of current outcomes will become more negative. When such reasoning is applied to Proposition 2, the following hypothesis can be stated:

> Hypothesis 12: In *patrón*-campesino relationships, campesinos tend to actively seek improved outcomes in these or alternative relationships when their cognitive capacity increases.

Cognitive capacity can be measured in terms of literacy, education, experience outside the community, and participation in mass communication. It will be proposed that cognitive capacity is increased by processes such as migration, expanding communication and transportation networks, and travel.[1] These last processes can thus be used as indirect measurements of changes in cognitive capacity, or "resocializing experiences" (Galjart, 1972: 12).

Low levels of literacy and education, as has been argued in Chapter 7, have traditionally restricted the cognitive capacity of campesinos. Campesinos, in turn, tend to be aware of this handicap, as education appears to be one of their primary goals for which utmost sacrifices are made (Wagley, 1964: 41; Tullis, 1970: chap. 6; Cotler, 1970a: 556). In a number of studies, increased education among the younger campesinos has been directly linked with the formation of class movements and organizations. After the revolution of 1952, the syndicates of the Cochabamba valley in Bolivia greatly benefited from a new generation of campesinos that had received schooling (and, on the side, radical indoctrination) in the 1930s and 1940s (Dandler, 1971: 42–43, 53–54, 102; Malloy, 1970: 197). In a number of Peruvian rural communities studied by Tullis and Alberti, young villagers with schooling were the ones who fermented discontent among their elders (Tullis, 1970: chap. 6; Alberti, 1970b: 184–85). One landowner, returning to his estate after a long absence, indignantly asked a village teacher: "What have you done to these Indians? Before they used to kneel down and kiss my hand; now they are all insolent" (Alberti, 1970a: 123).

Expanding channels of communication provide opportunities for increased cognitive capacities. It should be noted first, however, that in some cases traditional channels have been influential in spreading discontent and rebellion among campesinos. In Mexico, traveling *cancioneros* sang the news and stories of folk heroes who had fought and died battling the rich, protecting the poor, and chased by the police. Before and during the revolution of 1910 word of such real or legendary events was spread in the *corridos* (narrative folk ballads) at every market, fiesta, cockpit, and cantina (White, 1969: 109, 125–26). A similar tradition of folk ballads and peasant poetry existed in Brazil. Here the songs and pamphlets of *violeiros*, *cantadores*, and *folhetinistas*[2] spread word of the deeds of bandit heroes as well as of Julião's peasant leagues from hamlet to hamlet (Julião, 1962: 33–41; Moraes, 1970: 481; Davies, 1969).

Increased exposure to mass media is not always associated with increased participation in campesino movements. Venezuelan data indicate that rural union activists have no more exposure to media than other campesinos, although they do have greater personal contact with noncampesinos (Mathiason, 1966: 148). In a comparison between the indigenous community of Sicuani and a hacienda in Paucartambo, Cotler (1970a: 552–57) found that the villagers of Sicuani, although much more exposed to mass media and outside connections, had much less faith in the government programs than the more isolated, less literate and more fatalistic *colonos* on the hacienda (apparently as a consequence of different successes in organized movements and different policies of the government in intervening in labor conflicts in the two communities).

Although current evidence does not contradict the thesis that improved communication among campesinos and between campesinos and individuals in the larger society contributes to the emergence of campesino movements, few studies are directly addressed to the problem. A number of authors have related the development of rural unrest in Brazil to the process of proletarianization, whereby the tenants and sharecroppers, traditionally scattered over the large estates and isolated from one another, were converted into wage earners and gathered in compact settlements along the roads—a process that furthered communication and the shared expression of discontent (Furtado, 1964: 152; Forman, 1971: 4–5; Lopes, 1966: 200; 1964, 16). Increased communication among Chilean *inquilinos* and their increased exposure to mass media (newspaper, radio) have been related to the formation of a syndicate by Petras and Zemelman (1969: 6, 18). But such propositions, plausible as they may be, will remain speculative until a relation between communication and campesino organization can be empirically demonstrated.[3]

Considerably more evidence—albeit not very systematic—is available that campesino movements are preceded by increased contacts of villagers with neighboring towns and villages as well as with the larger cities through commercial or political activity, personal connections, travel, and migration.[4] While a good deal of evidence is available to show the empirical connection between such contacts and experiences on the one hand and the formation of campesino movements on the other, the utilization of such evidence as a measure of increased cognitive capacity remains a matter of postulation, as no direct measurement of cognitive capacity at the individual level is available and thus cognitive capacity cannot be related to the propensity to join campesino movements.

In Chile, a change in the attitude of the *inquilinos* toward traditional social relations has been traced to increased contacts of the tenant-laborers with friends and relatives who had migrated to the cities; this phenomenom was, in turn, associated with voting for leftist parties (Petras and Zeitlin, 1970: 511–13) and the formation of campesino syndicates (Petras and Zemelman, 1969: 9). Furthermore, Petras and Zeitlin (1967) found that the percentage of votes for leftist parties in rural districts increased in inverse proportion to the proximity of the districts to mining towns in which a more radical political climate prevailed. Data from Galjart (1972) show that campesino syndicates (excepting those sponsored by government agencies) occurred most frequently in communities with close proximity to urban centers. It should be emphasized, however, that this relationship may well be due to political factors, rather than increases in cognitive capacity. When *yanconas* on Peruvian haciendas were no longer restricted by their landlords from visiting neighboring villages, towns, and markets (often even on behalf of their *patrón*), they became aware of alternatives to their status quo and dissatisfied with their current situation (Alberti, 1970a: 117; Tullis, 1970: 94, 125). The early growth of campesino syndicates in Bolivia's Cochabamba valley was also fostered by the proximity and easy accessibility of towns and market centers, where campesinos freely went to deliver goods or to work at the townhouse of their *patrón* and to participate increasingly in markets as free producers, artisans, and even middlemen (Dandler, 1971: 25–27, 38).

Various forms of migratory experience have been found to contribute to an awakening of campesinos. Petras and Zeitlin, for example, have suggested that seasonal migration has an effect on political radicalism among agricultural workers in Chile. They noted that wage laborers tend to be hired as complements to the permanent labor on the larger *fundos*, as "outsiders" (*afuerinos*) who often leave their families temporarily to seek additional work to supplement their livelihood. They often travel great distances, work in all sorts of industrial and agricultural jobs, and get exposed to radicalism and unionism in the mines, nitrate fields, or factories (1970: 514–15). Petras and Zeitlin argue,

The very fact that they work for wages, and have worked for many *patrones*, and that they have no reciprocal obligations to a particular *patrón* other than the cash nexus, means that they are unlikely to be subject—to any extent comparable to that of the *inquilinos*—to patriarchal domination or to develop particularistic loyalties. (1970: 515)

Petras and Zeitlin's ecological analysis of presidential election results reveals that the proportion of votes for the *Frente de Accion Popular* (FRAP) under Salvador Allende was greatest in districts with the highest proportion of agricultural wage laborers (1970: 517–27).

A number of Peruvian studies reveal that migration into an area was associated with peasant militancy. The valley of La Convención, after it had been depopulated by a malaria epidemic that lasted for over a decade until the late 1940s, became flooded with immigrants in the two decades before the outbreak of campesino rebellion; between 1940 and 1960 the population increased by over 100 percent, and in 1964–1965 less than one-third of the campesinos living in the valley had been born there (Craig, 1967: 28–30). In the coastal Chancay valley, Matos Mar (1967: 12–13) observed that the tenant-workers who were born in the valley were considerably less militant (and more preferred for administrative posts by the owners) than those who had immigrated to the valley from the highlands.[5]

Leaders of campesino movements have frequently been persons who migrated into the community from the outside. The role of outsiders such as teachers and lawyers has already been discussed in the section on brokers, but indigenous leadership has also been prominently furnished by immigrants with experience abroad (Rojas in Bolivia) or at universities (Blanco and others in Peru) (Craig, 1969: 288; Alberti, 1970a: 121; Tullis, 1970: 94).

Returned migrants have generally made large contributions to innovativeness and campesino organizations in Latin America (for general observations, see Wagley, 1964: 46). In Mexico, Emiliano Zapata had been in the army and worked in Mexico City for a while, and Primo Tapía from Michoacán had been a *bracero* in the United States (Huizer, 1967: 9, 55). In the Mantaro valley of Peru, villagers returning from towns and cities brought their education or their experience with labor syndicates in the mines to their community to become the leaders and most active followers in the nascent rural labor movements; one of them received his most thorough training in a prison where he had extensive contact with jailed labor organizers (Alberti, 1970b: 184–85, 187; Tullis, 1970: 112, 125, 140). In Venezuela the local leadership of the *Federación Campesina* was prominently composed of campesinos who had returned home after some years of experience in urban politics and unionism (Powell, 1969: 83–84). However, returning migrants do not invariably contribute to innovation and campesino movements. In a comparison of a Bolivian and an Ecuadorian village, Buechler (1970) found that returning migrants were mediators of social change only in the former; he suggested as a plausible explanation that in the Ecuadorian village the traditional power and authority structure was still intact and enforced by the government, while in Bolivia the revolutionary government allowed and fostered political and social reorganization at the local level.

STUDIES IN INFORMATION THEORY

While the preceding analysis suggests that a change in cognitive capacity can be associated with a number of campesino movements, such association should only be expected when the increase in cognitive capacity is not accompanied by a simultaneous expansion of the opportunities available to campesinos. In other words, there should be cognitive inconsistency in regard to capabilities and opportunities. A number of studies have come out of the Peru project of Cornell University that examine campesino movements in relation to inconsistencies between cognitive capacities and opportunities. Craig (1967), Weldon (1968), Alberti (1970a; 1970b), and Tullis (1970) have approached the problem in terms of the information-processing theory developed by Frank Young. In terms of this theoretical framework, human behavior involves structures of meaning and information. Meanings are symbolized by actions, sounds, languages, and artifacts, and these symbols can be structurally ordered so that they form variables that explain and predict human behavior (Weldon, 1968: 3). The strategic variables in this scheme are a social system's capacity for information processing, or differentiation, solidarity, and relative centrality. *Capacity for information processing* refers to a social system's ability to utilize a diversity of information, or to handle diverse and complex meanings in a symbolic structure; this capacity is reflected in the *differentiation* within a social system (Weldon, 1968: 3; Tullis, 1970: 12–14) and can be measured through enumeration of different symbols (artifacts, roles, voluntary organizations). *Solidarity* refers to the degree to which a system tends to process information "according to an integrated format or more concretely, the degree to which meaning sectors of a symbolic structure—no matter how differential—show overall unity" (Young, cited by Weldon, 1968: 3). Solidarity implies a "coordination of minds" in the interpretation of symbols among members of a community with regard to certain issues, and "the more unified the interpretation of the symbols on those issues, the more united the village will tend to be" (Tullis, 1970: 15). Solidarity has been measured through perceived unity in the village (Craig, 1967) or joint class action (Tullis, 1970). *Relative centrality* is a system's position in relation to other systems with which it interacts. It is measured by sociogramlike techniques assessing the position of a community within a network of villages, describing the net flow of institutional transactions between communities (who goes to school, church, or market in which village, and so forth) (Weldon, 1968: 4; Alberti, 1970a: 54–55). Tullis (1970: 16–18) argues that a community's relative centrality within an intervillage network determines the degree to which it has an opportunity to process whatever information it is capable of processing; he therefore used the term *relative opportunity* in his own analysis, denoting a broader concept that includes a variety of opportunities and restrictions such as constraints by a *hacendado*.

These concepts all refer to processes and structures at the systemic or institutional level, not to individual dispositions and capacities. We shall, therefore, have to make a number of assumptions to utilize the studies cited for evaluating the theory of this study; these assumptions allow us to measure psychological properties of individuals (with which our thesis is concerned) in terms of the systemic properties of the communities for which we have data:[6]

1. The greater the capacity for information processing in a social system (differentiation), the greater the average cognitive capacity of the members of the community.

2. The greater the relative centrality or relative opportunity of a social system, the greater the opportunity for the individual members of the community to handle given information and symbols and to perform given actions.

3. The greater the solidarity of a social system, the greater the number of members in a community who identify with the community as a whole and are prepared to get involved in joint or cooperative actions.

According to Hypothesis 12, campesinos will actively seek improved outcomes from a traditional relationship if their cognitive capacity increases while outcomes remain the same or deteriorate. If the opportunity to act in terms of the new definitions is low, however, there will develop an inconsistency between capacity and opportunity. Under conditions of such a *structural bind* (Tullis, 1970: 19; Alberti, 1970b: 201), solidarity expressions (for example, campesino organizations) are expected to develop. This thesis was tested and supported by Weldon, who found that "under conditions of lower intervillage solidarity, the greater the discrepancy between a community's differentiation (high) and its relative centrality (low), the greater will be its solidarity" (1968: 2). Alberti (1970b), in a general interpretation of campesino movements in Peru and using the findings of Tullis (1970), Craig (1967), and his own investigations (1970a), also explains the development of campesino solidarity in terms of a structural bind involving high capacity (differentiation) and low opportunity (relative centrality). The most important developments he saw as contributing factors to structural binds were population increases (reducing opportunity), social differentiation (new occupations and middlemen, building of schools, formation of *patronatos escolares*—equivalents of the North American PTA—political and administrative activities), new experiences and reference sources (returning migrants, work in mines, union contacts, education, ideological influences), and intransigence of landowners (refusing moderate demands, enacting greater restrictions, thereby keeping opportunities discrepant with capacities) (Alberti, 1970b: 201–12).

The structural bind model has been refined by Tullis (1970) to account for variations in the degree of militancy of campesino movements. Tullis added the variable of *subordination* (the degree to which solidarity movements are blocked by real or imaginary acts of coercion and other forms of repression) and hypothesized that (1) villages with high structural binds will manifest intense (militant) expressions of solidarity in their actions and rhetoric when they are also highly subordinated, and (2) villages with structural binds will manifest moderate (nonradical) expressions of solidarity when they are not highly subordinated (1970: 35–36). To test these hypotheses, Tullis examined solidarity movements in two village systems—gathering his information through both quantitative and qualitative (historical) procedures. The villages in one system were highly subordinated because they were within the restrictive domains of haciendas. Structural binds developed in this system due to the emergence of new brokers (teachers, lawyers, politicians), new ideologies imported by these brokers and by migrants returning from the mines and from schools, village schools, and village organizations, as well as to intransigent reactions and restrictions by the *hacendados*. Campesino movements developing in these villages were suppressed and became militant (Tullis, 1970: chaps. 6, 7). A second village system consisted of free indigenous communities that were less exposed to the constraints of the haciendas, and access to national institutions (cultural, economic, political) was easier for them than for the villages in the first system. Measuring capacity by the number and type of village organizations, solidarity by the presence of cooperative and joint activities, and relative centrality through sociogramlike procedures, he found that solidarity expressions were associated with structural binds (high capacity, low centrality), but that these expressions were moderate in comparison with those encountered in the first system (1970: chap. 8).

CHANGES IN PERCEPTIONS

Three aspects of changing perceptions may be related to the emergence of campesino movements. First, campesinos may change their general interpretation of the world and of their position in it in such a manner that alternatives to given relationships with the *patrón* appear increasingly viable and realistic; second, they may perceive models for their own conduct that render new alternatives more plausible for them; and third, their expectations (perceptions of future outcomes) in regard to alternatives may become more positive. Thus, Proposition 5 can be converted into another hypothesis:

Hypothesis 13: In *patrón*-campesino relationships, campesinos will actively seek improved outcomes in these or alternative relationships if
a. they redefine their situation in such a manner that they perceive themselves as having greater powers than before to explore alternatives,
b. they perceive successful models for their own conduct, and/or
c. their expectations of success in their actions become more positive than before.

Information that pertains to redefinitions of the situation by campesinos is implicit in the studies of Tullis, Alberti, and Craig, but direct evidence on changing existential definitions is rather scarce. However, Petras and Zemelman (1972) offer some excellent data and interpretations of campesino consciousness associated with the takeover of the *fundo* Culiprán in Chile. They distinguish between three possible phases in peasant consciousness: (1) "paternalistic consciousness" in which peasants relate to their particular good *patrón* as individuals, (2) "trade union consciousness" in which peasants perceive their common grievances against a particular bad *patrón*, and (3) "political consciousness" in which peasants relate themselves as a class to a contrasting class of landlords in universalistic categories (1972: 62–63). The extensive statements by the peasants (1972: 107–45) reveal that none of them had reached the stage of political consciousness: within the group there is a good deal of differentiation, as some exhibit essentially paternalistic views, others trade union consciousness, and one a relatively advanced level between trade union consciousness and political consciousness. Essentially four changes in perceptions led to the development of trade union consciousness and revolt on the *fundo*: (1) a memory of earlier revolts on the *fundo* that were unsuccessful but established a dormant tradition that was still part of the older *inquilinos* of the estate; (2) an awareness of declining economic returns and a breakdown of paternalistic relations (as was discussed in Chapters 10 and 11), (3) the perception that the current owner was a particularly bad *patrón* who did not treat his *inquilinos* well. Significantly, the peasants and their leaders indicated that they would not have taken over the *fundo* under a good *patrón*. One follower of the movement remarked to the investigators:

The *patrón* we had here was the worst possible. He didn't fulfill his obligations to us . . . if the *patrón* had treated the *inquilinos* well, we wouldn't have done anything. . . . But if they have a good *patrón* they shouldn't do it [take over the *fundo*]. It's only right to do it to the bad *patrones*, but there are *patrones* who are good to the *inquilinos*. They give them all kinds of *regalías*, so that all the workers do is screw the *patrón*, that's all. No, I don't think I would help them. And if the *patrón* is good to them then it's unjust, and they shouldn't try to bother him. (1972: 128–29)

(4) the keen awareness of the peasants that they had the assistance and leadership of prominent politicians who protected them from police intervention and pressured the government to expropriate the estate under the agrarian reform laws. The current leader of the movement, for example, indicated, "You always have to ask for help from Congress, because if the Congressmen aren't on your side, you're lost. We, for example, abeyed Sentor Altamirano" (1972: 136). And as the former leader of the movement put it:

At first the Christian Democrats told us that they'd give us support, but they didn't deliver. So we took the *fundo* by ourselves, with the help of two from Santiago; there were two men from Santiago with us. If we hadn't had them, or the support of the politicians. I don't think the people would have had the courage to take the land. They were the ones who came to give us encouragement and make all the plans. Sure some people's knees were knocking. (1972: 118)

These statements indicate that the peasants of this estate had not reached the stage of class or political consciousness. But they did perceive their condition as being bad enough to legitimize revolt against their particular bad *patrón* once they could be sure of support from influential allies. The takeover of the estate was motivated less by a general peasant-class consciousness, although the need for group solidarity was asserted by the participant, than by particular perceptions of appropriate actions within a situationally specific context.

Dandler has provided some useful data on the rural movements in Ucureña, Bolivia. In that community, changing self-images and pride had been generated by the early achievements of the syndicate and by the successful implementation of a school program (Dandler, 1971: 101–2); enthusiastic responses by the campesinos to the plays of protest theater groups revealed their changing perceptions of themselves within the *latifundia* (Dandler, 1971: 84–85). Perceptions of the hacienda and the *patrón* changed in the early 1940s from a distinction between good and bad *patrones* to an undifferentiated view in which, according to one informant, "all *patrones* and administrators exploited us in the same manner" (Dandler, 1971: 167). For all the Bolivian campesinos the Indian Congress of 1945 became a turning point in their attempt to establish their class identity; and for the over one thousand participants from numerous provinces it became an exhilarating experience, providing them with a sense of participation and pride (Dandler, 1971: 111–14).

Changing perceptions of politics, from paternalistic favoritism to clientelistic bargaining, from blind following to deliberate choice, are reflected in this testimony by a Puerto Rican cane worker:

Here we have a thing—it's like with religion. There are people who say that they continue being a Republican because they must be grateful to some old leader for such and such a thing. And many vote out of gratitude for one or another leader this way. Do you see how it is? We have a lady here with whom you still can't touch on this matter of the Republicans. She says that Don Rafael Martínez Nadal did a great favor for a son of hers and that she can't stop being a Republican even though Martínez is long dead. And they go along this way—"My papa was a Republican, and I can't change"—"My father was this and that, and I am the same." As they say, "I must honor his bones."

Now as I told you before, the Popular Party forecast the laws they would put into operation. They explained to people what was happening, what the government in power was like. They talked to the people in a way that was easy to understand. Before, at political meetings the leaders would hold forth, and it was truly eloquent oratory, truly lovely. But what we heard we did not understand—orations about the mists, the seas, the fishes, and great things. Then, when Muñoz Marín came, he didn't come speaking that way. He came speaking of the rural worker, of the cane, and of things that were easier to understand. And the people could go along with him, understanding and changing. And so they learned to trade the mists and the sea for the plantation trees and for the land they were going to get if they gave the Popular Party their votes.

The first time I heard Don Luis Muñoz Marín speak it was in the barrio they call Coquí, in Salinas. . . . That night Don Luis was explaining to the people thus: "In this election you give me your vote, and I promise you the following things. And if I don't keep my promise, then vote against me in the next election." It was an easy thing to understand; the people understood. And one saw a great enthusiasm among the people because the party was just beginning, and everywhere they had meetings there were lots of people. (Mintz, 1960: 186)

Models for conduct can be provided by individual leaders for their followers or by the campesino movements of one community for the campesinos in the neighboring communities. The significance of leadership has already been treated in connection with the emergence of new brokers. The impact of campesino organizations in one community upon the developments in other communities has been observed in a number of studies. Craig (1967: 36–37) noted that the successful protest-petition (*reclamo*) of one hacienda in the valley of La Convención, Peru, served as a model and as encouragement for similar movements on other estates. Alberti (1970a: 134) reported that in the Mantaro valley in Peru the organizational success of one village attracted villagers from the surrounding area. Matos Mar (1967: 7) noted that in the Chancay valley the success of a rural syndicate on one hacienda greatly stimulated similar efforts on others, and related observations have been made in Bolivia (Dandler, 1971: 43–44) and Brazil (Julião, 1962: 30).

While these observations indicate the existence of behavioral models for campesino movements, they do not allow the conclusion that the existence of models per se led to perceptions of new behavioral alternatives. In fact, it appears reasonable to assume that conceptions of resistance and organizations already exist among campesinos before they act; it is the perception that movements in one community have a measure of success that is more likely to precipitate actions in other communities, as the expectation rises that they will be successful, too.

The significance of expectations predicting success in the development of campesino movements can be indicated by the characteristic spurt of land invasions, petitions, and other forms of organization after the election of presidents believed to be favorable to the desires of the campesinos. Such movements often go beyond the goals or means the new government might endorse. For example, such a situation developed in Chile (Galjart, 1972: 9), especially after the election of Salvador Allende to the presidency. In the past, similar events took place when López Michelsen was elected in Colombia in 1934 (Gilhodès, 1970: 417). In Peru in 1963, the first hundred days of the Belaúnde government were marked by spontaneous invasions throughout the highlands (Cotler and Portocarrero, 1969: 311). In Bolivia, the victory of the MNR in 1952 encouraged widespread peasant unrest in the Cochabamba valley that eventually led to the agrarian revolution; already the presidency of Villaroel had raised the expectations of the campesinos and encouraged general organizational activity among them after 1943 (Dandler, 1971: 106, 125). An *inquilino* on a Chilean *fundo* expressed his expectations when after a period of political repression

there was a change of President. We began to take heart when Mr., how is he called that . . . Mr. Eduardo Frei came forth, that had to help us . . . "Now Mr. Frei will help us" we told each other. At the same time in this period the Socialist Party didn't come around any more. Only the Christian Democratic and the Communist parties came around, they came around propagandizing for the election of deputies and senators. Thus we took further courage and we said: "Now we have to organize ourselves anew again." (Petras and Zemelman, 1969: 4)

Hopes and future expectations have been found to be associated with union participation in Venezuela, as Table 6 shows, but the data from which this table was constructed were gathered at a time when the FCV had already proved itself through its success in land

TABLE 6. *Relation between Perception of Personal Future and Union Participation (in percent) for Asentados and Non-Asentados in Venezuela*

	Asentados		Non-Asentados	
Attend Union Meetings?	Yes	No	Yes	No
In the next five years, personal situation will:				
Improve	89	81	93	63
Be the same or worse	11	19	7	37
TOTAL	100	100	100	100
N	96	43	57	79

SOURCE: Powell, 1969: 92.

reforms. The positive association between union participation and expectations reflected in the table is most marked among the non-*asentados*, in other words, those who have not yet benefited from the reforms but can expect to in the future.

The importance of realistic expectations for the mobilization of campesinos has also been emphasized by Huizer (1972: chap. 2). But in addition to being realistic, Huizer points out, expectations also have to entail prospects for changes that are radical enough to make a real difference in the status of the campesinos. On the basis of his own experiences, Huizer suggests that initial campesino distrust and resistance to cooperative endeavors in community development projects can be overcome when the campesinos are convinced that they are not once more being coopted into governmental pseudoreforms. It is in spite of such difficulties and constraints that peasants have frequently been convinced to attempt, for example, cooperative projects under conditions of extreme limitations, constraints, and polititcal and economic counterpressures from the landowners (Sharpe, 1977: chaps. 9, 10).

CHANGES IN EVALUATIONS

According to Proposition 4, campesino movements are expected to develop when changes in values, goals, or exchange rates induce campesinos to do without the traditional benefits of the *patrón*, to pay less for these benefits, to demand greater benefits from the *patrón*, or to seek greater benefits elsewhere.

In the literature surveyed for this study, no evidence was found that changing evaluations per se could account for campesino movements. What has sparked campesino movements in Latin America, apart from changes in power and economic relations, seems to be less a change in values than a failure of the old relationships between landlords and campesinos to meet the perceived needs and traditional values of the latter. There is good reason to believe that the vast majority of the campesinos were never satisfied with their subordinate position. They may have been grateful to good *patrones*, and they may not have sought new alternatives for a long time—but they hardly were content with their situation, as numerous uprisings have testified; most of them always dreamed the impossible dream of a better life. While it is plausible to assume that leaders, returning migrants, and other forms of communication with the larger society have had an ideological impact, it has never been demonstrated that campesino movements are set into motion by new values and goals. What has changed are the traditional relationships with the landholders (which made accommodation to his demands less attractive), perceptions of new alternatives, and opportunities to take advantage of these alternatives. Ideological indoctrinations from political parties have occurred, but it appears that any ideology has been acceptable to the campesino as long as it pragmatically helps him in achieving what he always wanted: land, education, and dignity. His goals tend to be rather limited: education, land, and a variety of concrete benefits to better his life (Cotler, 1970a: 556). After he has achieved his goals, he wants to be left alone. After the pioneering peasant league of Galiléia, Brazil, achieved the desired titles to the lands, it declined and lost its interests in agrarian struggles. By 1961 it was reduced to "a few dozen members who mostly fought among themselves because this one had a jeep and that one had a pick-up truck, etc." (Moraes, 1970: 478). Ideological commitments by campesinos may be inconsistent from the point of view of the larger political parties, depending on what views are most meaningful for their concrete interests (Mathiason, 1966: 140, 154–55; Newbold, 1957: 352). "The average *campesino,* by and large, does not look very far beyond his own fences" (Mathiason, 1966: 155), but once he has raised his demands, a failure of *patrón* or government to respond has led to militancy. Militant movements, especially the more successful ones, have tended to espouse agrarianist and indigenist ideologies (in Mexico and Bolivia), or they may have verbalized the ideological commitments of their political sponsor; however, such manifestations of ideology have never represented new values on the part of the peasants.[7] The more recent revolutionary strategies and concientization of Latin American peasants have been violently repressed (in Chile, 1973) or maintained at the level of controllable and isolated minorities within the rural population. It is, hence, inappropriate to analyze changes in peasant consciousness independently of the structural constraints and opportunities within which they are promoted as well as limited (Sharpe, 1977: chaps. 7, 10; Pearse, 1975: 219–21). "Concientization" as such has never been an independent force in the formation of peasant revolutionary movements.

CHAPTER 15

Modernized Mechanisms of Domination and Exploitation

The peculiar deference patterns involved in paternalism have been frequently transplanted into relationships with new brokers. R. N. Adams, for example, suggests that government paternalism has been substituted for the traditional patterns in many places (1967a: 186–87); in comparing relations among laborers on two Puerto Rican sugar plantations, he notes that the more militant labor organization was on the plantation that was privately owned and where the government could intervene on behalf of the laborers, whereas on a government-run plantation paternalism still prevailed, precisely because the government *was* the *patrón* whose favors were needed by the workers (R. N. Adams, 1964: 70–71). In Brazil, Galjart (1964; 1965) argues that the peasant movement was essentially not a manifestation of "class struggle" in the Marxian sense, but rather the movement of a clientele (following) behind leaders and agencies that manipulated the peasants for their own ends and gave them rights and protection as favors from above, a view reflected by other writers as well (A. Leeds, 1964; Hewitt, 1969: 395–96; Forman, 1970: 14–15; for a conflicting view, see Huizer, 1965). Anthony Leeds indicates that already in the early 1950s some rural workers believed that outside organizers took advantage of them: "The communists are always out to use you for their own purposes and get as much out of you as they can. I wouldn't be a communist, even if I could see any advantages in it" (1957: 457). "The communists use others for their own ends, and drop them when they have finished with them" (1957: 486). A Puerto Rican caneworker, active in union affairs, expressed related feelings:

If it were up to me to make the nominations for union offices, I would never pick people mixed up already in politics. I would always keep the two apart. . . . They should pick men who are free, free of politics, who are not mixed in that. The politican often has the idea of capturing a portion of the people for his own political benefit, and he is not thinking of the workers'

187

interest. You understand what I mean? It may be that he is a candidate, and he presents himself as a labor leader though he isn't a labor leader at all, but needs the worker's support for the moment. (Mintz, 1960: 200)

But other peasants take a more positive attitude toward new paternalistic relations. A member of Julião's league explained:

"I want a defense in life, for medicine, if one should fall sick among us . . . for advice." His opinion of Francisco Julião was clear. "He is the Prince of Life, who is going to give us the resources to live." When queried as to how this would be done, the peasant quipped, "I don't know because I am ignorant. I am waiting for an explanation and then will follow." (Forman, 1971: 13)

Julião's style in dealing with his followers was quite congruent with the paternalistic styles to which the latter had been accustomed, as is witnessed by Moraes's description:

He had the patience and humility to work well with the peasants, the energy to defend them without tiring, the openhandedness to distribute the favors and money that the peasants needed so badly, and a political style sufficiently paternalistic to permit him to relate himself successfully to peasants accustomed for generations to the paternalism of the great landowners. . . .

The peasant arriving at Julião's home suffered no sense of dislocation from the familiar atmosphere of the *fazenda* (plantation). The physical surroundings were virtually the same, with one substantial difference: in Julião's home the peasant was a guest who sat about, ate and slept with absolutely no sense of discomfort, at times sojourning for several days, to work out a solution to his problems or to enjoy protection from the pursuit of the police or the landowner. In addition the peasant was able to converse for hours with the "boss" or "chief" (Julião), who often attended his guests in pajamas, utterly free of any trace of stiff protocol. Although the peasant may not have resolved any of his problems, for all the long journey to the capital, he returned to his village satisfied, deeply pleased for having met this rich man, this "Doctor" who treated him as an equal, with respect and great kindness. . . . Peasants went forth from his house spreading the word wherever they passed of the "graciousness of Dr. Julião," each day raising still higher the personal prestige of Julião among the dispossessed. (1970: 470–71)

Numerous examples from other countries could be cited for similar reactions; for example, in Bolivia participants of the Indian congress in 1945 reported enthusiastically that the sympathetic President Villaroel "promised that he would become our father and protector, and if necessary, would die for us" (Dandler, 1971: 113).

The persistence of paternalism in campesino movements is reflected in the continuity of intraclass conflicts at all levels in Latin American societies. Traditionally, interclasss alliances have com-

peted and battled with factions of a similar socioeconomic composition for spoils and privileges, as outlined in Part II of this study.
Thus, landowners and politicians at all levels of the sociopolitical
hierarchy of a country would seek to be in on the distribution of
privileges, and the peasants in their following would battle each
other in the interest of their protectors. In northeast Brazil, peasants could find themselves fighting each other as outlaws, *capangas,* or members of the police forces in alliance with one of the
rivaling political bosses. In Colombia, liberal peasants would engage conservative peasants in bloody battles, as followers of their
upper-class sponsors. Rivalries within and between campesino
organizations reflect a similar pattern in which individual leaders
and their followers compete against each other, rival sponsors
compete for the campesino followings, or rival organizations compete for a territory. Rivalries between different peasant and rural
workers' organizations in Brazil have already been referred to
above; furthermore, the *ligas camponêsas* have been beset by
internal conflicts over leadership and strategy (Moraes, 1970:
483–89). After its initial growth, the syndicate of the valley of La
Convención was split between the more moderate original grass-
roots leaders and the radical followers of Trotskyite Hugo Blanco
(Craig, 1967; 1969). In Bolivia, the leader of the Cochabamba
syndicate (José Rojas) was involved in various intrigues and coups
after 1953 to assert his leadership of the movement (Dandler, 1971:
215–22); in the Cochabamba valleys as well as other areas of the
country new *caciques* (political bosses) emerged among the campesino leaders and used violence to assert their control, using the
armed support of their followers; civil wars were often imminent
(Malloy, 1970: 211–13; Antezana, 1960). In Venezuela, competition developed after 1945 between campesino unions sponsored by
the ruling AD and those sponsored by other groups (Huizer, 1967:
213–14; Powell, 1971). Instances like these point to the conclusion
that as long as campesinos have little autonomous power, they will
be inclined to fight each other in order to gain privileges handed
down from their political patrons. What is new in recent developments is the fact that there are new protectors who may have an
interest in manipulating the campesinos for their own ends but
whose class interests may not necessarily be in conflict with those
of their campesino followers.

In order to critically assess the campesinos' potential for expressing their class interests and mobilizing toward an emancipatory path, it is helpful to critically examine the underlying concepts, since both the terms *interest* and *emancipation* contain a

variety of descriptive and normative connotations. One difficulty in defining group interests in general is the discrepancy between interests that are subjectively perceived at a given time by the members and that motivate their conduct on the one hand, and the normative implications of a structural analysis on the other. A dilemma that particularly applies to many peasants is that by virtue of their desire for landed property they identify themselves with the very values against which they rebel; once peasants have obtained the land they fight for, class differentiation is likely to emerge among them. Another problem in conceptualizing peasant interests rests in the differential significance between status improvements within the existing economic and political structure and the radical transformation of this same order. Clearly, it is possible to claim that Latin American campesino movements have been engaged in class struggles, have furthered the interests of their members, and have contributed to their emancipation. Some authors have even gone as far as to suggest that peasants have become a class for themselves, as Marx conceived the term, in countries such as Brazil (Huizer, 1965) and Venezuela (Powell, 1971: 58–59). In the following, a few general characteristics of an emancipated peasant "class for itself" will be sketched.[1] The progress of campesino movements will then be assessed in terms of these criteria; they are:

1. Campesinos are autonomous political actors determining and negotiating their own destinies.

2. The concern of campesino movements is for the class as a whole, not for individual members or subgroups.

3. "Class consciousness" entails a broad vision of macrosocietal structures of domination and alienation, rather than a limited perception of absolute or relative deprivation within the peasantry or some of its subgroups.

4. Campesino movements are directed at a radical transformation of the macrosocietal structures that subjugate the campesinos, rather than at the mere redress of group-specific grievances within the existing structures.

5. Landlords are collectively perceived as members of an opposing class, rather than being individually defined as particular good or bad *patrones*.

While these idealized conditions are approached at varying degrees by historical realities, they are useful standards of comparison.

MACROPOLITICAL TRANSFORMATIONS IN LATIN AMERICA: POTENTIALS AND LIMITATIONS OF RADICAL TRANSFORMATION

The overthrow of the traditional landed oligarchies in twentieth-century Latin America has principally represented the ascent of the urban and industrial bourgeois that was able to promote its position through tactical alliances with peasant and working-class organizations.[2] While, within these alliances, peasants had strong positions during certain periods (the Mexican, Bolivian, and Venezuelan revolutions) in some areas, these positions did not remain strong in the long run of historical developments. While the new regimes generally recognized the feasibility of incorporating the popular classes into new regimes, they tended to seek simultaneously the cooperation of capitalist entrepreneurs, especially those of their own nationality.

These strategies entailed inherently contradictory interests and led to varying combinations of nationalism, populism, and corporatism.[3] Outstanding examples of these new approaches are the *Estado Novo* of Getulio Vargas in Brazil, the *Justicialismo* of Juan Domingo Perón in Argentina, the regime of the PRI and its earlier formations in Mexico, the MNR in Bolivia after 1952, and the current Peruvian regime. These types of governments were founded on the basic premise that the socioeconomic development of Third World nations can take a "Third Route" between capitalist exploitation and socialist revolution via a system of vertical alliances between different social classes. The unifying foundation of such a path was seen in political and economic nationalism; it was assumed that, within the unique historical context of imperialism, the interests of different social classes were not contradictory but complementary. Hence, the semicorporatist national state had the crucial function of controlling and balancing different class interests. According to this model, it was declared that class struggle was suspended in the national interest. Thus, struggles between social classes with inherently contradictory interests were temporarily suspended. Contradictory class interests where hidden under the ideology of a common national interest without, however, being resolved in the long run. In terms of traditional concepts of political development, the popular classes were utilized for incorporation as participants in the given political system. The basic foundation of the political systems within the context of class relations was, however, not fundamentally challenged. As a result, national-populist political structures have always entailed a precarious balance of diverse interests. The mobilization of peasants and industrial workers entails a shifting political balance, but without affecting the traditional mechanisms for obtaining, distributing, and maintaining political power. Thus, incorporation of the lower classes into national politics—which benefited individual families—also had the function of legitimizing social structures that had not emancipated campesinos and industrial workers as social classes. Furthermore, the national-populist governments continued to operate under a series of weaknesses and inherent contradictions (Mayorga, 1974; Cotler, 1974; Trip, 1974). These contradictions were founded precisely on a situation in which class conflicts were not resolved but only accommodated within a politico-economic system whose stability was inherently precarious—even in the spectacularly constant rebalancing process of Mexican politics since the 1920s (Kaufman Purcell and Purcell, 1980). Within such systems, all groups continue to maintain their separate interests but submit—more or less voluntarily, and with greater or lesser benefits—to the balancing mechanisms supervised in the last resort by the national government. Within this structure of accommodation across class lines, there tends to be a continuous fluctuation of power; the stability of the system depends on the capability of the government to limit the expression of excessive class interests. Radical peasant and labor demands in such a system would limit the government's ability to attract private—national or foreign—capital. Hence, radical peasant and workers' movements tend to be controlled through co-optation or repression in the populist political structure.

There are other models of Latin American political structures that entail different strategies of resolving the contradictory needs for capitalist investments as well as lower-class acceptance within the substructure of the capitalist periphery. These alternatives include capitalist liberalism, socialism, and dictatorships under conservative governments. Chile, under the government of Frei, tended to represent the liberal capitalist model. While the policy of Frei's government was founded less on alliances across class lines within a corporate state, it incorporated a measure of nationalism and of "arranged" class conflicts within carefully observed limits. This model has permitted a certain degree of free competition between social classes, but always only within the rules of the game. No one class could emancipate itself at the expense of others. It is in this context that the coup d'etat against the more radical government of Allende in Chile (1973) has to be understood. In this respect, the liberal capitalist and national-populist governments share a fundamental premise that defines the opportunities as well as the limits of popular mobilization.

Finally, two other alternatives can be identified as responses to contradictory class relations. In conservative military dictatorships, the number of which has tended to increase in the 1970s, popular mobilization is either directly repressed or politically manipulated without consideration of class interests. On the opposite end, there have been attempts to establish radical socialist regimes (in Guatemala under Arévalo and Árbenz, in Cuba under Castro, in Chile under Allende, possibly in Brazil under Goulart, and in Nicaragua since 1979). Apart from Cuba and Nicaragua, these socialist governments have been overthrown through military coups supported by the U.S. government. Thus, extensive peasant mobilizations have principally occurred under liberal capitalist and national-populist regimes—regimes that did not completely repress peasant mobilizations but rather defined and enforced their limitations.

In the following section, the contemporary mechanisms of peasant domination will be examined. In general terms, it will be argued that the very conditions under which peasant mobilizations have been stimulated since the second half of the nineteenth century have also defined the limitations of these movements. Contemporary, modernized mechanisms of domination are due to changing political and economic equations; but such shifting balances have not entailed an emancipation of Latin American peasants as a social class.

MODERNIZING THE MECHANISMS OF DOMINATION

A fundamental question concerns the relationships between the decline in the dominant position of the traditional landlords and the potential for peasant emancipation. The model of the closed triangle, for example, represents an ideal-typical focus on peasants whose self-interests have become identical to an interest in class solidarity within the integrated structural context of the larger society (see Chapter 11). It should be noted, however, that other alternatives besides the open and closed triangles are not only conceivable but, indeed, have been historically observable (Singelmann, 1975b): the traditional open triangle may simply replace the traditional dominant broker with a more modern substitute (Figure 4); competing brokers, including government agents, may create competitive conflicts among their compesino followers (Figure 5); the outcomes of conflicts between peasants and landlords over governmental support (Figure 6) cannot be predicted a priori; and the traditional landlords may compete with new brokers for domination of the campesinos (Figure 7).

Such modernized mechanisms of domination can be classified in terms of (1) a dependence on new intermediaries, (2) continued particularization of class relations, and (3) the continuous possibility of repression as the ultimate mechanism of control.

Dependence on new intermediaries. It has been argued that the new intermediaries in rural Latin America have been able to mobilize peasants, or assume the leadership of locally emerging movements, precisely because they represent functional alternatives to the traditional *patrones* by offering to the campesinos concrete benefits and services that previously had been controlled by the landlords. While such new brokers may merely replace the old ones, they tend to compete among each other for their clients and thus provide alternatives among which the peasants have a greater freedom to choose. Furthermore, the class interests of the campesinos do not need to be in contradiction with the class interests of the brokers any more. But a crucial problem lies in the observation that the interests of campesinos and new brokers tend to be not identical but complementary within a short-run perspective. In the long run, however, this complementarity is limited by the self-interests of different social classes within the economic context of peripheral capitalism (Stavenhagen, 1969; Baran, 1970). Latin American alliances between peasants, industrial laborers, and members of the rising middle class have typically represented pragmatic reactions to temporary political constellations, rather than inherently identical class interests. Historically, there have been a number of violent confrontations between such groups. In Mexico, urban industrial workers formed the *Batallones Rojos* to fight the peasant armies of Zapata and Villa during the revolutionary decade. Although they formed revolutionary alliances in the 1950s, Bolivian peasants and mine workers have maintained delicate mutual relations, involving in the 1960s violent confrontations; and, after the military takeover, they formed contrasting oppositions and supports for the ruling junta. Such conflicts between social groups that, according to Marxian theory, have theoretically identical class interests are based on political structures that prompt the seeking of particularized interests and in which governments can dispose of institutionalized benefits in manners that divide the lower classes. This pattern of divide and rule is founded on the inherent tendency of clientelist political structures to promote the satisfaction of self-interest within a

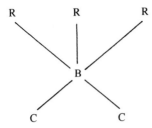

FIGURE 4. Open triangle with new broker.

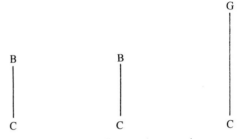

FIGURE 5. Competing brokers and competing campesinos
(G = government).

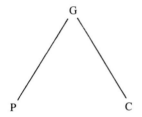

FIGURE 6. Landowners (P) and
campesinos (C) competing for
governmental policies and
legislation (G).

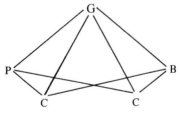

FIGURE 7. Single-power domain of
landowners (P) competing with
multiple-power domains of new
brokers (B).

network of temporary alliances across class lines. Hence, ambitious leaders have always had the opportunity to manipulate peasant movements in their personal interests; frequently, they have offered merely symbolic services to their clients in order to use their support to promote their own political interests.[4]

One example of such manipulation is the *charrismo*[5] in the Mexican *Confederación Nacional Campesina* (CNC) (Huizer, 1970a). On the other hand, the mobilization of peasants as clients has been dependent on the leadership's ability to provide concrete benefits that were valued sufficiently to satisfy given immediate peasant needs. Such benefits have included, in varying amounts, land, credit, political protection, and other necessities (Singelmann, 1973c). At the same time, however, such exchanges have generally—although with significant but short-range exceptions—created new dependencies due to the relatively weaker bargaining positions of the campesinos. Such dependence has been reflected in relations between peasants and their legal assistants (Whyte and Williams, 1968); it is also manifested in the temporal correlation between the growth of campesino organizations and the ascendance of favorable political regimes in Venezuela, Guatemala, Mexico, Brazil, Peru, Chile, and Bolivia.[6] Furthermore, this process is manifested by the resurgence of peasant land invasions—spontaneous or sponsored by the government—when presidents are elected who are expected to be sympathetic to such endeavors; cases in point are the ascendance of presidents Lopez Michelson in Colombia (1936), Belaúnde in Peru (1963), or Allende in Chile (1970).[7] A further manifestation of new dependencies of campesinos is the subordination of agrarian reform programs to political fluctuations within a given party in power. This process is manifested in the gradual deradicalization of the agrarian policies in Venezuela under the Acción Democrática (Powell, 1971), or by the ascendances and declines of drastic agrarian policies in Mexico before and after 1940 (Huizer, 1970c). Finally, new dependencies are manifested in the paternalistic attitudes of campesinos toward their *padres, jefes,* or *principes de la vida,* who give them their lands as favors.[8]

It has been generally observed (Galjart, 1967) that the new intermediaries serve similar functions to the traditional *patrones*. Heath (1973) notes "new patrons in old roles" and "old patrons in new roles" who maintain the continuity of traditional *patrón*-client relations in the Bolivian countryside. The current military government in Peru has transformed the traditional haciendas and plantations into rural cooperatives; but they are managed by political bureaucrats, appointed by the federal government, who play the roles of the traditional *patrones* (Cotler, 1974: 178) and manage enterprises in which the campesinos as formal coowners are no more emancipated economically than they were as clients of the traditional *patrones* (Petras and Havens, 1979; Guillet, 1979: 202).

It may be argued that the new patterns of paternalism are temporary excesses that can eventually be controlled and lead to a peasant emancipation according to critical criteria. But such arguments obscure the problem that the new *patrones*, while in many cases sincerely motivated, can become renegades who take egotistical advantage of their leadership when the campesinos are without an independent political and economic base. Indeed, many peasant leaders and other political or economic intermediaries have assumed precisely the traditional functions of domination and exploitation. So far, the new intermediaries have promoted, in the long run, new patterns of incorporating peasants into existing structures of domination; but there has been little change in the generic structure of domination itself (Eisenstadt and Roniger, 1980: 76–77). While it is important to recognize that many peasant movements have entailed a revolutionary potential, all radical peasant movements in Latin America (with the exception of Cuba and Nicaragua) have been eventually repressed, co-opted, or maintained in relative isolation. It has been precisely in those areas where the most radical peasant mobilizations have threatened previous balances that the most radical repressions have been observed. In this sense, the assassination of Emiliano Zapata in 1919 and the Chilean coup of 1973 are representative of the obstacles to revolutionary transformation in Latin America.

Particularization of class relations. As has been pointed out above, the traditional structures of domination founded on unilateral dependence and coercion resulted in the particularization of class relations in terms of individualized relations between *patrones* and clients. This enabled the *patrones* to divide their subordinates and prevent the formation of collective class consciousness. Hence, the new patterns of dependency entailed new ways of dividing and conquering in Latin America. In place of the traditional good and bad *patrones*, the twentieth century witnessed an increasing importance of good and bad presidents at the macropolitical level with similar implications for the peasant communities at the local level (Gillin, 1960: 37–38). In Brazil, Galjart (1964; 1965) emphasizes the protection and favors that peasant leagues and rural labor unions received from the government of Goulart. The Bolivian peasant leaders under Villaroel and Paz Estenssoro were recognized as padres by their followers, and Paz

Estenssoro had particular charisma because he gave land to the campesinos (Heath, 1969: 189). Mexico's President Làzaro Càrdenas has frequently been treated as a mystical figure supporting peasant movements. Peruvian peasants in the Valle de Mantaro trusted President Odría simply because he was born and raised in the region (Tullis, 1970: 116, 126–27). There have been many other good presidents and their bad equivalents, and the effect of the good presidents is identical to that of the good *patrones* (Feder, 1969a: 399–403): they can easily transform themselves into bad *patrones* or be replaced by bad successors, because their benevolence is founded precisely on their own decisions without enforceable obligations to well-organized peasant communities. Furthermore, it is precisely the occasional rule of good presidents that may correspond to a process of variable reinforcement that strengthens the hopes and confidence of peasantries in existing social structures. Thus, peasants may be tempted to work within the system and promote the election of good presidents, rather than seek substantial structural transformations.

Just as the traditional landlords distributed strategic benefits among their confidants (*hombres de confianza*), presidents who have sympathized in various degrees with the interests of the campesinos tended to strategically distribute assistance and protection among those groups who supported the party in power. As a result, the *hombres de confianza* of the traditional *patrones* have reappeared at the highest level of national politics in the form of the official peasant and labor leaders accepted by the president and the party in power. This confidence on the part of the government has been the key to the successes of the peasant and labor leaders accepted by the government: they have access to the highest political positions that determine the distribution of benefits to the lower classes.

However, in the long run this process has weakened peasant mobilizations. First, it has tended to divide peasants into groups, on the one hand, organized and/or patronized by the government and, on the other, who received lesser, unsatisfactory benefits or were linked to the opposition parties. Officials or government-allied peasant organizations have generally obtained greater privileges in terms of patronage, services, material benefits, and protection against repressive controls. The crucial aspect of these processes is not that all members of such subsystems of the peasantry benefit collectively from these exchanges, but that these individuals or groups are formally free and have advantages in competitive horizontal relationships within the general class of the peasantry. As a result, different organizations have competed for peasant support and for corresponding access to political resources. On the other hand, governments or parties in power have frequently formed their own or semiofficial peasant organizations as a political base, as has been the case in Chile (under President Frei), Guatemala (under Arévalo and Árbenz), Mexico, Bolivia (after the 1952 revolution), and Venezuela (after 1945). In each of these countries, there have also been competing campesino organizations that intended to mobilize peasants in attempts to establish independent political movements.[9] There have also been conflicts, occassionally violent, between different Brazilian peasant organizations; there is some evidence that President Goulart was going to organize these various groups under his own control before being overthrown during the coup of 1964 (Hewitt, 1969; Moraes, 1970; Price, 1964). Chilean campesinos were highly factionalized during the government of Frei (1964–1970)—precisely during the period in which the Chilean government was opened for the first time in a process of political modernization under which peasants obtained increasing freedom for political mobilization (Winn and Kay, 1974:137–38). In all of these countries it was well understood that the establishment of many peasant organizations was basically motivated by an interest in establishing bases for political parties, reestablishing the declining influence of the Catholic Church over the rural lower classes, or preventing peasant organizations from falling into the hands of communist parties.[10] These processes have tended to maintain the tradition of factional competition between groups within the same social class of the rural population (Landsberger and Hewitt, 1970: 562–65). The vertical solidarities between patrones—although they may be "new intermediaries"—and peasant clients remain a significant obstacle to horizontal class solidarization among the peasantry. The contradiction between class interest and individual self-interests has so far not been resolved.

The second implication of clientelistic social relations as an obstacle to peasant emancipation has been the link between trusted peasant syndicates (*de confianza*) and the interests of national governments. The clientelistic exchanges between official peasant organizations and the political parties in government have generally created oligarchical political machines at both levels, whose basic interests lie in maintaining their political control. Such balances tend to be maintained under delicate political equilibria that balance out a complexity of shifting political interests. They necessarily entail *charrismo* and corruption of the ideological principles. These processes entail exchanges in which peasants support governments in return for the chance to receive special benefits or assistance in time of need. This process, from which a given proportion of peasants obtain individual benefits, has achieved a high degree of perfection in Mexico (Anderson and Cockroft, 1969; Adie, 1970; Reyna, 1974; Kaufman Purcell and Purcell, 1980; Villegas, 1975), but it can generally be observed in Latin American areas where peasants have a degree of freedom to form political organizations (Fals-Borda, 1972: 131–33). Thus, the co-optation of traditional *hombres de confianza* has been replaced by large-scale co-optation of peasant movements. Such a process encourages peasants to seek personal benefits at the expense of class emancipation and thereby tends to maintain given macro-structural patterns of domination and exploitation by "marginally incorporating" (Martínez Ríos, 1974) peasants within the process of development.

Repression. Violent repression has traditionally constituted the fundamental basis of peasant subordination. The developments in the twentieth century represent not so much a change in this foundation as an increasing flexibility in different forms of control, which permits limited forms of peasant mobilization to relieve political pressures that could promote an explosive, violent peasant response.

In Latin America, large-scale and often violent peasant mobilizations have led to, or been promoted by, the new forms of sociopolitical integration discussed above, but without in the long run strengthening either the economic status or the political positions of the rural population. In countries such as Chile, Paraguay, and Guatemala, peasant mobilization can only exist clandestinely. In Colombia and Ecuador, peasant movements have been tolerated within clearly defined limits.

The more sophisticated techniques of domination entail the process of co-optation in connection with political modernization. Under that condition, most fully perfected in Mexico, coercion remains only the ultimate mechanism of control; but it represents nevertheless a significant, and feared, element in the political process that enters into the calculation of political opposition to the ruling party. In Peru, the development from a purely repressive government to one that increasingly institutionalized co-optation began under the government of Belaúnde but became the central emphasis under the military rule of Velasco Alvarado (Petras and Laporte, 1971; Cotler, 1974). Under a number of military governments, peasant demonstrations are controlled and completely manipulated by the government, as is illustrated by the Guatemalan election of 1974, where armed campesinos marched to the capital cheering for Langerud, the candidate of the military (*Excelsior,* Mexico, 5 March 1974). In Brazil, peasant organizations in the 1970s were controlled by the government. When peasants, legally organized under the direction of Manoel da Conceicão, seriously confronted abusive landlords in the Brazilian state of Maranhão (1968), the movement was violently repressed; their leader was incarcerated and violently tortured (USLA, 1973a; 1974). Bolivian peasant organizations entered a nonintervention treaty with the military governments of the 1970s. But when peasants from the Cochabamba Valley protested against rising costs of living in 1974, General Banzer used this as a pretext for an attack in which several hundreds of unarmed campesinos were killed. In Mexico, uncorruptible peasant leaders who present a serious threat to regional political balances risk imprisonment, torture, or death.[11] In Guatemala, independent peasant organizations are repressed not only by governmental forces, but also by various vigilante groups who, under clandestine protection from high-ranking military officers, have assasinated a variety of suspected communists. These groups include *Mano Blanca* (White Hand), *Ojo por Ojo* (Eye for Eye), and also *Escuadrones de Muerte* (Death Squadrons), which follow organizations under the same name in Brazil and Uruguay. They officially seek to kill small delinquents; in reality, however, these groups are highly politicized (Klare and Stein, 1974).

What has changed in the twentieth century, then, is not the use of repressive techniques of domination but the more systematic involvement of governmental agencies in them, under active U.S. military aid.[12] It is correct to assert that peasant mobilizations in twentieth-century Latin America have been promoted and strengthened through the weakening of the traditional landowners within a macrostructural and international process of ascending social groups who are competing for power or governmental support. Within this shifting process, there have been larger societal supports for peasant mobilizations with different degrees of radicalism and authentic social commitments. But when the governments themselves, for the purpose of political or economic stability, have taken the place of old *patrones* without establishing a radical macrostructural transformation, peasants in most Latin American countries have not been able to effectively resist the adapted forms of domination.

Conclusions

In Parts I and II of this study an exchange-theory model of traditional *patrón*-campesino relations was developed, and a number of propositions were derived from this model to explain and predict the development of campesino movements under conditions of change in one or more of the parameters. In Part III, evidence about the major campesino movements was surveyed in order to assess the utility of the theory and propositions formulated in Parts I and II. Finally, a critical assessment was offered concerning the emancipatory potential of Latin American peasant movements. The historical evidence suggests that an exchange-theory perspective that overcomes the conceptual limitations of a strictly behavioristic approach and enables scholars to grasp a significant dimension of social processes involving peasant resistance to exploitation. This approach also offers a point of departure for critically analyzing peasant mobilizations in terms of their potential, and their limitations under given historical conditions, for emancipating peasants as a social class. It should be emphasized again that a more complete assessment of this latter issue requires a systematic focus on political processes in connection with tendential developments in different and interrelated issues of production—an issue that requires specific attention to the theoretical focus of this book. Nevertheless, the present analysis offers some suggestions concerning the theoretical issues and historical dimensions of peasant emancipation.

CHANGING SOCIAL STRUCTURES AND THE EMERGENCE OF CAMPESINO MOVEMENTS IN LATIN AMERICA: AN INTERPRETATION

Traditional *patrón*-campesino relationships in Latin America have involved unilateral exchanges in which the landlord has a virtually absolute monopoly over institutional coercion and economic resources within his domain. This domain may have included not only the *colonos* residing on his estate but also independent communities or smallholders within the region in which his influence prevailed. The *colonos* living on the haciendas were completely dependent on their *patrón* for their livelihood, for protection, and for assistance in dealing with authorities outside the hacienda. The *colonos* were thus linked with the larger society only in an indirect manner, as various constraints kept them in isolation under the tight control of the landowner. For the individual *colono*, little could be gained from exchanges with his peers, since the resources and benefits most vital to him were controlled and sparsely provided by the landlord. Due to the extent of the *colono's* dependence on the *hacendado* and his inferior bargaining position, he had little to offer in return for the *patrón's* services except his acceptance of unspecified obligations to demonstrate his obedience and loyalty—obligations that could be invoked at the *patrón's* discretion when he needed extra services, informants, votes, or armed support. Extra favors granted by the *patrón* to individual subordinates established particularistic ties of loyalty, gratefulness, and intensified dependence to the *patrón*. Within the larger political structure of the society, the landholder would generally belong to one of the political factions that battled each other for the spoils of the government. Within this political structure, patronage networks would extend from the very top of the political hierarchy through the regional and local *caudillos* down to the campesino followers. Lines of cleavage and conflict were drawn primarily not between classes, but between blocs or factions that tended to be identically composed of individuals and groups from all socioeconomic levels battling each other at their own status level. This situation pitted peasant against peasant, *hacendado* against *hacendado, caudillo* against *caudillo*. The interest of the *colonos* on a hacienda was, therefore, to see that their *patrón* fared well politically and belonged to the "ins"—only then could he effectively provide for their security and livelihood. Thus, the well-being of their *patrón* was more important for a group of *colonos* than the well-being of their peers on a hacienda belonging to a rival *hacendado;* their particular group interests were incompatible with their class interests.

Within the domain of the hacienda, a similar situation prevailed that encouraged atomism and conflict among the campesinos. Where the good things of life were scarce and under the control of the *hacendado*, individual campesinos could gain most from seeking the favor of the *patrón* in order to receive a few extra privileges. These privileges were sparsely dispensed by the *patrón* so that the campesinos had to compete for them among each other. Gaining the trust of the *patrón* through loyalty, deference, and special services became thus imperative for the individual campesino; the particularistic relationships that resulted from this necessity motivated the campesino to act in ways that fostered the interests of the *hacendado* at the expense of the interests of his fellow campesinos; again his self-interests were incompatible with his class interests.

Given his dependence and powerlessness, the individual campesino had little chance to improve his traditional relationships with the *patrón* through directed action. His response to subordination and low status was cognitive—manifested in various forms of lowered expectation, fatalism, pessimism, the magnification of external constraints (if there was room for magnification), or the justification of his inferiority in terms of the favors done to him by his *patrón*. Such adaptations appear to have been mainly in terms of perceptual rather than evaluative adjustments, and they probably have reinforced submissive behaviors even in the face of changing power relations. As has been pointed out by Thibaut and Kelley (1967: 90–95), individuals who perceive themselves as having great control over their sociophysical environment tend to overestimate their abilities to obtain good outcomes, while individuals with little power tend to underestimate the range of outcomes available to them. But overestimates of one's ability are likely to be corrected by experience, whereas underestimates tend to remain uncorrected, since the individual with low power is not likely to attempt to achieve outcomes above his unrealistically low level of expectations.

In view of century-long suppression and deprivation, the campesinos' perceptual adjustment to subordination must be viewed as a realistic and rational response that made it possible for them to explain the world around them and guide their actions through a life that was full of traps and insecurities. Departures from the taken-for-granted routines were risky and could lead to death. Abandoning the protection of the *patrón* and the organization of horizontal solidarity movements would bring uncertainty and danger, as the process of legal recognition had uncertain results and took a long time, during which the landlord could punish the rebels with impunity. Secret organization was also risky, as informers from within the ranks always had to be expected to warn the *patrones* of an imminent rebellion before it could gain momentum.

The structure of constraint and power in which the campesino had to eke out a livelihood for his family in the past fits well the model of triadic exchange and unilateral dependence outlined in Chapter 3. The distribution of control over coercive, political, economic, and institutional resources has traditionally been conducive to paternalistic solidarities between campesinos and landholders, which have then been reinforced by a variety of psychocultural configurations (Chapters 4 to 7).

Furthermore, horizontal solidarities within the campesino community have been kept weak by these same vertical solidarities. Exchanges between campesinos have yielded low returns in comparison to the returns that *some* peasant could expect from their paternalistic relationships with the landlords, and social relations in the campesino community have often been tenuous and conflict prone.

Campesino movements have generally developed under the conditions specified in the theory developed in the first two parts of this study. Some of the most pertinent factors may be listed:

1. Breakdown of the traditional isolation of the hacienda domain, and breakdown of the institutional-political controls *hacendados* have held over the campesinos.

2. Availability and accessibility of new suppliers for the benefits traditionally supplied by the landlord; emergence of new *patrones* and brokers who could integrate the peasantry into the larger society by circumventing the old landlord.

3. A deterioration in the campesinos' socioeconomic position due to proletarianization, economic depressions and transformations, and the inability or unwillingness of the *patrones* to continue supplying paternalistic or customary services to the campesinos.

4. Macrosctructural transformations in the larger society that detrimentally affected the powers and resources of the landed elite and strengthened new sectors and power contenders that could gain from alliances with campesinos.

5. Ascension to power of a party or government that was willing (or needed) to grant concesssions (or favors) to organized campesinos.

6. Experience by the campesinos of gains that could accrue from horizontal solidarity in their community.

7. Increases in the cognitive capacity on the part of campesinos in general and of leaders in particular, due to exposure to new reference sources (city, national politics, labor syndicates, schooling, travels, migration).

8. Changes in the perceptions of campesinos related to their powers and capabilities: "definitions of the situation," availability of successful models for conduct, and raised expectations.

These generalizations provide some of the general parameters of campesino mobilization in Latin America. It is well at this point to remember Giorgio Alberti's (1972: 330) propositions that, first, "no *single* characteristic of the peasantry will do in the attempt to explain peasant movements" (my italics) and, second, a correlational analysis of variables must be a historical analysis of processes. The processes to be analyzed are the social interactions of campesinos and *patrones* from which campesino movements emerge, take shape, succeed, and fail. Based on his own studies in the Yanamarca Valley of Peru, Alberti (1972: 329–30) suggests a general four-stage model of peasant mobilization that summarizes the preceeding propositions and puts them into a historical as well as an interactive perspective:

Stage 1: the *hacendado* has full control over the life of the peons and is at the heart of the regional power structure (traditional pattern).

Stage 2: emergence of new economic groups in the region and changes in the economic structure of the area. New power contenders challenge the political position of the landowners, but the latter retain their hold over the peons in the domains of their estates.

Stage 3: a new regional elite displaces the traditional *hacendado* class; entrance of national politics into the rural areas, development of new political alternatives as the *hacendadados* manage to share political control by virtue of their established connections and traditions. Thus, social relations on the hacienda persist as if nothing has changed around the estates. Some of the peons have participated in the general change process by working in mines and returning to the estates, participating in union activities outside the haciendas, or establishing *patrón*-client relationships with political sponsors. They have developed a "new consciousness" and become discontented with the traditional social structure of the haciendas.

Stage 4: Total loss of economic and political control of the *hacendado* class, which reacts to economic difficulties by attempting to squeeze more labor out of the peons. This serves as a precipitating factor for a rebellion that is supported by politicians and bureaucrats at the national level.

The changes involved in these processes have primarily affected the objective structure of constraints and opportunities within which the traditional exchanges between campesinos and *patrones* take place. But they have also modified the cognitions of campesinos. In either case, the changes have created cognitive imbalances among the campesinos to which they could have responded either by changing some of their cognitions—as they have done in the past—or by acting upon the environment that was perceived in a new manner. As has been proposed, the campesinos' responses are most likely to be active, rather than cognitive, when their political position has gained relative to that of the landholders. This is manifested primarily in the active responses to changes in the national power structures and in the seeking out of alternative *patrones*.

Exchange and power relations between *patrones* and campesinos do not exist in a macrostructural vacuum. Rather, as Blau (1964a) argues, changes in the national polity or society differentially affect the outcomes and bargaining positions of actors and can thus give rise to imbalance and cognitive inconsistencies on the micro level. Furthermore, it is the nature of these macrostructural changes that determines the nature of the campesinos' response to such disequilibrium. In the light of the extreme dependence and powerlessness that have traditionally been combined with cognitive adaptations, discouraging innovation and aggression against the *hacendado*, it is generally not enough that the campesino changes his values (if they need changing at all) in order to revolt. Nor is it enough that objective conditions improve so that alternative courses of action can be taken. Rather, there must be a drastic and increasingly unviable rupture in the campesino's traditional routines before he can take deliberate action to change his situation. Under conditions of scarcity and dependence, stability of outcomes is more important in guiding the campesino's behavior than the deliberate calculation of means, ends, and consequences, because "an adaptive solution . . . is provided by routines that obviate these complex cognitive activities and automatize the procedures for gaining adequate outcomes" (Thibaut and Kelley, 1967: 28); it is only when the traditional routines break down or "at certain critical junctures in the lives of the [campesinos] when major alternatives with long-term . . . consequences are clearly perceived" (Thibaut and Kelley, 1967: 62; see also 29; Berger and Luckmann, 1966: 23–24) that traditional modes of conduct are apt to be altered. Ruptures that challenge the taken-for-granted occur when traditional adaptations cease to bring the expected outcomes. A significant and felt deterioration in terms of economic returns, disintegrating paternalism, or increased demands can stir the campesinos to rebellion. Or the offerings of new patrons with demonstrable power and ability to dispense tangible benefits may increase the campesino's readiness to risk a departure from the status quo. Dramatic demonstrations of success on the part of some rural syndicates or of the political sponsor may convince the campesino. Furthermore, experiences that enable campesinos to transcend the narrow cognitive horizon of the isolated community make them look at their lives through a new perspective. This makes it possible for the campesinos to take advantage of whatever institutional resources may be mobilizable in their society for their own benefit. In general, these different types of imbalances tend to occur simultaneously and thus reinforce each other in their impact upon the campesinos. But the most crucial process appears to be a shift of the balance of force and power that strengthens the position of the campesinos and their emerging allies. Such a shift makes the campesinos' traditional cognitive responses to subordination decreasingly plausible to them and increases the realistic expectation that aggressive action can successfully redress the old and new grievances.

PERSPECTIVES ON PEASANT EMANCIPATION

While these changes are significant in stimulating the development of campesino organizations, it is equally important to recognize the continuity with the traditional social structures that is reflected in campesino movements. This continuity lies in the persistence of paternalistic leadership patterns to which Latin American nations have been accustomed. Campesino leaders at all levels in many ways are still protectors and providers for their followers, and they are able to play this role because of the brokerage function they perform in the larger political structure. It is still important to be in with the group that controls spoils and patronage at all levels of the governmental hierarchy. Interclass vertical alliances linking campesinos with local, regional, and national power figures are still much in evidence. While campesinos have frequently acted as a class vis-à-vis the government (for example, in Mexico and Bolivia), conflicts within given classes often continue to place campesino against campesino, organizer against organizer, and politician against politician. Campesino organizations and leaders often compete with one another for spoils, patronage, and clients.

While continuity has thus been built into the very patterns of change, the situation of the Latin American campesino has been modified in two important ways. First, he has increasingly been freed from the constraints that traditionally prevented him from moving outside the boundaries of the hacienda and from freely utilizing political resources. Second, the new *patrones*, between which he is freer to choose, do not necessarily have interests opposed to his own class interests. Campesino politics have been moving toward a clientelistic model in which the campesino offers organizational, armed, and electoral support to the highest bidder, who, in turn, uses this support as a means to induce favors and obligations from higher-ranking political figures for the benefit of his campesino clientele. The degree to which campesinos are the manipulators or the manipulated varies with the extent of the institutional and coercive powers. In virtually all cases, however, it appears that the campesinos need the new *patrones* and the governmental support, while they, in turn, are needed by their *patrones* and by the government. While it should be emphasized that these patterns of interdependence are clearly unilateral and in favor of the *patrones*, this situation has created a more flexible political system in which campesinos can mobilize themselves to make certain "legitimate" demands; but at the same time their militancy must be contained within a tolerable range, which varies directly with the degree of political and military autonomy the campesinos have. At the one extreme of the continuum campesinos have complete autonomy and thus completely determine governmental policies; this pattern would represent a stage of class emancipation for the campesinos. But any situation involving less than that kind of autonomy is conducive to tactics seeking limited and group-specific improvements within the existing social structure, rather than a radical change of that structure in order to eliminate the very conditions of domination and alienation. Historically, Latin American campesino movements by virtue of their limited power within the larger society have not succeeded in transcending the co-optative mechanisms of modern politics. Bolivia after the revolution of 1952 perhaps represents a situation where the government was most dependent on campesino support, while the history of the Guatemalan movement is a good illustration of an organization completely dependent on the fortunes of the national government. The Venezuelan case may come closest to a relatively bilateral exchange between campesino organizations and governments. All of these cases are variations of basically similar sociopolitical structures that differ only in terms of the degree of campesino power. This perspective gives us a handle for analyzing campesino movements by the degree to which they represent genuine class struggle or merely a subtler form of false consciousness. In the face of low political power, following a protector, even if he is self-seeking, may in the short run appear as the most meaningful immediate alternative for the campesino, regardless of what his objective class interests are in the long run. As his control over institutional and coercive resources increases, he could increasingly mold the activities of his leaders and sponsors in his own interest without having to pay for such a privilege with the renunciation of intraclass solidarity. The problem is that, apart from relatively temporary fluctuations, the Latin American campesino of the twentieth century has not been able to attain or maintain the needed control over means of coercion. After a decade of hope in the 1960s, the 1970s have witnessed a period in which independent campesino movements were repressed, manipulated, or co-opted throughout the continent. Perhaps, with the benefit of hindsight, this could have been expected as the immanent logic of political structures that have been bent but have not radically changed, that have overcome old traditions only to revive them in new forms, and that dispose of a U.S.-supported military apparatus by attempting to maintain such continuity.

The focus of this book has been to critically analyze historical developments up to the 1970s and to explore those dimensions of social change and political mobilization that have taken place without necessarily promising peasant emancipation or the transformation of peasants into qualitatively different social classes.

It should be emphasized that the arguments presented here are not addressed to the question whether radical peasant revolutions are inherently impossible in contemporary underdeveloped countries in general and in Latin America in particular. Indeed, as has been discussed in Chapter 1, peasant revolutions have had significant historical impacts in the nineteenth and twentieth centuries. In Latin America, peasants have played crucial roles in establishing socialist programs in Cuba and since 1979 in Nicaragua. Furthermore, the contradictions inherent in peripheral capitalist development—in connection with drastic population growth, limited creation of urban-industrial employment, and persistent maintenance of noncapitalist dimensions in rural and urban labor relations (Pearse, 1975: 256–57, 264; Griffin, 1969: chap. 1; Migdal, 1974: chap. 8, 224)—raise the question whether these problems stand in the way of capitalist development along the lines of the classical transformation of the peasant majority into urban-industrial laborers and employees. If these dilemmas continue to threaten precarious societal balances, which may increasingly fall back on coercive controls, revolutionary changes may be inevitable.

Notes

1. For a general overview of Latin American peasant movements in the twentieth century, see the volumes edited by Landsberger (1969a), Stavenhagen (1970), and Huizer (1972).

2. For an extremely thorough collection of the literature, see Skocpol (1979: 296–97, fns. 18–20).

3. For a detailed analysis of exchange theory, see Chapter 2.

4. The traditional structures of exchange and power will be discussed in detail in Chapter 5.

5. The concept of dependence entails the notion that (1) peasants need the benefits from a landlord more than the landlord needs the services of the given peasant, and (2) peasants have no (acceptable) alternatives to the landlords for meeting these needs.

6. Balance is conceptualized not in terms of lacking contradictions or equality, but as a situation in which given structural relations tend to be maintained in spite of possible resistance by some of the participants. For a critical analysis of the contradictions emerging in Latin American haciendas, see Duncan and Rutledge, eds. (1977), which focuses on increasing difficulties in rebalancing traditional rural-class relations since the nineteenth century.

7. For a recent and comprehensive analysis of patron-client relations, see Eisenstadt and Roniger (1980). For a more detailed discussion, see Chapters 5 and 6.

8. On the "open triangle" and the problems of "closing," see Cotler (1969), Whyte (1970), Dandler (1969; 1971), Alberti (1970b), as well as the critical analysis by Singelmann (1975b). See also the analysis of power and exchange as factors in the development of peasant solidarity. The notions of exchange and power have already been incorporated in some of Tullis's theoretical discussions (1970), and Alberti (1970a: 1972) has analyzed peasant movements on one Peruvian hacienda in terms of the power and exchange paradigm proposed by Blau. Tullis's and Alberti's contributions have been important in motivating the present study and providing empirical data relevant for the proposed theory.

9. See the debate between Galjart (1964; 1965) and Huizer (1965).

10. Of course, the concept of "objectification" (*Versachlinchung*) is a Marxian concept that has been applied, for instance, in describing the "fetishism of commodities." Ideologies and other cultural factors as objectified cognitions mediate the relationships between objective conditions and subjective actions. See Berger and Luckmann's (1966) extensive discussion of "objectivation."

CHAPTER 2

1. For a detailed statement of Homans's approach to exchange theory, see Homans (1958; 1961). For some extensions and critical appraisals of Homans's theory, see Abrahamson (1970), Blau (1964b), Alexander and Simpson (1964), and Singelmann (1972; 1973).

2. Initially, network approaches have been emerging in anthropology (see the reprints of Firth, 1964, as well as Wolfe, 1978). A pioneering formulation of network analysis can be found in Bott (1957). For discussions of general theoretical issues and case analyses, see Boissevain and Mitchell, eds. (1973), Leinhardt, ed. (1977), Holland and Leinhardt, eds. (1979), Anderson and Willer, eds. (1980), and Barth (1966).

3. This contradictory coexistence of legitimation and inequity in the status quo of institutional structures is best summarized by Blau: "Vested interests and powers create rigidities in social structures, and so does the institutionalization of social arrangements through which they are perpetuated beyond the life span of individuals. Social institutions are crystallized forms of organized social life that have their base in historical traditions and that are supported by major cultural values internalized in childhood and passed on from generation to generation. Traditional institutions, endowed by profound values with symbolic significance, tend to defy innovation and reform even when changes in social conditions have made them obsolete. Powerful groups whose interests are served by existing institutional arrangements defend them against attack and fortify them. Institutions meet the need for social order and stability at the cost of rigidities and inequities that often cause serious hardships. Vigorous social opposition is required to produce a change in institutions, and it constitutes a countervailing force against institutional rigidities" (1964a: 335).

4. See Thoden Van Velzen (1973), Heckathorn (1979a), Willer (1980b: table 5), Southard (1980: figs. 1 and 3), Emerson (1972, vol. 2; 1969: 396–98), and Caplow (1968). See also Kapferer's (1969: 212) definition of exchange in terms of network analysis.

CHAPTER 3

1. The scope of Person's power over Other refers to the number of life spheres in which Person can manipulate Other's environment and direct his behavior. When the scope is low, Person can manipulate few aspects of Other's environment (for example, fire him from his job); a large scope of power can theoretically go as far as a domination in which Person exerts total control over all relevant spheres in the life of a subordinate. Such total control is only possible when Person can effectively control Other's access to needed benefits and block the availability of alternative sources from which Other could receive the needed benefits. Power and dependence relationships exist of course in a larger macrostructural context; the actual or potential links each interactant can have with "outsiders" affect the very nature of microrelationships. When the scope of the domination in a relationship is extremely large, powerholders can effectively block direct relationships between their subordinates and third parties from the outside while reserving a monopoly over such outside contacts for themselves. Conversely, when the subordinates gain access to previously unaccessible outside relationships from which they can receive needed benefits, they

improve their bargaining position in confrontations with the powerholder. As will be discussed later, traditional *patrón*-campesino relationships resemble the model of landlord monopoly and campesino isolation, while the emergence of alternative *patróns* for the campesinos has been a crucial factor in their mobilization against the landlord.

CHAPTER 4

1. The following section is based on Konetzke (1965), Mörner (1970; 1973; 1975), and Stein and Stein (1970), unless cited otherwise. For the forms and policies of land settlement, see Konetzke (1965: 42–68); for Indian policies and laws regulating the exaction of labor and tributes from the Indians, see pp. 165–72 (slavery), pp. 173–95, 204–8 (*encomienda* and *repartimiento*), pp. 195–204 (*naboria* and *yanacona*). For further historical analyses of case studies and for a regional focus, see Florescano (1971) Florescano, ed. (1975), Bauer (1975), and de la Pena (1975).

2. For different perspectives on types of landlord and labor-peasant relations such as plantations, haciendas, sharecropping, and combined arrangements, see Florescano, ed. (1975), Mörner (1975), Duncan and Rutledge, eds. (1977), Laclau (1977), and Frank (1969).

3. On the traditional patterns of land monopolies and labor exploitation, see the comparative analysis of Griffin (1969: esp. 68–74; 1976: 124). On the balancing dimensions of these patterns, see Barraclough's (1973: 7–9) discussion of the "old," "dynamic equilibrium" based on "absolute coercive controls," as well as Pearse's analysis of traditional balances in landlord domination over peasants (1975: chap. 7). Pearse showed how these balancing mechanisms adjusted to changing political structures (colonial independence and the freeing of native landholders from governmental controls) and economic crises in the 1930s and 1940s when landlords adjusted to increasing outside economic pressures by attempting increased abuses and exploitation of the peasants. The tendencies toward changing economic patterns resulting from this pressure (Pearse, 1975: chap. 3) are discussed in Chapter 10.

4. The extent of land concentration increases when regional breakdowns are used for each country. Thus in the Brazilian coastal sugar zone, 88.7 percent of the area belonging to agricultural establishments is owned by large-scale producers holding 7 percent of all establishments, while those 84 percent of the establishments owned by small-scale producers cover 5.3 percent of the total area under cultivation (Wilkie, 1964: 4). Comparable figures from Bolivia a few years before the revolution of 1952 indicate that smallholdings constituted 69 percent of all agricultural establishments but covered only .41 percent of the total area in possession of rural owners, while 91.95 percent of the total area was owned by large landholders owning 7.67 percent of all establishments (Heath, Erasmus, and Buechler, 1969: 35). Figures for Guatemala before the 1944 takeover indicate that a small group of plantation owners who constituted 2.1 percent of the total population of the country owned 72.2 percent of the known arable land (Pearson, 1969: 323). For a detailed discussion of current patterns and trends in Latin America, see the CIDA studies for individual countries and Feder's (1971) penetrating analysis.

5. Descriptions of such arrangements can be found in S. Schulman (1955), Tannenbaum (1960: 82–83), CIDA (1965: 38–41, 135–51, 158–68; 1966a; 1966b: 125–31; 1966c: 112–13), Pearse (1970: 20–21), Cotler (1970a:

543–45), Erasmus (1967: 353–56), Hobsbawm (1969: 39–41), Tullis (1970: chap. 6), Martínez (1963a; 1967), Palacio (1957a; 1957b; 1960; 1961).

6. For a detailed description of such dependency relations on an Ecuadorian hacienda, see CIDA (1965b: 173–74, 238–39). In one of the cases, villagers were forced to work in order to retrieve clothes and hats taken as forfeits from them by the hacienda (1965b: 239). Forfeits were also used in prerevolutionary Bolivia to keep the resident labor force on the estates (Heath, Erasmus, and Buechler, 1969: 99). On the extreme and accelerating patterns of rural poverty under peripheral capitalist development since the midtwentieth century, see Chapter 10.

7. See also Migdal's general analysis on "stress relieving" mechanisms of domination (1974: chaps. 2–4) and Sharpe's (1977: chap. 7) excellent case study of debt and dependence in a peasant village.

8. For an excellent overview of the issues discussed in this and the following sections, see Feder (1971: chaps. 13, 14).

9. Maria Brandao, describing certain types of residents on Brazilian *fazendas* who receive food and housing in return for their permanent availability for work on the estate, stated, "The smaller the monetary relationship between the owner and the worker, the greater are the obligations of the worker towards the owner" (CIDA, 1966a: 250). In this context, Homans's discussion of money as a "generalized reinforcer" is pertinent. Money can be used to obtain many different kinds of rewards, whereas the specialized reinforcements encountered on traditional *latifundias* provide little opportunity for barter.

CHAPTER 5

1. Authors often emphasize that "the *hacienda* is a way of life rather than a business" (Tannenbaum, 1960: 82) without considering the commercial aspects. As has been pointed out by various authors (summarized by Frank, 1969: 231–47), the haciendas arose in response to the needs of mining and urban centers that required agricultural products. It was only when mining decayed in the late sixteenth and early seventeenth centuries that the haciendas turned inward. The commercial orientation of the large estates is most obvious in the case of plantations, but was never absent in other types of agriculture. Whether or not the traditional hacienda was a capitalist enterprise depends on the observer's point of view. Traditionally, much of the profits were not reinvested, were wasted through conspicuous consumption and the underwriting of upper-class life-styles. But, as Vitale (1968) has pointed out, colonization in Latin America has never been feudal in the European sense but was part of a larger capitalist world economy that needed the extraction of raw materials for the international market. For an authoritative account of the Mexican large hacienda and its historical origins, see Chevalier (1970); Whetten (1948: 90–108). For recent interpretations of historical data on colonial and postcolonial landed estates in Latin America, see Florescano, ed. (1975), and Duncan and Rutledge, eds. (1977).

2. In Mexico before the revolution and in several contemporary Latin American countries, estates have been found in excess of 1 million acres (Tannenbaum, 1960: 78; Silva-Herzog, 1959: 122–24).

3. It is not uncommon to find advertisements such as the one found in a Bolivian newspaper in 1948, offering a hacienda for sale with 500 acres of land, 50 sheep, much water, and 20 peons (Tannenbaum, 1960: 82).

4. *Moradores* are resident plantation workers who may have the use of a

small plot. For an account of the isolation characterizing many estates in Brazil and the consequences this has for the dependence of the *moradores*, see CIDA, 1966a: 155–59.

5. For examples of the internal organization of large estates, see Feder (1969a: 404–5; 1971: 120–24), H. W. Hutchinson (1957: 49, 70), CIDA (1965: 183–326), Vázquez (1963), and Heath, Erasmus, and Buechler (1969: 101–2).

6. For the most recent and comprehensive review of the literature on *patrón*-client relations, as well as an attempt to integrate previous analyses within a systematic theoretical perspective, see Eisenstadt and Roniger (1980).

CHAPTER 6

1. For the background of the movement, see USLA (1973a; 1973b; n.d.).

2. These excerpts are taken from USLA (1973a). For a full text of the letter, see USLA (n.d.), in the author's files. Da Conceição's tortures have become notorious in the courts. For excerpts from the court transcripts, see USLA (1974).

3. For data on U.S. police training and counterinsurgency assistance, see Murtha (1973) and Klare and Stein (1974). For data on U.S. military assistance to Latin American and other Third World countries, see Klare (1974).

4. For example Guillén-Martínez in his brilliant analysis of the Colombian class structure and politics in the nineteenth century suggests that the labor of the subjected Indians served as a resource to the *gamonales* and enabled the latter to participate in the competition for control over the national administration, which yielded immense benefits. He states: "The owner [sic] of the bureaucratic machine disposes automatically over the fruits of this semi-servile peasant labor and the large landowners, and allies himself with the government functionaries to maintain this dual power in the hands of one group; in the meantime, a rival group, with identical composition, emerges to challenge him for the rich spoils" (1963: 84. My translation). For perceptive analyses of *caudillismo*, see Wolf and Hansen (1967), Tannenbaum (1960: 66–76, 86–89), Beezley (1969), Moreno (1971), and Chevalier (1962).

5. For a more detailed interpretation of the *cangaceiros*, see Vianna (1949, vol. 1), Singelmann (1974), and Chandler (1978). See also Eisenstadt and Roniger's observations (1980: 76).

6. For the friends—bread, for the enemies—the stick.

7. The discussion of *coronelismo* during the First Republic has been based chiefly on Nuñes Leal (1948: chaps. 1–2).

8. See also the general discussion by Tannenbaum (1960: 136–72) and the descriptions by Landy (1959: 54–56) and Fals-Borda (1955: 241–44). The two large Uruguayan parties that resemble one another completely carry the unimaginative names of *Colorados* (Colored) and *Blancos* (White). As for the peasantry, ideology, if relevant at all, appears also to be subsumed under pragmatic considerations. Campesinos in Venezuela have responded in survey interviews with inconsistent ideological statements and a large percentage of "don't knows" (Mathiason, 1966: 141); Newbold's interviews with imprisoned campesinos after the 1954 coup revealed (not very surprisingly) that ideological catchwords had little meaning for them; the most common statements he heard were to the effect that they were poor, knew

nothing, favored whichever government was in power, wanted to return home to their families and work, and were good Catholics (Newbold, 1957: esp. 352). These findings, however, should be taken *cum grano salis*, as this was precisely the kind of responses that would most likely lead them back into freedom. For an excellent discussion of clientelism and peasant politics in Latin America, see Powell (1970), Greenfield (1966; 1969), Lopes (1964; 1966), Hicks (1971), and Walker (1970). Actually, the processes of clientelistic politics are more complex than has been described here. Especially, there are usually several intermediary positions between patrons and their clientele. A local or regional politician in Brazil, for example, is usually linked to his clientele through his *cabo eleitoral* (something like a ward heeler) to whom the voters are clients and who himself is a client to the politican he works for. The function of the *cabo eleitoral* in the *favelas* (squatters' settlements) of contemporary Rio de Janeiro has been described in detail by E. Leeds (1970). For the benefits a local boss could obtain for his rival followers in northeastern Brazil, see Galjart (1964: 6–8).

9. This kind of situation is emerging in several Latin American countries today, notably Chile, Venezuela (Powell, 1969), and perhaps Peru. In urban areas lower-class voters tend to be free from the powers of the *patrones* and, while not necessarily losing their dependence on some protectors for obtaining urban services and legal aid, they are able to bargain with different sponsors and promise their votes to those politicians who provide the greatest benefits in return. This process of playing the game of milking competing politicians for all they can provide has been well described for the *favelas* (slum settlements) in Rio de Janeiro by E. Leeds (1970). In those societies where peasants are relatively free to cast their votes for whomever they want, clientelistic bargaining with competing politicians and parties seems to be the rule. See the excellent article by Powell (1970).

10. For a general discussion of the emergence of new brokers in Latin America, see Wagley (1964: 45–48). An excellent interrelation of pertinent historical developments in Mexico since the Spanish conquest is offered by Wolf (1965). The general relationships between clientelism and the brokerage function are succinctly discussed by Powell (1970: 413–16). Blondel (1957) has also made a relevant contribution in describing the conflicts between *novos políticos* (new politicians) and *chefes tradicionais* in a Brazil community.

11. The current figure should be around 186 (August 1980).

12. The relationship between official and unofficial violence in northeast Brazil has been described in greater detail, within the context of social banditry, by Singelmann (1973a).

13. It is precisely the advent of lawyers that developed some more genuine concern for the campesinos, together with their political leverage, which helped the development of peasant movements in the last two decades. This has been notable in Peru and Brazil, where Francisco Julião is the outstanding example.

14. For example, the current agrarian reform law in Colombia provides that "appropriately used" *latifundist* property can only be expropriated when the social conditions of the tenants and workers make it appear to be absolutely necessary (*Der Spiegel*, 1971: 96).

15. For examples, see S. Schulman (1966), CIDA (1966c: 437), Paulson (1964: 49–58), and Smith (1969). An excellent discussion of the problem of counterreform has been provided by Feder (1970; see also 1969a). Other

accounts of inefficient, unenforced, and damaging laws and regulations can be found in Barraclough and Domike (1970: 74–79), CIDA (1966a: 67–68, 266, 329–32), Wilkie (1964: 4–5), Gilhodès (1970: 418–20), Huizer (1972: chap. 2), and Hirschman (1965: chaps. 1, 2). It should be noted that Hirschman is generally more optimistic about the possibility of social reform in Latin America than the other authors cited.

CHAPTER 7

1. One problem with such causality is that frequently the cultural variables that are said to determine behavior are actually inferred from these very behaviors, so that the explanation becomes circular. When approached in terms of mutual determination, given behaviors are situationally meaningful for individual actors, regardless of whether the ultimate causes are cultural or structural.

2. Concern is here with the traditional ideal-typical parameters. The discussion is still applicable to contemporary Latin America, although significant changes (to be discussed below) have taken place and even in the traditional contexts the limitations described have never been absolute. For a sample of data on current problems of literacy, language barriers, and cultural isolation, see Cotler (1970b: 418, 420–21; 1970a: 553), Patch (1960: 138), Heath (1969: 183), and Fromm and Maccoby (1970: 45–48).

3. The landholders, and often the campesinos, are usually aware of this. Tullis (1970: chap. 6), for example, reports the great desire of the villagers in several Peruvian highland communities to improve themselves (or their children) through education. They often undergo incredible sacrifices in time, money, and risks of expulsion to obtain a school and teachers. The landowners either blocked the establishment of schools in the villages from the outset or became suspicious of the effect of education once the schools have operated for a while. See also Heath, Erasmus, and Buechler (1969: 190) for examples from Bolivia.

4. The pragmatic character of this exchange between campesino and patron saint has been most systematically described in Foster's pioneering work on the "dyadic contract" in Tzintzuntzán, Mexico (1967a; 1967e). The general point has also been made for Brazil by B. Hutchinson (1966) and Kadt (1967). Ethnographic accounts of folk religion in various Latin American countries fit the "dyadic contract" model well. For Colombia, see Fals-Borda (1955: 223–24). It is interesting to observe in this context that different patron saints are venerated for different occasions with different needs, since each saint may be a specialist in certain fields. Saints who are repeatedly perceived as unresponsive may be abandoned in favor of more responsive ones. An informant told this writer in a Guatemalan village that a campesino had been overheard cursing a patron saint and throwing away his picture, saying: "I have offered you six candles so that you would heal my donkey. You took the candle but did not heal my donkey—this is the last time I ever make an offering to you."

5. The character orientations described by Fromm and Maccoby are not mutually exclusive but may exist in conjunction. The authors, therefore, scored their questionnaires in terms of "dominant," "secondary," and other orientations.

6. See also Cotler (1970b: 417).

7. Semenzato interviewed thirteen workers in the area, twelve of which were utterly pessimistic about their future. While this small group is obvi-

ously not a reliable random sample of rural workers in Brazil or even in the Itabuna region, the findings appear to be quite representative of rural workers under similar conditions in Latin America.

8. The *ejido* is a government-sponsored and directed rural cooperative program in which plots are assigned to individual members of the village community.

CHAPTER 8

1. For a summary of pertinent evidence in a number of Latin American and other rural communities, see Rubel (1966: 208–38).

2. Reina (1959) gives an interesting account of friendship patterns in Chinautla, Guatemala. Among the Ladinos, the *cuello* pattern implied practical utility as a mechanism of gaining economic or political advantage. Friendships in which the expected benefits were not forthcoming broke up easily. Among the Indians, the *camaraderia* involved very intimate personal relationships between a pair in which the intrusion of third individuals was precluded. Because of the emotionalism and the exclusiveness, tensions were easily engendered that could lead to a formal break similar to a divorce. Hostility between ex-*camaradas* appeared to be a recurrent phenomenon.

3. While acts to gain trust and favors from the landlord, for example, may be acceptable in the campesino community since they do not take anything away from others, such acts clearly elicit benefits that could have been obtained by others. Landlords do not gain anything by making available all benefits in sufficient amounts to everybody desiring them; rather, they benefit from their individual subordinate's need to outdo the others in order to gain these scarce benefits. Thus, competition among the campesinos for the landlord's favors may not engender as much hostility as do acts that threaten the positions of others within the campesino community. But the fact remains that the limited supply of paternalistic favors induces campesinos to act in ways that benefit the landlord at the expense of the interests of the campesinos as a class. For perceptive analyses of *patrón*-client relationships, see Wolf (1966b) and Greenfield (1966; 1969).

4. Kearney (1969) observes that in one area goods tend to exist in infinite amounts. This is the experience of intensified emotions during fiesta time. The experience of such emotions for an individual on this occasion does not tend to entail a loss for others. Fiestas are, therefore, the main occasion on which expressive solidarization takes place. Recently, Foster has been criticized by Huizer (1970b; 1972) for his alleged argument that it is the image of limited good that is a primary cause of the peasants' conservatism and resistance to change, when it should be more correctly interpreted as a consequence of repression. In a rejoinder, Foster points out that he himself has repeatedly discussed the structural constraints of peasant societies within which the image of limited good operates. It does appear, then, that scarcity provides the distinctive structural framework within which the image of limited good emerges, although for Foster the image was essentially an implicit cognitive organizing principle under which human conduct can be subsumed.

CHAPTER 10

1. As Wolf (1966a: 7–17) has noted, the lives of peasants tend to require precarious balancing acts to meet the conflicting demands of external domains and household needs. One characteristic response to the dilemma is underconsumption with concomitant conservatism and a reluctance to

engage in innovative activities (such as class conflicts), since "any novelty may undermine their precarious balance" (1966a: 16).

2. Among the large number of publications on dependency and peripheral capitalist development, particularly since the 1970s, see Amin (1974; 1975), Chilcote and Edelstein, eds. (1974), Müller (1975), and Laclau (1977). On some of the earliest reactions against traditional social theories of modernization and universal principles of economic development, see Frank's collected papers (1969).

3. On the transformation of agriculture and rural-class relations under peripheral capitalist development, see the essays on nineteenth-century agrarian transformations edited by Duncan and Rutledge (1977) and controversies in contemporary analyses, for example, Foweraker (1978), Vergopoulos (1975), Wallerstein (1977), Wolpe (1972; 1975), Portes (1978), Bartra (1974), and Singelmann (1980).

4. This is not to suggest that in Bolivia peasants only joined rural syndicates in response to outside organization. On the contrary, after the ascendance of the MNR in 1952 widespread land seizures and rural rebellions, both organized and spontaneous, probably forced the new government to take a militant procampesino stand in order to head off the movement it could not control at the time. It took considerable time until the government of Paz Estenssoro made a decisive turn toward radical agrarian legislation, political sponsorship, and organizational support for the peasant movement. Thus, in the Cochabamba valley, the peasant movement grew autonomously after 1952, whereas later, in other areas, campesinos were recruited by the spreading movement from outside their communities and with governmental sponsorship. For an overview of the issues and controversy, see Heath, Erasmus, and Buechler (1969), Heath (1965; 1969), Patch (1960; 1963), R. J. Alexander (1958), Dandler (1969; 1971).

CHAPTER 11

1. The opposition of the Chilean Catholic Church to more profound changes is reflected in its hostility to the Allende regime and its enthusiastic support of the military coup of September 1973. Characteristically, some friction between the clergy and the Pinochet regime developed only when the government removed a priest from the direction of the radio transmitter at the Catholic University in Santiago (*Excelsior,* Mexico, 30 March 1974: 3).

2. In Mexico, reports consistently indicate not only that priests in all ranks sought to influence the campesinos ideologically, but also that part were active in organizing counterguerrillas against campesino syndicates and sympathetic politicians as well as in supporting landowners in their claims and organization of "white" unions under their control (Huizer, 1967: 57, 67, 121–22). Today, posters and signs, sold in religious shops and frequently displayed, reflect this position in slogans such as "*comunismo, no—cristianismo, sí*."

3. The following discussion has been presented in Singelmann (1973b).

4. Landsberger has related the influence of urban sectors on campesino leadership to a low level of political modernization, hypothesizing: "The less modernized the society, the lower the rung of the organizational ladder from which outside leadership is recruited. Insofar as there is national leadership, it will be drawn *de facto* and until a relatively late stage of societal development, from urban middle classes, particularly intellectuals. Insofar as there is regional and local leadership, it will be recruited from the

local bourgeoisie, craftsmen, shopkeepers, lawyers, and lower clergy"
(1969a: 57). Within the framework of the present study, less emphasis is
placed on the role of intellectuals per se; what matters is their ability to
mobilize institutional resources and ideological support as lawyers, journal-
ists, university professors, clergymen, labor organizers, or parliamentarians; the fact that some of these are intellectuals is considered here as
incidental.

CHAPTER 12

1. This has been especially well documented for Brazil by Lopes (1964;
1966: chaps. 5–6) and Greenfield (1966). While Lopes focuses more on the
breakup of patrimonial relations in the countryside in the course of urbanization and industrialization, Greenfield points out the functions of the local
politicians in bringing in the votes to the highest bidder. The change from
paternalism to clientelism in local-level politics will be discussed in Chapter
15.

2. Brinton was greatly influenced by Pareto's theory of the circulation of
elites.

3. Guerrilla movements will be excluded from discussion in this study,
first, to limit the material surveyed to manageable proportions and, second,
because the influence of the urban intelligentsia in these movements war-
rants a separate study.

4. There have been debates about the original impetus for the campesino
movements. R. J. Alexander (1958: chaps. 4, 5) argues that the MNR
essentially gave the campesinos land, votes, and arms from above. Patch
(1960; 1963: 111, 117) maintains that in the Cochabamba valley the movements grew out of vigorous indigenous grass-roots support. It appears that
in the Cochabamba valley the rural syndicates did indeed develop autonomously and were able to put vigorous pressure on the new government
in 1952 (Dandler, 1969; 1971). It appears equally true that in most other
parts of the country rural syndicates developed only after organizers from
the government, miners, students, and other outside groups brought the
revolution to the countryside by supplying leadership, arms, the vote, and
food coupons. For this view, see Heath (1969), Malloy (1970: chap. 10),
Huizer (1967: chap. 5), and Dandler (1969; 1971).

5. This generalization corresponds to the findings of Tullis (1970), Alberti
(1970a; 1970b), and others in highland Peru that "moderate solidarity
movements" occur under conditions of low "structural binds" and "intense solidarity movements" occur under conditions of high structural
binds.

6. One *manzana* equals 1.73 acres.

7. Materials in this section have been presented on the basis of the works
by Moraes (1970), Hewitt (1963), Wilkie (1964), Galjart (1964; 1965),
Huizer (1965; 1967: 179–91), A. Leeds (1964), Price (1964), Gortaire Iturralde (1966a; 1966b), Julião (1962; 1968; 1969), CIDA (1966a), and Callado
(1968).

8. For more detailed studies of the Mexican revolution, see Huizer (1967:
3–140), Womack (1969), Millon (1969), Silva-Herzog (1959), Sotelo Inclán
(1970), and Díaz Zoto y Gama (1976). On contemporary aspects of peasant
mobilization and co-optation, see Gilly (1971), Bartra et al. (1975), Warman
(1973), and Stavenhagen et al. (1973).

9. Similar legal restrictions have been or still are common in other
countries, such as Brazil, Venezuela, Mexico, Peru, and Guatemala.

CHAPTER 13

1. The following section has been presented in Singelmann (1973b).

2. It is interesting to note Craig's (1967: 70, 72) findings that absences of internal land disputes appear to be preconditions for the perception of unity in a community. At the time of his study, various land surveys were undertaken by the government in order to redistribute the territories of former haciendas. These surveys gave rise to bitter conflicts among campesinos over their claims to certain plots. In the thirty-five communities surveyed by Craig, only eleven were reported to have no such disputes among the members.

CHAPTER 14

1. My argument is consistent with Lerner's thesis that geographical mobility, media participation, and in general "psychic travel" simplify and simultaneously expand perceptions and create a new, larger "vicarious universe" for the modernizing personality (Lerner, 1958: 52–54).

2. "The *violeiro* is a peasant who plays a special rural Brazilian guitar with twelve chords while singing improvised verses about the adventures of famous bandits, or simple peasants who rebel against the patterns of closed rural society. The *cantador*, in general, is a vendor of little pamphlets in which are published the 'histories' sung by the *violeiros*. In order to sell the little booklets at peasant fairs or festivals, the *cantador* recites the verse using a standard chant with little variation in the melody line. The *folhetinista* is the peasant poet who sets these stories to verse producing the little booklets at peasant fairs or festivals, the *cantador* recites the verse using a standard chant with little variation in the melody line. The *folhetinista* is the peasant poet who sets these stories to verse producing the little peasant pamphlets on a small press that he operates himself" (Moraes, 1970: 481, fn. 20).

3. Correlations between increases in media participation and other forms of communication on the one hand, and rural organization on the other, have been better documented in some cases; but these cases involve an increase in communications *after* campesino movements had already had some degree of success. Such cases are Venezuela (Mathiason, 1966: 148–49) and Bolivia (Patch, 1963: 124).

4. In this connection it is instructive to make a comparison with more systematic data from southern Italy that indicate that contact with emigrants produced egalitarian attitudes among peasants (Lopreato, 1967).

5. However, no evidence was offered in either report that militancy was directly associated with greater cognitive capacity among the immigrants. While such a connection is possible, the more likely explanation in this case is similar to that of Petras and Zeitlin (1970: 515): Resident peons who are born on the estate are more likely to be subject to paternalistic domination, whereas the newcomers in the valleys of La Convención and Chancay entered into more contractual and less particularistic relationships with the landowners and thereby did not owe them the traditional deference.

6. In this study, the term *system* will be adopted from the studies cited as an abstraction that refers to institutional interdependencies within a community. It highlights certain analytical properties but is not synonymous with *community*, the totality of real interactions among a social group. It will

not imply complete integration or the absence of conflict in a community.

7. For example, in the Cuban revolution it is difficult to separate the dimensions of popular peasant participation from the guerrilla movement based on nonpeasant leadership. Further significant development has recently taken place in Nicaragua, as well as in the precariously balanced relationships between conservative and leftist movements in El Salvador. In both these cases, it is impossible to separate increasing economic and political pressures from the dimension of changing perceptions or evaluations on the part of the peasants.

CHAPTER 15

1. This outline will follow the general conceptualization of Lukács (1970) and the criteria of political consciousness suggested by Petras and Zemelman (1972: 64–65).

2. The following two sections of this chapter have been largely based on Singelmann (1976), of which a large section, pp. 40–47, has been reprinted here in a free translation and slight revision by the author.

3. On populism in Latin American political development, see Tella (1965). On the problem of the "Third Route" in Latin America, see Mayorga (1974), Cotler (1974), and Trip (1974). On general issues related to the "Third Route," see Mansilla (1974).

4. On the aspect of manipulation in Brazil, see Galjart (1964; 1965), A. Leeds (1964), and Hewitt (1969). On Mexico, see Anderson and Cockroft (1969), Adie (1970), and Huizer (1970a); on Peru, see Cotler and Portocarrero (1969) and Dew (1969).

5. "El Charro" was the nickname of a railroad workers' union leader within the dominant party (PRI). Subsequently, the term *Charrismo* emerged in Mexico to indicate union structures in which the leadership selection was manipulated from above. The notion is applicable to leadership in many other Latin American peasant and labor unions.

6. The correlations between the rise and fall of peasant organizations and sympathetic governments has been documented, for example, in Brazil (Hewitt, 1969; Price, 1964), Guatemala (Murphy, 1970; Pearson, 1969), Venezuela (Powell, 1971), Chile (Menges, 1968), and Mexico (Fowler Salamini, 1978).

7. For exemplary case studies, see, on Colombia, Gilhodès (1970: 417); on Peru, Cotler and Portocarrero (1969: 311); on Chile, Galjart (1972: 9); and on Bolivia, Dandler (1971: 106).

8. For cases in point, see Petras and Zemelman (1972: 118, 136), Moraes (1970: 470–71), Forman (1970: 13), Heath (1969: 189), and Dandler (1971: 113).

9. For data on this political aspect, see, on Chile, Menges (1968); on Guatemala, Pearson (1969); on Peru, Cotler and Portocarrero (1969) and Petras and Laporte (1971); on Mexico, Huizer (1970b); on Venezuela, Powell (1971); on Bolivia, Heath (1969) and Dandler (1969; 1971).

10. See the general analysis by Landsberger and Hewitt (1970) on the origins of internal conflicts in campesino movements. Even in Chile under the government of Allende there were instances where peasants minimized their activities in collective—in contrast to their private—properties because as families they received greater benefits from their independent production (Winn and Kay, 1974: 158). See also Sharpe's observations on the Dominican Republic (1977: 214–15), Pearse's analysis of the inherent

limitations of Latin American peasant mobilization (1975: 159–61), and Fowler Salamini's (1978) analysis of the limitations of radical peasant mobilization in Mexico in the 1930s.

11. A famous case is the assassination in 1962 of Mexican peasant leader Rubén Jaramilla, who had been a charismatic leader of peasant resistance especially in the state of Morelos. But such assassinations, tortures, and arrests are common in contemporary rural Mexico. Peasant leaders of the Consejo Agrarista Mexicano (CAM), unwilling to be co-opted, were subject to arrests or shootings by forces of the federal secret police also during my fieldwork in Morelos (1975–1976). In contrast, the leader of the other faction within the movement was willing to compromise the movement and was subsequently rewarded with a position as a federal deputy, as were several other leaders of independent peasant organizations who had met as a group with President Echeverría in 1976 (field notes).

12. A large part of this aid has been delivered in a clandestine form. On the operations of the CIA in counterinsurgent activities and in sabotaging the socialist government of Allende in Chile, information is available in the newspapers around 1975. See also *Time*, 22 April 1974. Concerning USAID participation in vigilante operations, see Klare and Stein (1974: 21). On terrorist reactions against socialist movements, vigilante organizations, and general practices of military aid, see Klare and Stein (1974) and Murtha (1973).

Bibliography

Abrahamson, Bengt. 1970. "Homans on Exchange: Hedonism Revisited." *American Journal of Sociology* 76 (September): 273–85.
Adams, J. Stacy. 1965. "Inequality in Social Exchange." In L. Berkowitz, ed., *Advances in Experimental Psychology,* 2: 267–300. New York: Academic Press.
Adams, Richard N. 1960. "Social Change in Guatemala and U.S. Policy." In R. N. Adams et al., eds., *Social Change in Latin America Today*, pp. 231–84. New York: Random House.
———. 1964. "Rural Labor." In J. J. Johnson, ed., *Continuity and Change in Latin America*, pp. 49–78. Stanford: Stanford University Press.
———. 1967a. *The Second Sowing: Power and Secondary Development in Latin America.* San Francisco: Chandler.
———. 1967b. "Political Power and Social Structures." In C. Veliz, ed., *The Politics of Conformity in Latin America*, pp. 15–42. London: Oxford University Press.
———. 1975. *Energy and Structure: A Theory of Social Power.* Austin: University of Texas Press.
Adie, Robert F. 1970. "Cooperation, Cooptation, and Conflict in Mexican Peasant Organizations." *Inter-American Economic Affairs* 24: 3–25.
Alberti, Giorgio. 1970a. "Inter-Village Systems and Development: A Study of Social Change in Highland Peru." Ithaca: Cornell University Latin American Studies Program, Dissertation Series, no. 18.
———. 1970b. "Los movimientos campesinos." In R. G. Keith et al., eds., *La hacienda, la comunidad y el campesino en el Perú*, pp. 164–213. Lima: Franciso Moncloa Editores.
———. 1972. "The Breakdown of Provincial Urban Power Structure and the Rise of Peasant Movements." *Sociologia Ruralis* 12 (no. 3/4): 315–33.
Alexander, C. Norman, Jr., and Richard L. Simpson. 1964. "Balance Theory and Distributive Justice." *Sociological Inquiry* 24 (Spring): 182–92.
Alexander, Robert J. 1958. *The Bolivian National Revolution.* New Brunswick, N.J.: Rutgers University Press.
Amin, Samir. 1974. *El capitalismo periphérico.* Mexico City: Nuestro Tiempo.
———. 1975. "El capitalismo y la renta de la tierra: La dominación del capitalismo sobre la agricultura." In S. Amin and K. Vergopoulos, *La cuestion campesina y el capitalismo*, pp. 9–58. Mexico City: Nuestro Tiempo.
Anderson, Bo, and James D. Cockroft. 1969. "Control and Cooperation in Mexican Politics." *International Journal of Comparative Sociology* 7: 16–22.
Anderson, Bo, and David Willer, eds. 1980. *Social Exchange Networks: The Elementary Theory and Its Application.* New York: Elsevier.
Antezana, E. Luis. 1960. "La lucha entre Cliza y Ucureña." Pamphlet. Cochabamba, Bolivia.

————. 1969. "La reforma agraria campesina en Bolivia (1956–1960)." *Revista Mexicana de Sociología* 31 (April–June): 245–322.

Bailey, Norman A. 1967. "La violencia in Colombia." *Journal of Inter-American Studies* 9 (October): 561–75.

Banck, Geert A. 1973. "Network Analysis and Social Theory." In J. Boissevain and J. C. Mitchell, eds., *Network Analysis: Studies in Human Interaction*, pp. 37–43. The Hague: Mouton.

Banfield, Edward. 1958. *The Moral Basis of a Backward Society*. New York: Free Press.

Baracona, Rafael. 1964. *Rasgos fundamentales de los sistemas de tenencia de la tierra en el Ecuador*. Report, Inter-American Committee for Agricultural Development. Preliminary Version.

Baran, Paul A. 1970. "On the Political Economy of Backwardness." In R. I. Rhodes, ed., *Imperialism and Underdevelopment: A Reader*, pp. 285–301. New York: Monthly Review Press.

Barnes, J. O. 1969. "Networks and Political Process." In J. C. Mitchell, ed., *Social Networks in Urban Situations*. Manchester, Eng.: Manchester University Press.

Barnes Marshall, Katherine. 1970. "Cabildes, corregimientos y sindicatos en Bolivia despues de 1952." *Estudios Andinos* 1, no. 2: 61–78.

Barraclough, Solon. 1973. *Agrarian Structure in Latin America*. Toronto: D. C. Heath.

Barraclough, Solon, and A. Affouso. 1973. "Diagnóstica de la reforma agrarian chilena." In S. Barraclough et al., *Chile: Reforma agraria y gobierno popular*, pp. 9–92. Buenos Aires: Ediciones Periferia.

Barraclough, Solon L., and A. L. Domike. 1970. "Agrarian Structure in Seven Latin American Countries." In R. Stavenhagen, ed., *Agrarian Problems and Peasant Movements in Latin America*, pp. 41–94. Garden City, N.Y.: Doubleday.

Barraclough, Solon L., and José Antonio Fernández. 1974. *Diagnóstico de la reforma agraria chilena*. Mexico City: Siglo XXI.

Barth, Fredric. 1966. *Models of Social Organization*. London: Royal Anthropological Institute.

Bartra, Roger. 1974. *Estructura agraria y clases sociales en México*. Mexico City: Era.

Bartra, Roger, et al. 1975. *Caciquismo y poder político en el México rural*. Mexico City: Siglo XXI.

Bauer, Arnold J. 1975. *Chilean Rural Society*. New York: Cambridge University Press.

Beals, Ralph L. 1970. "Gifting, Reciprocity, Savings, and Credit in Peasant Oaxaca." *Southwestern Journal of Anthropology* 26 (Autumn): 231–41.

Beezley, William H. 1969. "Caudillismo: An Interpretive Note." *Journal of Inter-American Studies* 11 (July): 345–52.

Béjar, Hector. 1969. *Peru 1965: Notes on a Guerilla Experience*. New York: Monthly Review Press.

Bennholdt-Thomsen, Veronika. 1976. "Los campesinos en las relaciones de producción del capitalismo periférico." *Historica y Sociedad*, no. 10: 29–38.

Bequiraj, Mehmet. 1966. *Peasantry and Revolution*. Ithaca: Center for International Studies, Cornell University.

Berger, Peter L., and Thomas Luckmann. 1966. *The Social Construction of Reality: A Treatise in the Sociology of Knowledge*. Garden City, N.Y.: Doubleday.

Blanco, Hugo. 1972. *Land or Death: The Peasant Struggle in Peru*. New York: Pathfinder Press.

Blau, Peter M. 1964a. *Exchange and Power in Social Life*. New York: Wiley.

———. 1964b. "Justice in Social Exchange." *Sociological Inquiry* 24: 193–206.

Blok, Anton. 1973. "Coalitions in Sicilian Peasant Society." In J. Boissevain and J. C. Mitchell, eds., *Network Analysis: Studies in Human Interaction*, pp. 151–65. The Hague: Mouton.

Blondel, Jean. 1957. *As condicões da vida política no estado da paraíba*. Rio de Janeiro: Fundacão Getulio Vargas.

Boissevain, Jeremy. 1973. "Introduction." In J. Boissevain and J. C. Mitchell, eds., *Network Analysis: Studies in Human Interaction*, pp. vii–xiii. The Hague: Mouton.

———. 1974. *Friends of Friends: Networks, Manipulators and Coalitions*. New York: St. Martin's Press.

Boissevain, Jeremy, and J. C. Mitchell, eds. 1973. *Network Analysis: Studies in Human Interaction*. The Hague: Mouton.

Bott, Elizabeth. 1957. *Family and Social Network*. London: Tavistock Publications.

Bourque, Susan. 1971. "El sistema político peruano y las organizaciones campesinas: Un modelo de integración." *Estudios Andinos* 2, no. 1: 37–58.

Bourricaūd, François. 1961. "Syndicalisme et politique: La cas peruvien." *Sociologie du Travail* 4: 33–49.

Brinton, Crane. 1965. *The Anatomy of Revolution*. New York: Random House.

Buechler, Hans C. 1970. "Modelos didacticos en el analysis del campesinato boliviano y ecuatoriano." *Estudios Andinos* 1, no. 2: 5–18.

Buve, R. Th. J. 1972. "Protesta de obreros y campesinos durante el Porfiviato: Unas consideraciones sobre su desarrollo e interrelaciones en el este de México Central." *Boletín de Estudios Latinoamericanos* 13 (December): 1–20.

Callado, Antonio. 1968. "Las ligas campesinas del noreste Brasileño." In J. C. Bernadet et al., *Brazil hoy*. Mexico City: Siglo XXI.

Caplow, Theodore. 1968. *Two against One: Coalitions in Triads*. Englewood Cliffs, N.J.: Prentice-Hall.

Carlos, Manuel, and Bo Anderson. 1980. "Political Brokerage and Network Politics in Mexico: The Case of a Representative Dominance System." In B. Anderson and D. Willer, eds., *Social Exchange Networks: The Elementary Theory and Its Applications*. New York: Elsevier.

Carter, William E. 1964. *Aymara Communities and the Bolivian Agrarian Reform*. University of Florida Monographs, Social Sciences, no. 24. Gainesville: University of Florida Press.

Casillo Villegas, Daniel. 1975. *El sistema político mexicano*. Mexico City: Editorial Joaquín Morris.

Chadwick-Jones, J. K. 1976. *Social Exchange Theory: Its Structure and Influence in Social Psychology*. London: Academic Press.

Chandler, Billy James. 1978. *The Bandit King: Lampião of Brazil*. College Station: Texas A&M University Press.

Chevalier, François. 1962. " 'Caudillos' et 'caciques' en Amérique: Contribution a l'étude des liens personnels." *Bulletin Hispanique* 69: 30–47.

———. 1970. *Land and Society in Colonial Mexico*. Berkeley: University of California Press.

Chilcote, Ronald H., and Joel C. Edelstein, eds. 1974. *Latin America: The Struggle with Dependency and Beyond*. New York: Schenkman.

CIDA (Comite Interamericano de Desarrollo Agricola). 1963. *Inventory of Information Basic to the Planning of Agricultural Development in Latin America*. Washington, D.C.: Pan American Union.

CIDA (Centro Interamericano de Desarrollo Agrícola). 1965a. *Tenencia de la tierra y desarrollo socio-económico del sector agrícola: Guatemala.* Washington, D.C.: Unión Panamericana.

———. 1965b. *Tenencia de la tierra y desarrollo socio-económico del sector agrícola: Ecuador.* Washington, D.C.: Unión Panamericana.

CIDA. 1966a. *Land Tenure Conditions and Socio-Economic Development of the Agricultural Sector: Brazil.* Washington, D.C: Pan American Union.

———. 1966b. *Tenencia de la tierra y desarrollo socio-económico del sector agrícola: Colombia.* Washington, D.C.: Unión Panamericana.

———. 1966c. *Tenencia de la tierra y desarrollo socio-económico del sector agrícola: Perú.* Washington, D.C.: Unión Panamericana.

Clark, Ronald J. 1969. "Problems and Conflicts over Land Ownership in Bolivia." *Inter-American Economic Affairs* 22 (Spring): 3–18.

Cornblit, Oscar. 1970. "Levantamientos de masas en Perú y Bolivia durante el siglo dieciocho." *Revista Latinoamericana de Sociología* 6 (March): 100–141.

Correia de Andrade, Manoel. 1963. *A terra e o homem no Nordeste.* São Paulo: Editôra Brasiliense.

Cotler, Julio. 1969. "Pautas de cambio en la sociedad rural." In J. Matos Mar et al., *Dominación y cambios en el Perú rural.* Lima: Instituto de Estudios Peruanos.

———. 1970a. "Traditional Haciendas and Communities in a Context of Political Mobilization in Peru." In R. Stavenhagen, ed., *Agrarian Problems and Peasant Movements in Latin America,* pp. 533–88. Garden City, N.Y.: Doubleday.

———. 1970b. "The Mechanics of Internal Domination and Social Change in Peru." In I. L. Horowitz, ed., *Masses in Latin America,* pp. 407–44. New York: Oxford University Press.

———. 1974. "Politische krise und militärpopulismus in Peru." In H. C. F. Mansilla, ed., *Probleme des Dritten Weges: Mexiko, Argentinien, Bolivien, Tansania, Peru,* pp. 159–98. Darmstadt: Luchterhand.

Cotler, Julio, and Felipe Portocarrero. 1969. "Peru: Peasant Organizations." In H. Landsberger, ed., *Latin American Peasant Movements,* pp. 297–322. Ithaca: Cornell University Press.

Craig, Wesley. 1967. "From Hacienda to Community: An Analysis of Solidarity and Social Change in Peru." Ithaca: Cornell University Latin American Studies Program, Dissertation Series, no. 6.

———. 1969. "Peru: The Peasant Movement of La Convención." In H. Landsberger, ed., *Latin American Peasant Movements,* pp. 274–98. Ithaca: Cornell University Press.

Cunha, Euclides da. 1944. *Rebellion in the Backlands.* Chicago: University of Chicago Press.

Dandler, Jorge. 1969. *El sindicalismo campesino en Bolivia: Los cambios estructurales en Ucureña.* Serie Anthropología Social, no. 11. Mexico City: Instituto Indigenista Interamericano.

———. 1971. *Politics of Leadership, Brokerage and Patronage in the Campesino Movement of Cochabamba , Bolivia (1935–54).* Ann Arbor: University of Michigan Press.

Daniel, James M. 1965. *Rural Violence in Colombia since 1946.* Washington, D.C.: The American University.

Davies, James C. 1962. "Toward a Theory of Revolution." *American Sociological Review* 6 (February): 5–19.

———. 1969. "The J-Curve of Rising and Declining Satisfactions as a Cause of Some Great Revolutions and a Contained Rebellion." In H. D. Graham and T. R. Gurr, eds., *Violence in America,* pp. 671–709. New York: Signet Books.

Dew, Edward. 1969. *Politics in the Altiplano: The Dynamics of Change in Rural Peru*. Austin: University of Texas Press.

Díaz Zoto y Gama, Antonio. 1976. *La revolución agraria del sur y Emiliano Zapata su caudillo*. Mexico City: El Caballito.

Diégues, Manoel, Jr. 1954. *Populacão e açucar no nordeste do Brasil*. São Paulo: Comissão Nacional de Alimentaçao.

Dix, Robert H. 1967. *Colombia: The Political Dimensions of Change*. New Haven: Yale University Press.

Duncan, K., and I. Rutledge, eds. 1977. *Land and Labor in Latin America: Essays on the Development of Agrarian Capitalism in the Nineteenth and Twentieth Centuries*. Cambridge: Cambridge University Press.

Eisenstadt, S. N., and Louis Roniger. 1980. "Patron-Client Relations as a Model of Structuring Social Exchange." *Comparative Studies in Society and History* 22: 42–77.

Ekeh, Peter P. 1974. *Social Exchange Theory*. London: Heinemann Educational Books.

Emerson, Richard M. 1969. "Operant Psychology and Exchange Theory." In R. L. Burgess and D. Bushell, Jr., eds., *Behavorial Sociology*, pp. 379–406. New York: Columbia University Press.

———. 1972. "Exchange Theory, Part II: Exchange Relations and Network Structures." In J. Berger, M. Zeldich, Jr., and Bo Anderson, eds., *Sociological Theories in Progress*, vol. 2. Boston: Houghton Mifflin.

———. 1976. "Social Exchange Theory." In A. Inkeles, ed., *Annual Review of Sociology*, vol. 2. Palo Alto, Calif.: Annual Reviews.

Erasmus, Charles. 1965. "The Occurrence and Disappearance of Reciprocal Farm Labor in Latin America." In D. B. Heath and R. N. Adams, eds., *Contemporary Cultures and Societies of Latin America*, pp. 172–99. New York: Random House.

———. 1967. "Upper Limits of Peasantry and Agrarian Reform: Bolivia, Venezuela, and Mexico Compared." *Ethnology* 6 (October): 349–80.

———. 1968. "Community Development and the *Encogido* Syndrome." *Human Organization* 27: 65–74.

Fals-Borda, Orlando. 1955. *Peasant Society in the Colombian Andes: A Sociological Study of Sancío*. Gainesville: University of Florida Press.

———. 1972. *El reformismo por dentro en America Latina*. Mexico City: Siglo XXI.

Feder, Ernest. 1967. "Land Reform: A Twentieth Century World Issue." *América Latina* 10 (January–March): 96–134.

———. 1969a. "Societal Opposition to Peasant Movements and Its Effect on Farm People in Latin America." In H. Landsberger, ed., *Latin American Peasant Movements*, pp. 399–450. Ithaca: Cornell University Press.

———. 1969b. "Sobre la impotencia política de los campesinos." *Revista Mexicana de Sociología* 31 (April–June): 323–86.

———. 1970. "Counterreform." In R. Stavenhagen, ed., *Agrarian Problems and Peasant Movements in Latin America*, pp. 173–223. Garden City, N.Y.: Doubleday.

———. 1971. *The Rape of the Peasantry: Latin America's Landholding System*. Garden City, N.Y.: Doubleday.

———. 1974. "Notes on the New Penetration of the Agricultures of Developing Countries by Industrial Nations." *Boletín de Estudios Latinoamericanos y del Caribe* 16 (June): 67–74.

Fernandez y Fernandez, Ramón. 1973. *Cooperacion agrícola y organización económica del ejido*. Mexico City: Sep-Setenta.

Firth, Raymond. 1964. *Essays on Social Organization and Values*. London: Athlone Press.

Fitzgibbon, Russell H. 1950. "A Political Scientist's Point of View." *American Political Science Review* 44 (March): 118–29.

Florescano, Enrique. 1971. *Origen y desarrollo de los problemas agrarias de México: 1500–1821*. Mexico City: Era.

Florescano, Enrique, ed. 1975. *Haciendas, latifundios y plantaciones en América Latina*. Mexico City: Siglo XXI.

Fluharty, Vernon L. 1957. *Dance of the Millions: Military Rule and Social Revolution in Colombia*. Pittsburgh: University of Pittsburgh Press.

Foland, Frances M. 1968. *Newsletters to the Institute of Current World Affairs*. FMF 20, 21, 22, 23, 24. New York: Institute for Current World Affairs.

Ford, Thomas R. 1962. *Man and Land in Peru*. Gainesville: University of Florida Press.

Forman, Shepard. 1971. "Disunity and Discontent: A Study of Peasant Movements in Brazil." *Journal of Latin American Studies* 3 (March): 3–24.

Foster, George M. 1960–1961. "Interpersonal Relations in Peasant Society." *Human Organization* 19 (Winter): 174–78.

———. 1961. "The Dyadic Contract: A Model for the Social Structure of a Mexican Peasant Village." *American Anthropologist* 63: 1173–92.

———. 1962. *Traditional Cultures and the Impact of Technological Change*. New York: Harper & Row.

———. 1963. "The Dyadic Contract in Tzintzuntzán, I: Patron-Client Relationship." *American Anthropologist* 65 (December): 1280–94.

———. 1964. "Treasure Tales and the Image of the Static Economy in a Mexican Peasant Community." *Journal of American Folklore* 77 (January–March): 39–44.

———. 1967a. "The Dyadic Contract: A Model for the Social Structure of a Mexican Peasant Village." In J. M. Potter et al., eds., *Peasant Society: A Reader*, pp. 213–30. Boston: Little, Brown & Company.

———. 1967b. "Peasant Society and the Image of Limited Good." In J. M. Potter et al., eds., *Peasant Society: A Reader*, pp. 300–323. Boston: Little, Brown & Company.

———. 1967c. "Introduction: Peasant Character and Personality." In J. M. Potter et al., eds., *Peasant Society: A Reader*, pp. 2–14. Boston: Little, Brown & Company.

———. 1967d. "Introduction: What Is a Peasant?" In J. M. Potter et al., eds., *Peasant Society: A Reader*, pp. 296–99. Boston: Little, Brown & Company.

———. 1967e. *Tzintzuntzán: Mexican Peasants in a Changing World*. Boston: Little, Brown & Company.

Foweraker, Joseph L. 1978. "The Contemporary Peasantry: Class and Class Practice." In H. Newby, ed., *International Perspectives in Rural Society*, pp. 131–58. New York: Wiley.

Fowler Salamini, Heather. 1978. *Agrarian Radicalism in Veracruz, 1920–38*. Lincoln: University of Nebraska Press.

Frank, Andre G. 1969. *Latin America: Underdevelopment or Revolution*. New York: Monthly Review Press.

Freyre, Gilberto. 1946. *The Master and the Slaves: A Study in the Development of Brazilian Civilization*. New York: Knopf.

Fried, Jacob. 1962. "Social Organization and Personal Security in a Peruvian Hacienda Indian Community: Vicos." *American Anthropologist* 64 (August): 771–80.

Fromm, Erich, and Michael Maccoby. 1970. *Social Character in a Mexican Village*. Englewood Cliffs, N.J.: Prentice-Hall.

Fuenzalida, Fernando. 1968. *Estructuras tradicionales y economia de mercado*. Lima: Instituto de Estudios Peruanos.

Furtado, Celso. 1964. *Dialética do desenvolvimento*. 2d ed. Rio de Janeiro: Editora Fundo de Cultura.

————. 1965. "Political Obstacles to Economic Development in Brazil." In C. Veliz, ed., *Obstacles to Change in Latin America*, pp. 145–61. London: Oxford University Press.

Galjart, Benno. 1964. "Class and Following in Rural Brazil," *America Latina* 7 (July–September): 3–24.

————. 1965. "A Further Note on 'Followings': Reply to Huizer." *America Latina* 8 (July–September): 145–52.

————. 1967. "Old Patrons and New." *Sociologia Ruralis* 7, no. 4.

————. 1972. "Movilización campesina en América Latina." *Boletín de Estudios Latinoamericanos* 12 (June): 2–19.

Garcés, Juan E. 1974. *El estado y los problemas tácticos en el gobierno de Allende*. Mexico City: Siglo XXI.

Geschwender, James. 1968. "Explorations in the Theory of Social Movements and Revolution." *Social Forces* 42: 127–35.

Gilhodès, Pierre. 1970. "Agrarian Struggles in Colombia." In R. Stavenhagen, ed., *Agrarian Problems and Peasant Movements in Latin America*, pp. 407–51. Garden City, N.Y.: Doubleday.

Gillin, John. 1951. *The Culture of Security in San Carlos: A Study of a Guatemalan Community of Indians and Ladinos*. Middle American Research Institute, Publication no. 16. New Orleans: Tulane University Press.

————. 1960. "Some Signposts for Policy." In R. N. Adams et al., eds., *Social Change in Latin America Today*, pp. 14–62. New York: Random House.

Gilly, Adolfo. 1971. *La revolución interrumpida*. Mexico City: Ediciones "El Caballito."

Gómez, Sergio. 1973. "El rol del sector agrario y la estructura de clases." In S. Barraclough et al., *Chile: Reforma Agraria y Gobierne Popular*, pp. 179–218. Buenos Aires: Ediciones Periféria.

González-Casanova, Pablo. 1969. "Internal Colonialism and National Development." In I. L. Horowitz et al., eds., *Latin American Radicalism*, pp. 118–39. New York: Random House.

Gortaire Iturralde, Alfonso. 1966a. "Los sindicatos campesinos del Brasil: Una entrevista al Padre Franciso Lage Pessoa." *Comunidad* 1 (March): 69–76.

————. 1966b. "Francisco Julião y las ligas campesinas del Brasil." *Comunidad* 1 (September): 63–70.

Gouldner, Alvin W. 1960. "The Norm of Reciprocity: A Preliminary Statement." *American Sociological Review* 25: 161–78.

Greenfield, Sidney M. 1966. "Patronage Networks, Factions, Political Parties, and National Integration in Contemporary Brazilian Society." Paper presented at the annual meeting of the American Anthropological Association, Pittsburgh, 17–20 November.

————. 1969. "An Analytical Model of Patronage." Paper presented at the annual meeting of the American Anthropological Association, Pittsburgh, 17–20 November.

Griffin, Keith. 1969. *Underdevelopment in Spanish America*. Cambridge, Mass.: MIT Press.

————. 1976. *Land Concentration and Rural Poverty*. London: Macmillan.

Grindle, Merilee Serril. 1977. *Bureaucrats, Politicians, and Peasants in Mexico: A Case Study in Public Policy*. Berkeley: University of California Press.

Guillén-Martínez, Fernando. 1963. *Raíz y futura de la revolución*. Bogotá: Ediciones Tercer Mundo.

Guillet, David. 1979. *Agrarian Reform and Peasant Economy in Southern Peru*. Columbia: University of Missouri Press.

Gurr, Ted R. 1968. "A Causal Model of Civil Strife: A Comparative

Analysis Using New Indices." *American Political Science Review* 62: 110–24.

Guzmán Campos, German, O. Fals-Borda, and E. Umaña Luna. 1962. *La violencia en Colombia: Estudio de un proceso social*. Vol. 1. Bogotá: Ediciones Tercer Mundo.

Harris, Marvin. 1956. *Town and Country in Brazil*. New York: Columbia University Press.

Heath, Dwight B. 1965. "Revolution and Stability in Bolivia." *Current History* 49: 328–35, 367.

————. 1969. "Bolivia: Peasant Syndicates among the Aymara of the Yungas—a View from the Grass Roots." In H. Landsberger, ed., *Latin American Peasant Movements*, pp. 170–209. Ithaca: Cornell University Press.

————. 1973. "New Patrons for Old: Changing Patron-Client Relationships in the Bolivian Yungas." *Ethnology* 12 (January): 75–98.

Heath, D. B., C. J. Erasmus, and H. C. Buechler. 1969. *Land Reform and Social Revolution in Bolivia*. New York: Praeger.

Heckathorn, Douglas. 1978. A Paradigm for Bargaining and a Test of Two Bargaining Models." In *Behavioral Science* 23.

————. 1979. "The Anatomy of Social Network Linkages." *Social Science Research* 8: 222–52.

————. 1980. "A Unified Model for Bargaining and Conflict." *Behavioral Science* 25.

Hewitt, Cynthia N. 1969. "Brazil: The Peasant Movement of Pernambuco, 1961–64." In H. Landsberger, ed., *Latin American Peasant Movements*, pp. 374–98. Ithaca: Cornell University Press.

Hewitt Alcantara, Cynthia. 1974. "The Social and Economic Implications of Large-Scale Introduction of New Variety of Food Grains." Mimeograph. Geneva: UNRISO.

Hicks, Frederic. 1971. "Interpersonal Relationship and *Caudillismo* in Paraguay." *Journal of Interamerican Studies and World Affairs* 13: 89–113.

Hingers, R. H., and D. Willer. 1979. "Prevailing Postulates of Social Exchange Theory." In S. G. McNall, ed., *Theoretical Perspectives in Sociology*, pp. 169–86. New York: St. Martin's.

Hirschman, Albert O. 1965. *Journeys toward Progress: Studies of Economic Policy-Making in Latin America*. Garden City, N.Y.: Doubleday.

Hobsbawm, Eric. 1967. "Peasants and Rural Migrants in Politics." In C. Veliz, ed., *The Politics of Conformity in Latin America*, pp. 41–65. London: Oxford University Press.

————. 1969. "A Case of Neo-Feudalism: La Convención, Peru." *Journal of Latin American Studies* 1 (May): 31–50.

Holland, W. Paul, and S. Leinhardt, eds. 1979. *Perspectives on Social Network Research*. New York: Academic Press.

Holmberg, Allan. 1966. "Some Relations between Psychological Deprivation and Culture Change in the Andes." Mimeograph. Ithaca: Cornell University Center for International Studies.

Homans, George C. 1958. "Social Behavior as Exchange." *American Journal of Sociology* 63: 597–606.

————. 1961. *Social Behavior: Its Elementary Forms*. New York: Harcourt, Brace and World.

Horowitz, Irving L. 1969. "The Norm of Illegitimacy: The Political Sociology of Latin America." In I. L. Horowitz et al., eds., *Latin American Radicalism*, pp. 3–28. New York: Random House.

Huizer, Gerrit. 1965. "Some Notes on Community Development and Social Research." *America Latina* 8 (July–September): 128–44.

————. 1967. "Peasant Organizations in the Process of Political Modernization: The Latin American Experience." Paper presented at the Conference on Urbanization and Work in Modernizing Areas, St. Thomas, Virgin Islands, 2–4 November.

———. 1969. "Movimientos campesinos y reforma agraria en América Latina." *Revista Mexicana de Sociología* 31 (April–June): 387–416.

———. 1970a. "Emiliano Zapata and the Peasant Güerrillas in the Mexican Revolution." In R. Stavenhagen, ed., *Agrarian Problems and Peasant Movements in Latin America*, pp. 376–406. Garden City, N.Y.: Doubleday.

———. 1970b. " 'Resistance to Change' and Radical Peasant Mobilization: Foster and Erasmus Reconsidered." *Human Organization* 29 (Winter): 303–13.

———. 1970c. "Peasant Organizations in Agrarian Reform in Mexico." In I. L. Horowitz, ed., *Masses in Latin America*, pp. 445–502. New York: Oxford University Press.

———. 1972. *The Revolutionary Potential of Peasants in Latin America.* Lexington, Mass.: Lexington Books.

Hutchinson, Bertram. 1966. "The Patron-Dependent Relationship in Brazil." *Sociología Ruralis* 6: 3–30.

Hutchinson, Harry W. 1952. "Race Relations in a Rural Community of the Bahian Reconcavo." In C. Wagley, ed., *Race and Class in Rural Brazil*, pp. 16–81. Paris: UNESCO.

———. 1957. *Village and Plantation Life in Northeastern Brazil.* Monograph of the American Ethnological Society. Seattle: University of Washington Press.

———. 1961. "The Transformation of Brazilian Plantation Society," *Journal of Inter-American Studies* 3: 201–12.

Johnson, John J., ed. 1973. *Continuity and Change in Latin America.* Stanford: Stanford University Press.

Jongmans, D. G. 1973. "Politics on the Village Level." In J. Boissevain and J. C. Mitchell, eds., *Network Analysis: Studies in Human Interaction*, pp. 167–217. The Hague: Mouton.

Julião, Francisco. 1962. *Que são as ligas camponesas?* Rio de Janeiro: Editora Civilizacão Brasileira S.A.

———. 1968. *Cambão: La cara oculta de Brasil.* Mexico City: Siglo XXI.

———. 1969. *Ligas campesinas: Octubre 1962–Abril 1964.* Cuernavaca: CIDOC.

Kadt, Emanuel de. 1967. "Religion, the Church, and Social Change in Brazil." In C. Veliz, ed., *The Politics of Conformity in Latin America*, pp. 192–220. London: Oxford University Press.

Kapferer, B. 1969. "Norms and the Manipulation of Relationships in a Work Context." In J. C. Mitchell, ed., *Social Networks in Urban Situations*, pp.181–244. Manchester, Eng.: Manchester University Press.

Katzin, Donna. 1973–1974a. "Four Killed, Others Imprisoned." *USLA Reporter* (December–January): 12–13.

———. 1973–1974b. "The Charges." *USLA Reporter* (December–January): 13–14.

Kaufman Purcell, Susan, and John F. H. Purcell. 1980. "State and Society in Mexico: Must a Stable Polity be Institutionalized?" *World Politics*, 19 January.

Kay, Cristóbal. 1976. "Chile: Agrarian Reform 1965–1973." *América Latina* 17: 18–31.

Kearney, Michael. 1969. "An Exception to the 'Image of Limited Good.' " *American Anthropologist* 71: 880–90.

Kellert, Stephen, L. K. Williams, W. F. Whyte, and G. Alberti. 1967. "Culture, Change and Stress in Rural Peru: A Preliminary Report." *Milbank Memorial Fund Quarterly* 45: 391–415.

Klare, Michael. 1974. "Dealing Arms in the Third World." *NACLA Latin America and Empire Report* 8: 24–31.

Klare, Michael, and Nancy Stein. 1974. "Police and Terrorism in Latin America." *NACLA Latin America and Empire Report* 8 (January): 19–23.

Kling, Merle. 1968. "Toward a Theory of Power and Political Instability in Latin America." In J. Petras and M. Zeitlin, eds., *Latin America: Reform or Revolution?*, pp. 76–93. Greenwich, Conn.: Fawcett.

———. 1969. "Violence and Politics in Latin America." In I. L. Horowitz, J. de Castro, and J. Gerassi, eds., *Latin American Radicalism: A Documentary Report on Left and National Movements*, pp. 191–206. New York: Vintage.

Knox, John B. 1963. "The Concept of Exchange in Sociological Theory: 1884–1961." *Social Forces* 41: 341–46.

Konetzke, Richard. 1965. *Süd- und Mittelamerika I: Die Indianerkulturen Amerikas und die Spanisch-portugiesische Kolonialherrschaft.* Frankfurt: Fischer.

Kula, Witold. 1976. *An Economic Theory of the Feudal System: Towards a Model of the Polish Economy 1500–1800.* London: NLD.

Laclau, Ernesto. 1977. "Feudalism and Capitalism in Latin America." In E. Laclau, *Politics and Idealism in Marxist Theory: Capitalism, Fascism and Populism*, pp. 15–50. London: NLD.

Landsberger, Henry. 1969a. "The Role of Peasant Movements and Revolts in Development." In H. Landsberger, ed., *Latin American Peasant Movements*, pp. 1–61. Ithaca: Cornell University Press.

———. 1969b. "Chile: A Vineyard Workers' Strike—A Case Study of the Relationship between Church, Intellectuals, and Peasants." In H. Landsberger, ed., *Latin American Peasant Movements*, pp. 210–73. Ithaca: Cornell University Press.

Landsberger, Henry, and Cynthia Hewitt. 1970. "Ten Sources of Weakness and Cleavage in Latin American Peasant Movements." In R. Stavenhagen, ed., *Agrarian Problems and Peasant Movements in Latin America*, pp. 559–83. Garden City, N.Y.: Doubleday.

Landy, David. 1959. *Tropical Childhood: Cultural Transmission and Learning in a Puerto Rican Village.* Chapel Hill: University of North Carolina Press.

Laumann, Edward O., and Franz U. Pappi. 1976. *Networks of Collective Action: A Perspective on Community Influence Systems.* New York: Academic Press.

Leeds, Anthony. 1957. *Economic Cycles in Brazil: The Persistence of a Total Culture Pattern—Cacao and Other Cases.* Ann Arbor: University of Michigan Microfilms.

———. 1964. "Brazil and the Myth of Francisco Julião." In J. Maier and R. W. Weatherhead, eds., *Politics of Change in Latin America*, pp. 190–204. New York: Praeger.

———. 1965. "Brazilian Careers and Social Structure: A Case History and Model." In D. Heath and R. N. Adams, eds., *Contemporary Cultures and Societies of Latin America*, 379–404. New York: Random House.

Leeds, Elizabeth. 1970. "Games Favelas Play." Paper presented at the annual meeting of the American Anthropological Association, San Diego, 20 November.

Leinhardt, Samuel, ed. 1977. *Social Networks: A Developing Paradigm.* New York: Academic Press.

Lenski, Gerhard. 1966. *Power and Privilege: A Theory of Social Stratification.* New York: McGraw-Hill.

Lerner, Daniel. 1958. *The Passing of Traditional Society: Modernizing the Middle East.* New York: Free Press.

Lewis, Oscar. 1953. "Tepoztlán Revisited: A Critique of the Folk-Urban Conceptualization of Social Change." *Rural Sociology* 18: 121–34.

———. 1959. *Five Families.* New York: Basic Books.

————. 1960. *Tepoztlán: Village in Mexico.* New York: Holt, Rinehart and Winston.

Lopes, Juarez Rubens. 1964. "Some Basic Developments in Brazilian Politics and Society." Paper presented 12 November, at Vanderbilt University, Nashville, Tenn.

————. 1966. *Desenvolvimento a mudança social: Formação da sociedade urban-industrial no Brasil.* São Paulo: Faculdade de Árquitetura e Urbanismo da Universidade de São Paulo.

Lopreato, Joseph. 1967. *Peasants No More: Social Class and Social Change in an Underdeveloped Society.* San Francisco: Chandler.

Lord, Peter P. 1967. "El campesinado como factor político incipiente en México, Bolivia y Venezuela." LTC no. 35–S. Madison: University of Wisconsin Land Tenure Center.

Lukács, Georg. 1970. *Geschichte und Klassenbewusstsein.* Berlin: Luchterhand.

McCoy, Terry. 1967. "The Seizure of 'Los Cristales.' " *Inter-American Economic Affairs* 21, no. 1: 73–93.

Malloy, James M. 1970. *Bolivia: The Uncompleted Revolution.* Pittsburgh: University of Pittsburgh Press.

Mansilla, H. C. F. 1974. "Möglichkeiten und Grenzen des Dritten Weges." In H. C. F. Mansilla, ed., *Probleme des Dritten Weges: Mexiko, Argentinien, Bolivien, Tansania, Peru,* pp. 199–246. Darmstadt: Luchterhand.

Marini, Ruy Mauro. 1973. *Dialéctica de la dependencia.* Mexico City: Era.

Martínez, Héctor. 1963a. "Compadrazgo en una comunidad indígena altiplánica." *Perú Indígena* 10, nos. 22–23: 17–27.

————. 1963b. "La hacienda capana." *Perú Indígena* 10, nos. 24–25: 37–64.

————. 1967. "Tres haciendas altiplánicos: Chujuni, Cochela, y Panascachi." *Perú Indígena* 14: 96–162.

Martínez Ríos, Jorge. 1974. "Las invasiones agrarias en México o la crisis del modela incorporación-participación." *Revista Mexicana Agraria* 6: 7–56.

Marx, Karl, and Friedrich Engels. 1966. *Marx-Engels Studienausgabe.* 4 vols. Frankfurt: Fischer.

Mathiason, John E. 1966. "The Venezuelan Campesino: Perspectives on Change." In F. Bonilla and J. Silva Michelena, eds., *Studying the Venezuelan Polity,* pp. 120–55. Cambridge, Mass.: MIT Center for International Affairs.

Matos Mar, José. 1967. "Movimientos y organizaciones campesinas en el valle de Chancay." Proyecto: Los Movimientos Campesinas en el Perú desde Fines del siglo XVIII hasta nuestros dias, No. 2. Lima: Instituto de Estudios Peruanos.

Mayorga, René Antonio. 1974. "Das Scheitern des populistischen Nationalismus in Bolivien." In H. C. F. Mansilla, ed., *Probleme des Dritten Weges: Mexiko, Argentinien, Bolivien, Tansania, Peru,* pp. 69–125. Darmstadt: Luchterhand.

Meeker, B. F. 1971. "Decisions and Exchange." *American Sociological Review* 36 (June): 485–95.

Menges, Constantine C. 1968. "Peasant Organizations and Politics in Chile, 1958–1964." Mimeograph. Santa Monica, Calif.: Rand Corporation.

Meyer, Jean. 1973. *Problemas campesinos y revueltas agrarias (1821–1910).* Mexico City: Sep-Setentas.

Migdal, Joel S. 1974. *Peasants, Politics, and Revolution.* Princeton: Princeton University Press.

Millon, Robert P. 1969. *Zapata: The Ideology of a Peasant Revolutionary.* New York: International Publications.

Mintz, Sidney. 1960. *Worker in the Cane: A Puerto Rican Life History.* New Haven: Yale University Press.

Mintz, Sidney, and Eric Wolf. 1950. "An Analysis of Ritual Co-Parenthood (Compadrazgo)." *Southwestern Journal of Anthropology* 6 (Winter): 341–68.
———. 1967. "An Analysis of Ritual Co-Parenthood (Compadrazgo)." In J. M. Potter et al., eds., *Peasant Society: A Reader*, pp. 174–99. Boston: Little, Brown & Company.
Mitchell, Fanny. 1966–1967. *Newsletters to the Institute of Current World Affairs* (FM-8, 11, 12, 17). New York: Institute of Current World Affairs.
Mitchell, J. Clyde. 1969. "The Concept and Use of Social Networks." In J. C. Mitchell, ed., *Social Networks in Urban Situations*, pp. 1–50. Manchester, Eng.: Manchester University Press.
———. 1973. "Networks, Norms and Institutions." In J. Boissevain and J. C. Mitchell, eds., *Network Analysis: Studies in Human Interaction*, pp. 15–35. The Hague: Mouton.
Mitchell, Jack N. 1978. *Social Exchange, Dramaturgy and Ethnomethodology: Toward a Paradigmatic Synthesis.* New York: Elsevier North Holland.
Moore, Barrington, Jr. 1966. *The Social Origins of Dictatorship and Democracy: Lord and Peasant in the Making of the Modern World.* Boston: Beacon Press.
Moraes, Clodomir. 1970. "Peasant Leagues in Brazil." In R. Stavenhagen ed., *Agrarian Problems and Peasant Movements in Latin America*, pp. 453–501. Garden City, N.Y.: Doubleday.
Moreno, Francisco José. 1971. "Caudillismo: An Interpretation of Its Origins in Chile." In F. J. Moreno and B. Mitrani, eds., *Conflict and Violence in Latin American Politics*, pp. 24–42. New York: Thomas Y. Crowell.
Mörner, Magnus. 1970. "A Comparative Study of Tenant Labor in Parts of Europe, Africa and Latin America 1700–1900: A Preliminary Report of a Research Project in Social History." *Latin American Research Review* 5, no. 2: 3–15.
———. 1973. "The Spanish American Hacienda: A Critical Survey of Recent Research and Debate." *Hispanic American Historical Review* 53 (May): 183–216.
———. 1975. "La hacienda hispanoamericana: Examen de las investigaciones y debates recientes." In E. Florescano, ed., *Haciendas, latifundios y plantaciones en América Latina*, pp. 15–48. Mexico City: Siglo XXI.
Mulkey, M. J. 1971. *Functionalism, Exchange and Theoretical Strategy.* New York: Schocken.
Müller, Ronald. 1975. "The Multinational Corporation and the Underdevelopment of the Third World." In C. K. Wilber, ed., *The Political Economy of Development and Underdevelopment*, pp. 124–51. New York: Random House.
Murphy, Brian. 1970. "The Stunted Growth of Campesino Organizations." In R. N. Adams, *Crucifixion by Power*, pp. 438–78. Austin: University of Texas Press.
Murtha, Robert. 1973. "A.I.D. for the Torturers." *NSLA Reporter* 3 (September–October): 6–7.
NACLA. 1973. *New Chile.* New York: North American Congress on Latin America.
Nash, Manning. 1967. *Machine Age Maya: The Industrialization of a Guatemalan Community.* Chicago: University of Chicago Press.
Newbold, Stokes. 1957. "Receptivity to Community-Fomented Agitation in Rural Guatemala." *Economic Development and Cultural Change* 5 (July): 338–61.
Niehoff, Arthur, and J. C. Anderson. 1966. "Peasant Fatalism and Socio-Economic Innovation." *Human Organization* 25 (Winter): 273–83.
Nuñez del Prado, Oscar. 1965. "Aspects of Andean Native Life." In D. B.

Heath and R. N. Adams, eds., *Contemporary Cultures and Societies of Latin America*, pp. 102–23. New York: Random House.

Nuñes Leal, Victor. 1948. *Coronelismo, Enxada e Voto*. Rio de Janeiro.

Paige, Jeffery M. 1975. *Agrarian Revolution*. New York: Free Press.

Palacio, H. Gustavo. 1957a. "Relaciones de trabajo entre el patrón y los colonos en los fūndos de la provincia de Paūcartambo." *Revista Universitaria del Cūzco* 46: 45–72.

———. 1957b. "Relaciones de trabajo entre el patrón y los colonos en los fūndos de la provincia de Paūcartambo." *Revista Universitaria del Cūzco* 46: 173–222.

———. 1960. "Relaciones de trabajo entre el patrón y los colonos en los fūndos de la provincia de Paūcartambo." *Revista Universitaria del Cūzco* 49: 142–63.

———. 1961. "Relaciones de trabajo entre el patrón y los colonos en los fūndos de la provincia de Paūcartambo." *Revista Universitaria del Cūzco* 50: 67–140.

Paré, Louise. 1973. "Caciquisme et structure de pouvoir dans le Mexique rural." *Canadian Review of Sociology and Anthropology* 10, no. 1: 20–43.

Passos Guimarães, Alberto. 1964. *Quatro seculos de latifundio*. São Paulo: Editora Fulgor Limitada.

Patch, Richard W. 1960. "Bolivia: U.S. Assistance in a Revolutionary Setting." In R. N. Adams et al., eds., *Social Change in Latin America Today*, pp. 108–76. New York: Random House.

———. 1963. "Peasantry and National Revolution: Bolivia." In K. Silvert, ed., *Expectant Peoples: Nationalism and Development*, pp. 95–126. New York: Random House.

Paulson, Beldon H. 1964. *Local Political Patterns in Northeast Brazil: A Community Case Study*. Madison: University of Wisconsin Land Tenure Center. Research Paper no. 12.

Payne, James L. 1965. *Labor and Politics in Peru*. New Haven: Yale University Press.

———. 1968. *Patterns of Conflict in Colombia*. New Haven: Yale University Press.

Pearse, Andrew. 1970. "Agrarian Change Trends in Latin America." In R. Stavenhagen, ed., *Agrarian Problems and Peasant Movements in Latin America*, pp. 11–40. Garden City, N.Y.: Doubleday.

———. 1975. *The Latin American Peasant*. London: Frank Cass.

Pearson, Neale J. 1969. "Guatemala: The Peasant Union Movement, 1944–1954." In H. Landsberger, ed., *Latin American Peasant Movements*, pp. 323–73. Ithaca: Cornell University Press.

Peña, Sergio de la. 1975. *La formación del capitalismo en Mexico*. Mexico City: Siglo XXI.

Petras, James F. 1966. "Chile's Christian Peasant Union: Notes and Comments on an Interview with Hector Alarcon." Madison: University of Wisconsin Land Tenure Center, Newsletter no. 23 (March–July): 21–29.

Petras, James, and Eugene Havens. 1979. "Peasant Behavior and Social Change: Cooperatives and Individual Holdings." Mimeograph.

Petras, James, and Robert Laporte. 1971. *Peru: Transformacion revolucionaria o modernizacion?* Buenos Aires: Amorrortu Editores.

Petras, James, and Maurice Zeitlin. 1967. "Miners and Agrarian Radicalism." *American Sociological Review* 32 (August): 578–86.

———. 1970. "Agrarian Radicalism in Chile." In R. Stavenhagen, ed., *Agrarian Problems and Peasant Movements in Latin America*, pp. 503–31. Garden City, N.Y.: Doubleday.

Petras, James, and H. Zemelman. 1969. *Peasant Politics in Chile: A Case Study*. Madison: University of Wisconsin Land Tenure Center, LTC no. 65.

———. 1972. *Peasants in Revolt: A Chilean Case Study, 1965–1971*. Austin: University of Texas Press.

Portes, Alejandro. 1978. "The Informal Sector and the World Economy: Notes on the Structure of Subsidized Labor." *IDS Bulletin* 9, no. 4: 35–40.

Postan, M. M. 1972. *The Medieval Economy and Society*. Berkeley: University of California Press.

Powell, John Duncan. 1969. "Venezuela: The Peasant Union Movement." In H. Landsberger, ed., *Latin American Peasant Movements*, pp. 62–100. Ithaca: Cornell University Press.

———. 1970. "Peasant Society and Clientelist Politics." *American Political Science Review* 64 (June): 411–25.

———. 1971. *Political Mobilization of the Venezuelan Peasant*. Cambridge, Mass.: Harvard University Press.

Price, Robert E., 1964. *Rural Unionization in Brazil*. Research Paper no. 14. Madison: University of Wisconsin Land Tenure Center.

Quijano, Anibal. 1965. "El movimiento campesino del Perú y sus líderes." *América Latina* 8 (October–December): 43–65.

———. 1967. "Contemporary Peasant Movements." In S. M. Lipset and A. Solari, eds., *Elites in Latin America*, pp. 301–42. New York: Oxford University Press.

Redfield, Robert. 1930. *Tepoztlan: A Mexican Village*. Chicago: University of Chicago Press.

Reichel-Dolmatoff, Gerardo, and Alicia Reichel-Dolmatoff. 1961. *The People of Aritama: The Cultural Personality of a Colombian Mestizo Village*. Chicago: University of Chicago Press.

Reina, Ruben E. 1959. "Two Patterns of Friendship in a Guatemalan Community." *American Anthropologist* 61 (February): 44–50.

Reyna, José Luis. 1974. "Control político, estabilidad y desarrollo en México." Paper presented at I Congreso de la Sociedad Mexicana de Sociologia en Pátzcuaro, January.

Rogers, Everett M. 1969. *Modernization among Peasants: The Impact of Communication*. New York: Holt, Rinehart and Winston.

Rubel, Arthur J. 1966. *Across the Tracks: Mexican-Americans in a Texas City*. Austin: University of Texas Press.

Sayres, William. 1956. "Ritual Kinship and Negative Effect." *American Sociological Review* 21 (June): 348–52.

Schafer, Robert B. 1974. "Exchange and Symbolic Interaction: A Further Analysis of Convergence." *Pacific Sociological Review* 17: 417–34.

Schirmer, Ute. 1976. "Präkapitalistisches Mehrprodukt und kapitalistischer Profit: Zum Verhältnis zwischen Industrie und Agrarsektor im abhängigen Kapitalismus—der Fall Peru." Paper presented at the Lateinamerika-Kolloquium, Bielefeld, West Germany, 24–26 June.

Schofer, Lawrence. 1975. *The Formation of a Modern Labor Force: Upper Silesia, 1865–1914*. Berkeley: University of California Press.

Schulman, Irwin J. 1978. Review of J. M. Paige, *Agrarian Revolution: Social Movements and Export Agriculture. American Political Science Review* 72: 752–54.

Schulman, Sam. 1955. "The Colono System in Latin America." *Rural Sociology* 20 (March): 34–40.

———. 1966. "El reconocimiento del papel del campesino en la reforma agraria." *America Latina* 9, no. 3: 75–86.

Schwartz, David C. 1971. "A Theory of Revolutionary Behavior." In J. C. Davis, ed., *When Men Revolt and Why*, pp. 109–32. New York: Free Press.

Scott, James C. 1977. "Hegemony and the Peasantry." *Politics and Society* 7: 267–96.

Senghaas, Dieter. 1974. "Elemene einer Theorie des peripheren Kapitalismus." In D. Senghaas, ed., *Periphärer Kapitalismus: Analysen über Abhängigkeit und Unterentwicklung*, pp. 7–26. Frankfurt: Suhrkamp.

Sharpe, Kenneth Evan. 1977. *Peasant Politics: Struggle in a Dominican Village*. Baltimore: Johns Hopkins University Press.

Shazo, Peter de. n.d. "The Colonato System on the Bolivian Altiplano from Colonial Times to 1952." LTC no. 83. Madison: University of Wisconsin Land Tenure Center.

Siegel, Bernard. 1957. "The Role of Perception in Urban-Rural Change: A Bolivian Case Study." *Economic Development and Cultural Change* 5 (April): 244–56.

Silva-Herzog, Jesús. 1959. *El agrarismo mexicano y la reforma agraria*. Mexico City: Fondo de Cultura Económica.

———. 1960. *Brave historia de la revolución mexicana*. Mexico City: Fondo de Cultura Económica.

Simmons, Ozzie G. 1965. "Drinking Patterns and Interpersonal Performance in a Peruvian Mestizo Community." In G. Foster, ed., *Contemporary Latin American Culture: A Sourcebook*. New York: Selected Academic Readings.

Singelmann, Peter. 1972. "Exchange as Symbolic Interaction: Convergences between Two Theoretical Perspectives." *American Sociological Review* 37 (August): 414–24.

———. 1973a. "On the Reification of Paradigms: Reply to Abbot, Brown, and Crosbie." *American Sociological Review* 38 (August): 506–8.

———. 1973b. "Los movimientos campesinos en América Latina." *Problemas Internacionales* 20 (September–October): 86–92.

———. 1973c. "Interés propio e interés de clase: Algunas funciones de los movimientos campesinos en América Latina." *Revista Mexicana de Sociología* 35 (April–June): 383–97.

———. 1974. "Campesino Movements and Class Conflict in Latin America: The Functions of Exchange and Power." *Journal of Inter-American Studies and World Affairs* 16 (February): 39–72. Reprinted in *América Latina* 15: 75–103.

———. 1975a. "Political Structure and Social Banditry in Northeast Brazil." *Journal of Latin American Studies* 7, no. 1: 59–83.

———. 1975b. "The Closing Triangle: Critical Notes on a Model for Peasant Mobilization in Latin America." *Comparative Studies in Society and History* 17 (October): 389–409.

———. 1976. "Los movimientos campesinos y la modernización política en América Latina: Apuntes críticos." *Boletín de Estudios Latinoamericanos y del Caribe* (June): 34–53.

———. 1978. "Rural Collectivization and Dependent Capitalism: The Mexican Collective Ejido." *Latin American Perspectives* 5 (Summer): 38–61.

———. 1980. "Desarrollo del capitalismo periférico y la transformación de relaciones de clase rurales: El papel de cañeros campesinos en la industria azucarera mexicana." *Revista Mexicana de Sociología* (January [special issue]).

Sjoberg, Gideon. 1955. "The Pre-industrial City." *American Journal of Sociology* 60: 438–45.

Skocpol, Theda. 1979. *States and Social Revolutions*. Cambridge: Cambridge University Press.

———. 1980. "What Makes Peasants Revolutionary?" Paper presented at a symposium on peasant rebellions at Johns Hopkins University, Baltimore, in January.

Smith, John. 1969. "The Campesinos' Perspectives in Latin America." *Inter-American Economic Affairs* 23 (Summer): 47–66.

Snee, Carole A. 1969. *Current Types of Peasant-Agricultural Worker Coalitions and Their Historical Development in Guatemala*. Notebook 31. Cuernavaca: CIDOC.

Sonntag, Heinz Rudolf. 1972. *Revolution in Chile*. Hamburg: Fischer.
Sotelo Inclán, Jesús. 1970. *Raíz y razón de Zapata*. Mexico City: CFE.
Southard, Frank. 1980. "Normatively Controlled Social Exchange Systems." In B. Anderson and D. Willer, eds., *Social Exchange and Social Networks*. New York: Elsevier.
Spiegel, Der. 1971. "In Zehn Jahrhunderten." *Der Spiegel* 23: 95–96.
Spielberg, Joseph. 1968. "Small Village Relations in Guatemala: A Case Study." *Human Organization* 27 (Fall): 205–11.
Stavenhagen, Rodolfo. 1969. "Seven Erroneous Theses about Latin America." In I. L. Horowitz et al., eds., *Latin American Radicalism*, pp. 102–17. New York: Random House.
Stavenhagen, Rodolfo, ed. 1970. *Agrarian Problems and Peasant Movements in Latin America*. Garden City, N.Y.: Doubleday.
Stavenhagen, Rodolfo, et al. 1973. *Neolatifundismo y explotación*. Mexico City: Nuestro Tiempo.
Stein, Stanley J., and Barbara Stein. 1970. *The Colonial Heritage of Latin America: Essays on Economic Dependence in Perspective*. New York: Oxford University Press.
Stinchcombe, Arthur L. 1961. "Agrarian Enterprise and Rural Class Relations." *American Journal of Sociology* 65: 165–76.
Stokes, William S. 1952. "Violence as a Power Factor in Latin American Politics." *Western Political Quarterly* (September) : 449–69.
Tannenbaum, Frank. 1929. *The Mexican Agrarian Revolution*. New York: Macmillan.
———. 1960. *Ten Keys to Latin America*. New York: Random House.
Tella, Torcuato Di. 1965. "Populism and Reform in Latin America." In C. Veliz, ed., *Obstacles to Change in Latin America*, pp. 47–74. London: Oxford University Press.
Thibaut, John W., and Harold H. Kelley. 1967. *The Social Psychology of Groups*. New York: Wiley.
Thiesenhusen, William C. 1968. "Grassroots Economic Pressure in Chile: An Enigma for Development Planners." *Economic Development and Cultural Change* 16, no. 3: 412–29.
Thoden van Velzen, H. U. E. 1973. "Coalitions and Network Analysis." In J. Boissevain and J. C. Mitchell, eds., *Network Analysis: Studies in Human Interaction*, pp. 219–50. The Hague: Mouton.
Tocqueville, Alexis de. 1955. *The Old Regime and the French Revolution*. New York: Doubleday.
Trip, Günter Matthias. 1974. "Theorie and Realität: Zur Konzeption des Dritten Weges am Beispiel Mexico." In H. C. F. Mansilla, ed., *Probleme des Dritten Weges: Mexiko, Argentinien, Bolivien, Tansania, Peru*, pp. 11–26. Darmstadt: Luchterhand.
Tullis, F. LaMond. 1970. *Lord and Peasant in Peru: A Paradigm of Political and Social Change*. Cambridge, Mass.: Harvard University Press.
Tumin, Melvin. 1952. *Cash in a Peasant Society: A Case Study in the Dynamics of Cash*. Princeton: Princeton University Press.
USLA. n.d. "Once Again My Life Is in the Lord of the People." Pamphlet.
———. 1973a. "Peasant Leader in Danger." *USLA Reporter* 3 (April–May): 6–8.
———. 1973b. "Medici's Victims." *USLA Reporter* 3 (September–October): 4–5.
———. 1973c. "Stroessner vs. Agrarian Leagues." *USLA Reporter* 3 (September–October) : 12.
———. 1974. "Conceicão's Court Testimony." *USLA Reporter* 4 (February–April): 10–12.
Valderama, Mariano L. 1976. "Siete años de reforma agraria peruana." *Historia y Sociedad* 9: 5–20.

Vázquez, Mario C. 1963. "Autoridades de una hacienda andina peruana." *Perú Indígena* 10, nos. 24–25: 24–36.

Vergopoulos, Kostas. 1975. "El capitalismo disforme: El caso de la agricultura en el capitalismo." In S. Amin and K. Vergopoulos, *La cuestión campesina y el capitalismo,* pp. 59–137. Mexico City: Nuestro Tiempo.

Vianna, Oliveira. 1949. *Instituicões politicas brasileiras.* 2 vols. São Paulo: Livraría José Olympio Editora.

Villanũeva, Victor. 1967. *Victor Hugo y la rebelión campesina.* Lima: Juan Mejía Baca.

Villegas, Cosio. 1975. *La succesión: Desenlace y perspectivas.* Mexico City: Cuadernos de Juan Martíz.

Vinicius Vilaca, Marcos, and R. C. de Albuquerque. 1965. *Coronel, coroneis.* Rio de Janeiro: Edicoes Temp Brasileiro.

Vitale, Luis. 1968. "Latin America: Feudal or Capitalist?" In J. Petras and M. Zeitlin, eds., *Latin America: Reform or Revolution?*, pp. 32–43. Greenwich, Conn.: Fawcett.

Wagley, Charles. 1960. "The Brazilian Revolution: Social Changes since 1930." In R. N. Adams et al., eds., *Social Change in Latin America Today,* pp. 177–230. New York: Random House.

———. 1964. "The Peasant." In J. J. Johnson, ed., *Continuity and Change in Latin America,* pp. 21–48. Palo Alto: Stanford University Press.

Wagley, Charles, and M. Harris. 1965. "A Typology of Latin American Subcultures." In D. B. Heath and R. N. Adams, eds., *Contemporary Cultures and Societies of Latin America,* pp. 42–69. New York: Random House.

Walker Linares, Francisco. 1953. "Trade Unionism among Agricultural Workers in Chile." *International Labor Review* 68, no. 6: 509–23.

Walker, Malcolm. 1970. "Power Structure and Patronage in a Community of the Dominican Republic." *Journal of Inter-American Studies and World Affairs* 12: 485–505.

Wallerstein, Immanuel. 1976. *The Modern World System: Capitalist Agriculture and the Origins of the European World Economy in the Sixteenth Century.* New York: Academic Press.

———. 1977. "Rural Economy in Modern World-Society." *Studies in Comparative International Development* 12: 29–40.

Warman, Arturo. 1973. *Los campesinos: Hijos predilectos del régimen.* Mexico City: Editorial Nuestro Tiempo.

———. 1976. *. . . Y venimos a contradecir: Los campesinos de Morelos y el estado nacional.* Mexico City: CIS-INAH.

———. 1977. "La colectivización en el campo: Una crítica." *Cuadernos Políticos* 11 (January–March): 47–56.

Weldon, Peter D. 1968. *Social Change in a Peruvian Highland Province.* Ithaca: Cornell University Latin American Studies Program, Dissertation Series, no. 10.

Whetten, Nathan. 1948. *Rural Mexico.* Chicago: University of Chicago Press.

White, Robert A. 1969. "Mexico: The Zapata Movement and the Revolution." In H. Landsberger, ed., *Latin American Peasant Movements,* pp. 101–69. Ithaca: Cornell University Press.

Whyte, William F. 1970. "El mito del campesino pasivo: La dinamica del cambio en el Peru rural." *Estudios Andinos* 1, no. 1: 3–28.

Whyte, William F., and Lawrence K. Williams. 1968. *Toward an Integrated Theory of Development.* Ithaca: New York State School of Industrial and Labor Relations.

Wilkie, Mary. 1964. *A Report on Rural Syndicates in Pernambuco.* Rio de Janeiro: Centro Latino-Americano de Pesquisas em Sciencias Sociais.

Willer, David. 1980a. "Structurally Determined Networks of Social Action." In B. Anderson and D. Willer, eds., *Social Exchange Networks: The Elementary Theory and Its Application.* New York: Elsevier.

———. 1980b. "What Is Exact Theory?" Manuscript.

Williams, Lawrence K. 1969. "Algunos correlatos sico-sociales de sistemas de dominación." In J. Matos Mar et al., *Dominación y cambios en el Perú rural,* pp. 80–94. Lima: Instituto de Estudios Peruanos.

Winn, Peter, and C. Kay. 1974. "Agrarian Reform and Rural Revolution in Allende's Chile." *Journal of Latin American Studies* 6: 135–59.

Wolf, Eric. 1955. "Types of Latin American Peasantry: A Preliminary Discussion." *American Anthropologist* 57 (June): 452–71.

———. 1957. "Closed Corporate Peasant Communities in Mesoamerica and Central Java." *Southwestern Journal of Anthropology* 13 (Spring): 1–18.

———. 1965. "Aspects of Group Relations in a Complex Society: Mexico." In D. B. Heath and R. N. Adams, eds., *Contemporary Cultures and Societies of Latin America,* pp. 85–101. New York: Random House.

———. 1966a. *Peasants.* Englewood Cliffs, N.J.: Prentice-Hall.

———. 1966b. "Kinship, Friendship, and Patron-Client Relations in Complex Societies." In M. Banton, ed., *The Social Anthropology of Complex Societies,* pp. 1–22. New York: Praeger.

———. 1969. *Peasant Wars of the Twentieth Century.* New York: Harper & Row.

———. 1977. "Review Essay: Why Cultivators Rebel." *American Journal of Sociology* 83: 742–50.

Wolf, Eric, and Edward C. Hansen. 1967. "Caudillo Politics: A Structural Analysis." *Comparative Studies in Society and History* 9 (January): 168–79.

Wolfe, Alvin W. 1978. "The Rise of Network Thinking in Anthropology." *Social Networks* 1: 53–64.

Wolpe, Harold. 1972. "Capitalism and Cheap Labor-Power in South Africa: From Segregation to Apartheid." *Economy and Society* 1, no. 4: 425–56.

———. 1975. "The Theory of Internal Colonialism: The South African Case." In I. Oxaal et al., eds., *Beyond the Sociology of Development: Economy and Society in Latin America and Africa.* London: Routledge and Kegan Paul.

Womack, John, Jr. 1969. *Zapata and the Mexican Revolution.* New York: Random House.

Zemelman, Hugo. 1973. "La reforma agraria y las clases dominantes." In S. Barraclough et al., *Chile: Reforma agraria y gobierno popular,* pp. 147–78. Buenos Aires: Ediciones Periería.

Index

Allende, Salvador, president of Chile, 163, 184, 192, 193, 196. *See also* Chile
Alternative outcomes and peasant movements, 4
Argentina, 86

Belaúnde, Fernando, president of Peru, 157, 183, 196, 200. *See also* Peru
Benefits: declining and peasant movements, 123–33; imposed alternatives and peasant movements, 134; new supplies and peasant movements, 138–40; and paternalism, 136–38
Blanco, Hugo, Peruvian peasant leader, 143, 176, 189. *See also* Peru
Bolivia, 53–54, 68, 85, 88, 91, 108–9, 126–36 passim, 139–40 144–45, 155–56 167–76 passim, 185, 188, 191, 194, 196, 199, 201
Brazil, 49–60 passim, 71–74, 75, 78–99 passim, 104, 109, 126, 129, 131–37 passim, 141–43 passim, 149–52 passim, 158–60, 173, 174, 185, 189–201 passim
Brokerage: explanation of, 10–11; function of, 59; new, 140–41

Campesino, character structure of, 98–103. *See also* peasant
Cangaceiros: Brazilian social bandits, 86, 87; Lampião, 86
Caudillos, caudillismo, 70, 71, 87–88, 203
Chile, 66, 81, 82, 83, 97–98, 128,138, 141–43 passim, 149, 152, 161–63, 167, 174, 175, 180–81, 183, 185, 192–93, 196–200 passim
Church, Catholic: conservative bent of, 77; declining influence of, 199; support for peasant movements, 141–42, 143, 149–50, 199
Class consciousness, 12–13, 65, 146–47, 181, 185–86, 190, 197; and emancipa-

tion, 189–90, 192, 209–10; solidarity, obstacles to, 11, 106
Coercion: declining resources for and peasant movements, 148–50; persistence of, 67–68. *See also* Exchange, coercion and
Colonialism, economic contradictions of, 48–49; and formation of rural class structures, 43–46, 126, 129
Co-optation, 164, 169, 192, 199–200
Compadrazgo, 108–11
Coronels, coronelismo, 70, 71–74, 85, 86
Corporativism, 191–93
Cuba, 76, 193, 197, 222n

Dialectic analysis, 8–9, 22, 65, 191

Economic costs of peasant movements, 134
Economic resources and peasant movements, 133–34
Ecuador, 62, 68, 89, 90, 91, 102–3, 176, 200
Elections, 81–85; "electoral clan" in Brazil, 72; fraud in, 84; nonideological determinants of, 77–78, 215–16n
Elite intransigence and peasant movements, 151–52
Exchange: balance and imbalance, 10–12,21, 24, 29, 47; and brokerage, 10; coercion and, 10, 21, 34, 48, 118–19; consciousness and, 23–25, 33–37; cultural and institutional matrix of, 20–22, 114; dependence and, 12, 21, 30–31, 49, 51, 53–56, 66, 75, 117–20, 196, 204; as dialectics, 22–23, 29; dyadic contracts and, 93, 111–13; economic decline and, 125–31; as elementary behavior, 18–19; general principle of, 9, 28–29; and gifts, 63; micro- and macrostructure of, 9–10,

243

DATE DUE